The Sculptor and His Stone

The Sculptor and His Stone

Selected Readings on Hellenistic and Christian Learning
and Thought in the Early Greek Fathers

The Most Reverend Chrysostomos
Former Archbishop
and
Metropolitan Emeritus of Etna

with

Archimandrite Patapios,
Bishop Auxentios,
J. C. B. Petropoulos,
Constantine Cavarnos, and
the Reverend Gregory Telepneff

◆PICKWICK Publications • Eugene, Oregon

THE SCULPTOR AND HIS STONE
Selected Readings on Hellenistic and Christian Learning and Thought in the Early Greek Fathers

Copyright © 2016 Archbishop Chrysostomos. All rights reserved. Except for brief quotations in critical publications or reviews, no part of this book may be reproduced in any manner without prior written permission from the publisher. Write: Permissions. Wipf and Stock Publishers, 199 W. 8th Ave., Suite 3, Eugene, OR 97401.

Pickwick Publications
An Imprint of Wipf and Stock Publishers
199 W. 8th Ave., Suite 3
Eugene, OR 97401

www.wipfandstock.com

ISBN 13: 978-1-4982-3122-0

Cataloguing-in-Publication Data

Chrysostomos, Archbishop of Etna

    The sculptor and his stone : selected readings on Hellenistic and Christian learning and thought in the early Greek Fathers / Archbishop Chrysostomos et al.

    xii + 162 p. ; 23 cm. Includes bibliographical references.

    ISBN 13: 978-1-4982-3122-0

    1. Hellenism. 2. Fathers of the church, Greek. 3. Orthodox Tradition. 4. Philosophy, Ancient. I. Title.

BR128.8 C49 2016

Manufactured in the U.S.A.   01/06/2016

This work is dedicated to the memory of Werner Jaeger, whose pivotal writings about Greek *paideia* culminated, at the end of his life, in a demiurgic study of the encounter between the wisdom of the classical Greek sages and the teachings of the early Greek Fathers.

Contents

Acknowledgements | ix
Contributors | xi
Introduction | 1

CHAPTER 1   Man and His Universe in Hellenistic Thought and the Greek Fathers | 9
—*The Reverend Gregory Telepneff and the Most Reverend Chrysostomos*

CHAPTER 2   Body, Soul, and Spirit in the Greek Ancients and in the Greek Fathers and Their Theological Legacy in Eastern Orthodox Christianity* | 21
—*The Most Reverend Chrysostomos*

CHAPTER 3   The Greek Fathers and Secular Knowledge | 53
—*The Most Reverend Chrysostomos and Archimandrite Patapios*

CHAPTER 4   The Transformation of Hellenistic Philosophical Nomenclature in the Greek Patristic Tradition | 66
—*The Most Reverend Chrysostomos and Archimandrite Patapios*

CHAPTER 5   The Notion of Rhetoric in the Eastern Orthodox Patristic Tradition | 81
—*Bishop Auxentios*

Contents

CHAPTER 6 The Concept of Philosophy in the Hellenic Tradition | 94
—*Constantine Cavarnos*

CHAPTER 7 Images of the Invisible Beauty: Plotinian Aesthetics and Byzantine Iconography | 119
—*Archimandrite Patapios*

CHAPTER 8 In Defense of Piety: Respect for Words and Respect for *"The Word"* | 131
—*J. C. B. Petropoulos*

CHAPTER 9 Free Will, Character, and Responsibility in Classical Greek Thought, the Greek Fathers, and Modern Existentialism | 137
—*Constantine Cavarnos*

CHAPTER 10 The Ancient Greek Heritage | 149
—*Constantine Cavarnos*

CHAPTER 11 The Hellenic Heritage in Byzantium | 156
—*Constantine Cavarnos*

Acknowledgements

I WOULD LIKE TO thank the Institute for Byzantine and Modern Greek Studies for permission to use six essays that appear in the present collection in expanded and at times extensively modified form: chapter 1, "Man and His Universe in Hellenistic Thought and the Greek Fathers," which appeared in Archbishop Chrysostomos, *God Made Man and Man Made God* (Belmont, MA: IBMGS, 2010); chapter 3, "The Greek Fathers and Secular Knowledge," originally a chapter in Archbishop Chrysostomos, J. C. B. Petropoulos, *et al.*, *A Patristic Reader* (Belmont, MA: IBMGS, 2010); chapter 6, "The Concept of Philosophy in the Hellenic Tradition," which was first published in Constantine Cavarnos, *The Hellenic-Christian Philosophical Tradition* (Belmont, MA: IBMGS, 1989); chaper 9, "Free Will, Character, and Responsibility in Classical Greek Thought, the Greek Fathers, and Modern Existentialism," which was first published in Constantine Cavarnos, *Philosophika Meletemata* (Belmont, MA: IBMGS, 1979); and chapters 10 and 11, "The Ancient Greek Heritage" and "The Hellenic Heritage in Byzantium," which were originally published in Constantine Cavarnos, *The Hellenic Heritage* (Belmont, MA: IBMGS, 1999).

I am also indebted to the editors of the periodical *Glossa* for permission to reprint the article "The Transformation of Hellenistic Philosophical Nomenclature in the Greek Patristic Tradition," which appeared in that periodical in 2006 (vol. 2, no. 1) and appears here as chapter 4.

Equal gratitude I owe to the Center for Traditionalist Orthodox Studies, which allowed me to reprint chapter 5, "The Notion of Rhetoric in the Eastern Orthodox Patristic Tradition," originally published in my book, *Contemporary Traditionalist Orthodox Thought: A Second Volume* (Etna, CA: C.T.O.S., 1998), and chapter 8, "In Defense of Piety: Respect for Words and Respect for 'the Word,'" which appeared as an article in *Orthodox Tradition* (vol. 3, no. 3, 1986).

Acknowledgements

Finally, I would like to thank Rowman and Littlefield Publishers for permission to reprint the second chapter in my book *A Guide to Orthodox Psychotherapy: The Science, Theology, and Spiritual Practice Behind It and Its Clinical Applications* (Lanham, MD: University Press of America, 2006), which appears here in revised form as chapter 2, under the title "Body, Soul, and Spirit in the Greek Ancients and in the Greek Fathers and Their Theological Legacy in Eastern Orthodox Christianity."

Metropolitan Chrysostomos

Contributors

The Most Reverend Chrysostomos, who holds multiple undergraduate and graduate degrees in history and psychology, received his doctoral degree at Princeton University. He has held professorships in psychology at the University of California and Ashland University and was a visiting lecturer in Eastern Christian thought at the Ashland Theological Seminary and Visiting Professor of Patristics and the Psychology of Religion at the Theological Institute of Uppsala University, in Sweden. As a Fulbright Scholar in Romania, and subsequently Executive Director of the U.S. Fulbright Commission in that country, he taught Byzantine history at the University of Bucharest, consumer behavior at the University of Iași, and the theology of ecclesiastical art at the Ion Mincu University of Architecture. A former visiting scholar at the Harvard Divinity School, Pembroke College (Oxford University), the University of Washington, Seattle, and the Graduate Theological Union at Berkeley, His Eminence was most recently the Larson Fellow in Health and Spirituality at the Kluge Center of the United States Library of Congress. He is the author of numerous books and scholarly articles and chief translator of the English version of the four-volume Greek collection of the writings of the ascetic Fathers of the Christian East, the *Evergetinos*. In retirement, he is Senior Research Scholar at the Center for Traditionalist Orthodox Studies (C.T.O.S.) in Etna, California.

Archimandrite Father Patapios, a graduate of Cambridge University in Classics and Philosophy, received his doctoral degree in patristics at the Graduate Theological Union (G.T.U.), Berkeley, where he was a Newhall Teaching Fellow. Former Lecturer in sacred languages at the St. Joseph of Arimathea Anglican Theological College, he is now Academic Director of the C.T.O.S. His most recent publications are, with Archbishop Chrysostomos, *Manna from Athos: The Issue of Frequent Communion on the Holy

Contributors

Mountain in the Late Eighteenth and Early Nineteenth Centuries (Peter Lang Publishers) and, with Archbishop Chrysostomos and Monk Chrysostomos, an annotated translation of St. Nicodemos the Hagiorite's *Christian Morality* (Institute for Byzantine and Modern Greek Studies).

Bishop Auxentios of Etna and Portland, a Princeton alumnus, received his doctoral degree in liturgics at the G.T.U., Berkeley, and is Director of the C.T.O.S. He is the author of *The Paschal Fire in Jerusalem: A Study of the Rite of the Holy Fire in the Church of the Holy Sepulchre* (St. John Chrysostom Press) and several other books and patristic and liturgical studies.

J. C. B. Petropoulos, a graduate of Harvard University, received his doctoral degree at Oxford University. He is Director of Harvard University's Center for Hellenic Studies in Nafplion, Greece, and Professor of Ancient Greek Literature at the Democritean University of Thrace. He is also a member of the advisory board of the C.T.O.S. His most recent publication is *Kleos in a Minor Key: The Homeric Education of a Little Prince* (Harvard University Press).

The late Constantine Cavarnos (d. 2011) received his AB, AM, and PhD degrees at Harvard University, taught at Harvard and other U.S. universities, and was President of the Institute for Byzantine and Modern Greek Studies in Belmont, MA. He was also a founding member of the advisory board of the C.T.O.S. An *Archon* of the Oecumenical Patriarchate, in his last several years he embraced monasticism and was tonsured to the Great Schema at the Monastery of St. Anthony the Great in Florence, Arizona. Professor Cavarnos authored more than fifty books and numerous scholarly articles, during his scholarly career, in philosophy, Greek classical studies, and Eastern Orthodox theology, hagiography, and history.

The Reverend Father Gregory Telepneff, a graduate of Yale University, received his doctoral degree in historical theology at the G.T.U., Berkeley. A retired married clergyman, he is a Senior Scholar at the C.T.O.S., former visiting scholar at the Harvard Divinity School, and former adjunct instructor at Anna Maria College in Paxton, Massachusetts. He is the author of several books and scholarly articles in patristic studies.

Introduction

THE DESIRE TO COMPILE a collection of writings on the early Greek Fathers and their attitudes towards classical learning has been germinating in my mind for almost five decades. This book, therefore, is conceptually the product of my composite intellectual and academic interests and activities over many years. The seed from which it springs was first planted when I was at the University of California, where as an undergraduate I studied church history under Professor Jeffrey Burton Russell, the distinguished medievalist, and where, as a graduate student with him and other mentors at two separate campuses of the university, I studied the history of the Byzantine ecclesiastical tradition. Later, as a doctoral student in psychology at Princeton University, my intense interest in concept formation and cognitive processes again turned my attention towards church history and patristic studies. It was at Princeton that I became an academic disciple of sorts of the Russian Orthodox theologian and patristic scholar, Father Georges Florovsky, who was teaching there after retiring from his professorial post at Harvard University. Florovsky, whose initial work in physiological psychology was published through the efforts of no less a figure than Ivan Pavlov in the last issue of the pre-revolutionary journal of the Russian Imperial Academy of Sciences, was no stranger to the world of psychology and learning theory. It would be perhaps cliché, yet inarguably true, to say that my friendship with him, therefore, was not just fortuitous, but serendipitous; indeed, with enthusiasm and vigor he helped me to refocus my psychological interests in learning and cognition on the Greek patristic tradition and arranged for me to publish some of the original research that grew out of my efforts.

A decade later, when I had resigned my first academic post (at the University of California) to become an Orthodox clergyman myself, it was one of Father Florovsky's colleagues at Harvard, the church historian

George Huntston Williams, who kindly helped me to secure the status of Visiting Scholar at the Harvard Divinity School in the Spring of 1983. My arrival at Harvard coincided with that of the late Henri Nouwen, the Dutch psychologist and Roman Catholic priest, who had just accepted a teaching post at the Divinity School. Father Nouwen's fascination with the nexus between psychology and religion, and especially as it was manifested in the lives of the desert Fathers, coincided with my own research interests: the derivation of a "patristic psychology" from a systematic examination of the writings, teachings, and spiritual experiences of the desert dwellers. Because of our common engrossment with the early Christian monastics, Nouwen and I continued to correspond after my departure from Harvard, and in addition to providing me with new insights into the psychology of religious experience, he made invaluable contributions to my thought about the classical Greek roots of the spirituality and theology of the desert Fathers and of the Greek patristic tradition in general.

It is not gratuitously or simply to acknowledge a debt of gratitude to Professor Russell and Fathers Nouwen and Florovsky that I have written the foregoing, even if I assuredly owe them such. Each one of these scholars, in his own way, broadened my perspective on classical learning and the epistemology of the early Christian Fathers. It was through interests spurred by Jeffrey Russell's writings on the early Christian world and its reception of classical Greek philosophy that I first encountered Werner Jaeger's three-volume work on classical *paideia* and his last published book, *Early Christianity and Greek Paideia*, which appeared in 1961.[1] The latter made Jaeger my *mentor bound in leather* by way of the written word. Father Florovsky, on his part, repeatedly urged me to study and to write about what he called the inseparability of classical Hellenism from Christianity, calling the former a cornerstone of the life and thought of the early Church and of the teachings of the Greek Fathers and affirming that Byzantine theology was an organic continuation of the patristic age.[2] Henri Nouwen, with whom I spoke and corresponded at length about the continuity of experience between the philosophical wisdom of the ancient Greeks and the spiritual or noetic enlightenment sought by the desert mystics and the Greek Fathers, helped me to look with ever greater perspicuity at this commonality of ethos between these two Greek traditions—one classical and one Christian—as part of a complementary but distinct view of the goal of

---

1. Jaeger, *Early Christianity and Greek Paideia*.
2. Florovsky, *Collected Works*, 4:20.

INTRODUCTION

human knowledge and learning. Consequently, to these individuals I owe the evolution of the present collection.

The nexus between ancient Greek philosophy and the Christian religion has been a matter of study and debate since the earliest Christian centuries, when these two foundational forces in Western civilization first encountered one another. Surprisingly, scholars and historians in the West have parsed the influence of Hellenism on Christian apologetics and the synthesis of the two traditions by the Greek Fathers according to a paradigm that has changed little—allowing, of course, for various refinements and minor thematic variations—up to modern times. It has been assumed, according to this model, that the fledgling Christian religion simply borrowed much of its form and content from the Greek mystery cults and other religious traditions, forming its anthropology and cosmology around the thinking of the ancients—Platonism and Aristotelianism in particular—and adroitly blending Hellenic philosophy and Christian doctrine into an intelligible simulacrum, through the "Christ narrative," of Jewish messianic visions, drawing from Old Testamental myths and epopees and from the language and imagery of the ancient world. This synthesis of Greek wisdom and Christian dogma, those who adhere to this thinking would argue, led to a hostility on the part of Christian apologists towards their philosophical progenitors, Christian theological writers having prepensely attributed to their synthesis of the Christian narrative and Greek wisdom a unique, universal quality. With the ascendancy of Holy Writ, or the canon of Christian Scripture, as the source of doctrine and authority in the new Christian religion, it was natural that the link between the ancients and the new people of the Christian realm should become increasingly blurred. Apologists for the nonpareil truth of Christianity increasingly dismissed what they came to dub "classical paganism." The Juggernaut of Christianity, with its inexorable dominance in the political and social life of the Western world, further created a tension between the waning dominance of Hellenistic thought and Christianity at a popular level, even if the philosophical methodology of the ancients has survived as the object of immense interest in Christian academic theology to this day.

Quite another perspective on the relationship between Christianity and the wisdom of the ancients, and especially the classical Greek philosophical tradition, has held sway in the Christian East since apostolic times, and it is reflected in a certain limited but symbiotic convergence of Hellenistic philosophical ideas with the theological precepts of the Greek

Fathers. According to this alternative model, the Greek philosophers, the Greek mystery cults, and other pre-Christian religions, though imperfect, of purely human and mundane provenance and thus spiritually barren and infecund, were nonetheless notional forerunners of Christian theology and religious practice. When conflated with the visionary insights of the Jewish prophets and of Jewish messianism, reckoned, by contrast, to be of divine origin and yielding foundational principles of revealed truth integral to Christian belief and experience, the imperfect and unfulfilled wisdom of the ancients served to pave the way for the unfolding of the *pleroma* of Christian teaching and its spiritually enlightening revelation. In their epistemological hierarchy, the Greek Fathers place great value on ancient wisdom as an access-point in approaching the mystery of spiritual cognitions (revealed or noetic truths); through sagacious insights and perceptions of an intellectual or dianoetic kind, one stands, as it were, in the antechamber of knowledge of a higher and mystical kind. One can effectively illustrate this relationship between the ancient Greek sage and the Christian adept in a passage from Homer's *Odyssey*, the second oldest extant piece of writing in the Western world (composed at the end of the eighth century BC), which, as we shall see, the Greek Fathers often cited, and in a similar pericope from the famous Epistle of the Apostle Paul to the Christians of Corinth (written shortly after the middle of the first century of the Christian era). Homer attributes to Telemachos, the son of Odysseus, the following statement about childish thought and the acquisition of intellectual ripeness: "ἤδη . . . νοέω καὶ οἶδα ἕκαστα . . . · πάρος δ' ἔτι νήπιος ἦα" (now I perceive and know each thing; whereas before I was childish).[3] In surprisingly similar language, St. Paul describes this same maturation, but with reference to spiritual discernment, in the following acclamation: "ὅτε ἤμην νήπιος, ὡς νήπιος ἐλάλουν . . . , ὅτε δὲ γέγονα ἀνήρ, κατήργηκα τὰ τοῦ νηπίου" (when I was a child, I spoke as a child . . . , but when I became a man, I did away with childish things).[4]

If the oft cited views of Tertullian (d. 225), who is frequently called the first Latin Father of the Christian Church and who rejected Greek philosophy and considered Plato, Aristotle, and other Greek thinkers nothing more than pre-Christian heretics, and indeed the *patriarchs* of heretics (*"patriarchae haereticorum"*),[5] lend force to the argument that Christianity

---

3. Homer, *Odyssey*, 20.309–10.
4. 1 Cor 13:11.
5. "De Anima," in *Patrologia Latina*, 2:651B.

Introduction

was disdainful of the Greek ancients, this is not true of the Greek Fathers. Though in certain Greek Fathers one may find at times even strident disapprobation of classical wisdom, the *consensus Patrum* in the East eschews any such notion, except as it is expressed in the affirmation of the lesser, yet complementary, status of the faculty of human learning in facilitating noetic enlightenment and the mystical knowledge of God to which it gives rise. The goal of Christian thought and life, as the Greek Fathers envision them, is the divinization of the human being (*theosis*) and the integration of his or her intellectual or dianoetic faculty with the νοῦς, or the spiritual faculty by which one experiences and understands revealed or higher truth. In the attainment of this latter primary goal, the secondary achievement of refining and expanding the mind to advance the reception of higher spiritual knowledge presupposes a synergy between the mental and the noetic, the worldly and the transcendent, and mundane learning and mystical (divine) knowledge. It is for this reason *par excellence* that the Greek Fathers often cite classical Greek writers, from Homer to thinkers of the so-called late Hellenistic period. Homer was, incidentally, hands down first and chief among the literary luminaries whom the Greek Fathers studied, praised, and cited, quoting him as they did the great Jewish patriarchs and prophets. Some of the more significant Saints of the Christian East—Gregory of Nyssa (d. *ca.* 395), Isidore of Pelusium (d. *ca.* 436), Basil the Great (d. 379), and John Chrysostomos (d. 407), to mention but a few—adorned their writings and homilies with Homeric citations. Even well into Byzantine times, the Greek Fathers reveled in the works of Greece's greatest epic poet. Thus a well-known maxim in Greek patristic studies: if one has not read and understood Homer, one cannot know and understand the Church Fathers. Correspondingly, if one cannot philosophize along with Plato and Aristotle, one cannot ascend to the heights of the clerisy of the Church. Hence, if the secular wisdom of the ancient Greeks was received by the latter with certain restraints, its natural incorporation into the enlightened doctrines of Christianity was a virtual canon of their theological discourse and rumination.

The high regard in which the Greek Fathers held the Greek ancients should not lead us to think, of course, that the restraints placed on the reception of Greek wisdom were simple window-dressing; in fact, they were essential and comprised certain ideational boundaries. Beholden and addicted as these Fathers were to the language, symbols, metaphors, similes, tropes, and magnificent rhetorical devices of the ancients, they did not use these indiscriminately. The Fathers were always eclectic in their appropriation of the ethos of Hellenism and drank through certain doctrinal filters from the wells of the ancients. It is often said, in this respect, that they "baptized" the richness of the classical tradition to adorn the spiritual splendor of the Christian message. Moreover, as the essays contained in this small volume will attest, the Greek Fathers did not share with the classical Greek world a common anthropology or cosmology; nor, to be sure, are the soteriological and eschatological ideas of the Eastern Church, on close examination, compatible with, let alone derived from, the teleological thinking of the Greek ancients. One must be sedulous to grasp this point, lest one slip back into the Western vision of a Christianity somehow grafted onto the trunk of philosophies from the Hellenic and Hellenistic periods. Likewise, it should not be assumed that, in the fervor with which they incorporated much from the ancients into the corpus of Christian apologetic works and theological expositions, the Greek Fathers somehow elevated the Greek philosophers and sages to the status of the Jewish prophets, to whom Eastern Christian writers attribute genuine spiritual enlightenment. At all times, despite their great admiration for its luminaries, the Greek Fathers saw the ancient Greek world as imperfect, in need of spiritual restoration, and, though wise, still bereft of spiritual perfection. That their *apparent* tergiversation with regard to classical wisdom rises *in reality* from within the core of Christian oeconomia is evidenced by an anecdote from the seventh century, recounted by St. Anastasios of Sinai. According to Anastasios, "ancient tradition" tells us that "a certain lawyer uttered many imprecations against Plato the philosopher. Plato, therefore, appeared to him when he was asleep, saying: 'O man, desist from cursing me, for you are harming yourself.' Plato," Anastasios continues, "went on to tell the lawyer that, 'when Christ descended into Hades, in truth no one believed in Him before I did.'"[6] In short, the Greek Fathers, while poignantly responsive to the wisdom of the ancients, at all times saw them through the prism of their Christian worldview—in this case, with something akin to theological paternalism.

I would like to conclude these introductory remarks by returning to the scholarship of Werner Jaeger, the dean, as it were, of the limited number of classical scholars who have moved beyond classical learning, or Greek *paideia*, to study what St. Clement of Rome, in the first century of the Christian era, called "παιδεία ἐν Χριστῷ," or Christian learning. The significance of Professor Jaeger's contributions to our understanding of Christian education is inestimable. His pivotal work on Christian learning and erudition

---

6. "Questions and Answers," Question 111, in *Patrologia Graeca*, 89:764BD.

INTRODUCTION

preoccupied him towards the end of his career, when he dedicated himself especially to the works of St. Gregory of Nyssa. These interests led him, despite his Protestant background and the fact that he received his secondary education in a Roman Catholic school (at the Gymnasium Thomaeum in Kempen, Germany), away from a Western paradigm in assessing the nature and theological ethos of the Greek Fathers, the consensus of whom he so perfectly expresses in many ways. He came to understand that they had as much Christianized the Hellenic witness, with their novel anthropology and radically different cosmology, as Greek *paideia* had Hellenized their Christianity with its richness of philosophical diversity, magnificence of expression, and what the Greek Fathers would call their "intuitions" about Christian revelation. In his perspicacity, Jaeger helped to pave the way for a meeting of the Classics and the Greek Fathers that moves beyond doctrinal and sectarian concerns, drawing us into a realm of common striving for the truth that neither overestimates the contributions of the ancients to Christian learning and culture nor imputes to Greek *paideia* an insignificant place in the expression and development of Clement's παιδεία ἐν Χριστῷ. Perhaps without full cognizance of the fruitfulness of looking at early Christianity through the eyes of the Greek patristic witness—and by no means, in so doing, denigrating or ignoring the Latin Fathers and their Western scions—Jaeger struck on that fulcrum on which one can so perfectly balance the search of the Hellenic sages for lofty philosophical wisdom against the nisus of the Greek Fathers to reach transcendent enlightenment.

The balance that emerges from Jaeger's last published work is the *deliberate aim* of the essays contained in this short book, which center on the classical Greek wisdom tradition as the Greek Fathers approached, understood, and selectively incorporated it into their search for *theosis* and the harmony of learning and spiritual knowledge. I believe, from a heuristic standpoint, that these essays collectively constitute a fruitful strategy, in the spirit of Professor Jaeger, for looking anew at the Greek classical world and Christianity through the eyes of the Greek Fathers, who were, as we must remember, the *direct inheritors* of the ancient Greek worldview.

Metropolitan Chrysostomos
Etna, California

Bibliography

Florovsky, Georges. *The Collected Works of Georges Florovsky*. Edited by Richard S. Haugh. 14 vols. Vaduz, Liechtenstein: Büchervertriebsanstalt, 1987–89.

Homer. *Opera*. Edited by Thomas W. Allen. 2nd ed. Oxford: Clarendon, 1919.

Jaeger, Werner. *Early Christianity and Greek Paideia*. Cambridge: Belknap Press of Harvard University Press, 1961.

Migne, J.-P., ed. *Patrologiae Cursus Completus, Series Graeca*. 161 vols. Paris: 1857–66.

———. *Patrologiae Cursus Completus, Series Latina*. 221 vols. Paris: 1844–64.

CHAPTER 1

Man and His Universe in Hellenistic Thought and the Greek Fathers

*The Reverend Gregory Telepneff and
the Most Reverend Chrysostomos*

THE RELATIONSHIP BETWEEN HELLENISTIC thought and the theology of the Greek Fathers is one that is frequently misunderstood by both Western theologians and not a few Eastern Orthodox theologians (and especially those in the West), not only because they look with an uncritical eye at classical Greek philosophy itself, but also because they often overlook the clear process of development, during the first few centuries of Christianity, that led to a remarkable unity of thought in the Greek patristic understanding of the cosmos and man. Thus it is that various theologians and church historians hold forth with sweeping, and even naïve and unctuous, pronouncements against the Platonic or Aristotelian (and, among the less careful, even Gnostic) foundations of this or that Eastern patristic notion. Indeed, even many an ingenuous scholar has elegized the Greek Fathers with tales of their woeful fall to the traps of Hellenistic paganism.

One cannot deny, of course, the existence of certain affinities between the corpus of patristic writings, both Eastern and Western, and Hellenism. Nor would we wish to disclaim certain general intuitions and experiences, as it were, held in common in these respective systems of thought. But the Greek Fathers, in borrowing language, images, and ideas from the Greek philosophers, maintained, in this process, views that are, on careful examination, quite at odds with the cosmology and anthropology of the Greek ancients. One might even say that their debt to Hellenistic thought is not so much that of *a student to his mentor* as that of *a sculptor to his stone*. The Greek Fathers built with the basic materials of Greek philosophy, but what they produced was different in form and in intent from that philosophy. Though they were beholden to the ancients and saw themselves standing in a tradition that linked Hellenistic wisdom to Christian enlightenment, the very vision of what it was that they were to form from the stone of their philosophical forefathers, in fact, flowed from a view of man and the universe that the Greek classical philosophers would have considered revolutionary.

The Greek Fathers believed and taught that God had acted through Israel and the Jewish people to prepare the human mind and heart for the coming of Christ. They also felt that the "fullness of time" rested in the Hellenes. Providence had appointed the Greeks, too, if not the Roman Empire itself, as a vehicle for the dissemination of Christianity. One would perhaps not wish to call this appointment a "covenant"; but certainly it was not, for the Greek Fathers, adventitious. There were, according to the Fathers, hints of Christian truth in Hellenism, and some of its ideas could be employed in the promulgation of the Christian faith. Thus, the Fathers were eclectic and not, as many suppose, syncretic in their incorporation of Hellenism into the task of Christian philosophizing or, more precisely, theologizing. St. Justin the Martyr, for example, though he characterizes Plato as a "Christian before Christ," emphasizes that many Platonic ideas about the soul and the world are incompatible with Christian teachings. St. Gregory the Theologian also suggested that, though Hellenistic language was useful to the Christian theologian, it had to be "baptized" and "transformed" to convey adequately the Christian experience. The "old skins" could not completely hold the "new wine." For the Greek Fathers, the final criterion in any decision to use the *tool* of Greek philosophy in teaching Christian truth was whether or not it conformed to Christian spiritual *experience,* the life and experience of the Faith. Hellenistic wisdom was never thought to be adequate in and of itself. St. Gregory of Nyssa summarizes what we have said, when he writes that "pagan philosophy says that the soul is immortal. This is a pious offspring. But it also says that souls pass from body to body and are changed from a rational to an irrational nature. This is a fleshly and alien foreskin. And there are many other such examples.... It acknowledges [God] as creator, but says He needed matter for creation. It affirms that He is both good and powerful, but that in all things He submits to the necessity of fate."[1] Ultimately, for Gregory of Nyssa Greek philosophy was as if "always in labor but never giving birth."[2]

1. *Life of Moses*, II.40, 63.
2. Ibid., II.11, 57.

Man and His Universe in Hellenistic Thought

I. P. Sheldon-Williams, in his general investigation of the relations between Christian and Hellenistic thought, very much supports what we have said about Hellenism and the Greek patristic tradition.³ He identifies, in particular, three Hellenistic ideas about the cosmos and the person that are at odds with early Christian (essentially Greek patristic) thought: the eternity of the cosmos, the inherently divine nature of the human soul, and the dualistic belief that the soul is a substance distinct from the body and, therefore, ultimately destined to a disembodied existence. The most compelling support for Sheldon-Williams's insights is the fact that the three major areas of divergence between Christian and Hellenic thought that he identifies mirror, and quite closely so, those very principles of Christian doctrine which Synesios of Cyrene, Christian Bishop of Ptolemais (*ca.* 410) and a former Platonic philosopher, had such difficulty accepting before his conversion. In his "105th Letter," Synesios cites what were initially for him problematic areas of Christian thought: the denial of the eternity of the world; the denial of the pre-existence of souls (a corollary to the doctrine of the soul's συγγένεια or inherent co-naturality with the divine); and the doctrine of the resurrection of the body. To be sure, his confession confirms, as Sheldon-Williams also contends with us, that the Hellenic world and the spiritual milieu of the Greek Fathers, at very least with regard to the foregoing important issues, were anything but a marriage of like *Weltanschauungen* and similar cosmologies and anthropologies.

The classical Greek doctrine of the eternity of the cosmos stands in total contradiction to the Christian belief that God created the world *ex nihilo*, and thus the nature of the universe is quite different for the Hellenistic thinker and the Greek Father. The primary ontological categories in Hellenistic thought, the intelligible and the sensible realms ("God" at the height of the intelligible), are foreign to patristic thought. The Church Fathers divide reality into Uncreated (God) and created realms, distinctions between the intelligible and noetic and the sensible and material belonging to the created realm.⁴ The dualistic ontology of the Hellenistic philosophers constitutes a metaphysics which is not only at odds with that of Christian ontology, but which, more specifically, cannot accommodate the Christian notion of redemption. The structure of Hellenistic ontology renders the Christian doctrine of redemption meaningless, since the Christian ontology of the Greek Fathers is decidedly Theocentric and thus rests on the

---

3. See his chapters in Part VI of Armstrong, ed., *Cambridge History*, 425–533.
4. Ibid., 426.

restoration of creation to its Creator.⁵ This ontology is inconsistent with an ontology focused on essentially intellectual elements.

Thus, because they believed in its essential immortality and incorruptibility, the pivotal Christian doctrine of an incarnational scheme to redeem the soul from sin and ontological corruption is absent from the thought of the ancient Greek philosophers.⁶ According to Hellenistic philosophy, the soul is enlightened by γνῶσις, which reminds it of, and recalls it to, its extant, but obscured, original and pristine state. The soul is not in need of the ontological renewal or transfiguration afforded by the Incarnation of God; nor is it necessary for one to overcome "sin." In the mind of the ancients, God and the *novus homo*, if the latter term even obtains in the Hellenistic tradition, were reached and attained through γνῶσις and intellectual contemplation; while, in Christian teaching, God in essence is never available to the intellect and spiritual revelation transcends the capacities of human knowledge as such.⁷

The Christian doctrine of enlightenment and the restoration of the soul also centers on divine Grace. Since the soul is not inherently immortal or divine, the human person must "acquire" something above and beyond human nature, in order to achieve salvation, enlightenment, the restoration of the soul, and communion with God. Moreover, the soul, according to the Greek patristic view, cannot acquire this "something" (knowledge or vision, if you will) by its own power. Instead, it must rely on a divine act, the Grace of divine revelation and the Grace of the Incarnation, by which potential perfection is offered to mankind in the ontological restoration of the human soul. Indeed, the difference between the Hellenistic (and especially Platonic) vision of human enlightenment and that of the Greek Fathers centers on two radically different views of God and the world, on a "Metaphysics of Intellect" and a "Metaphysics of Grace."⁸

5. Ibid.

6. John Romanides very persuasively argues that the idea of salvation from sin and ontological corruption is a fundamentally biblical concept in his essay, "Original Sin According to St. Paul." For those who wish to pursue the issue of restored human ontology, see Tsirpanlis, "Aspects of Maximian Theology."

7. Bouyer, Review of *Origins of the Christian Mystical Tradition*.

8. Compare Sheldon-Williams, in *Cambridge History*, 427. One might argue that later Hellenistic philosophers, such as Plotinos, come closer to a Christian metaphysics. Despite such contentions, however, even later Hellenistic thought ultimately purports that it is the "purified mind," reduced to a state of pure simplicity, which "reaches" God. A Christian concept of effective Grace is wholly absent from such a scheme. See in this regard Dörrie, "Was Ist 'Spätantiker Platonismus'?" esp. 293, 301ff.

Hellenistic somatology, finally, conceives of the body as an illusion which binds and frustrates the actions of the divine soul: a "prison," in Platonic parlance, holding man captive. Though careless observers often attribute such Hellenistic beliefs to the Greek Fathers, these beliefs in fact stand, as Sheldon-Williams rightly argues, in sharp and obvious contrast to Christian somatology and its doctrine of the "rehabilitation" of the body.[9] A fundamental element of Christian teaching is that the body will be resurrected with the soul at the *Parousia*, and no small number of Greek patristic writings is devoted to the explication and defense of this dogma. By the same token, since the "lower" psychic[10] and sensible faculties of the body participate in its general restoration, it is not only the body, but physical perception and the senses that are transformed in the spiritual life and fully regenerated at the General Resurrection. Christian *theosis*, or divinization, is fulfilled in the Resurrection, when the wholeness of the body and soul are restored. This patristic teaching could not be more greatly removed from the Hellenistic idea of enlightenment and the escape of the human soul from the chains of the body.

The late Protopresbyter Georges Florovsky has also dealt extensively in his writings with the relationship between patristic thought and Hellenism.[11] He emphasizes especially the transformation which Hellenistic thought underwent as it was incorporated into the thought of the Greek Fathers. In one characteristic passage, he writes that:

> Usually we do not sufficiently perceive the entire significance of this transformation which Christianity introduced into the realm of [Hellenistic] thought.... It is sufficient to point out just a few examples: the idea of the createdness of the world, not only in its transitory and perishable aspect but also in its primordial principles. For Greek thought the idea of "created ideas" was impossible and offensive. And bound up with this was the Christian intuition of history as a unique—once-occurring—creative fulfillment, the sense of movement from an actual "beginning" up to a final "end," a feeling for history which in no way at all allows itself to be linked with the static *pathos* of ancient Greek thought. And the understanding of man as person, the concept of personality, was entirely

---

9. Ibid., 426.
10. The patristic θυμός and ἐπιθυμία and the Hellenistic νοῦς and λογιστικόν.
11. See his *Collected Works*, "Creation and Creaturehood," "Redemption," "The 'Immortality' of the Soul," and "The Last Things and the Last Events," chaps. in vol. 3; "The Patristic Age and Eschatology," chap. in vol. 4.

inaccessible to Hellenism, which considered only the πρόσωπον or mask as person. And finally there is the message of Resurrection in glorified but real flesh, a thought which could only frighten the Greeks, who lived in the hope of future dematerialization of the spirit.... These are the presuppositions and categories of a new Christian philosophy....[12]

One of the most important differences between Hellenistic philosophy and Greek patristic thought cited by Father Florovsky is their divergent concept of time and history. This subject deserves our special attention, since it helps to focus the more general distinctions in cosmology and anthropology noted by Sheldon-Williams. Father Florovsky says specifically of time and history:

> Greek Philosophy was dominated by the ideas of permanence and recurrence. There could be but a disclosure [i.e., in history] of the pre-existing fulness. [Even] Aristotle made this point with a complete frankness: "What is 'of necessity' coincides with what is 'always,' since that which 'must be' cannot possibly 'not be.'... If, therefore, the 'coming-to-be' of a thing is necessary, its 'coming-to-be' is eternal.... It follows that the 'coming-to-be' of anything, if it is absolutely necessary, must be cyclical, i.e., must return upon itself.... It is in circular movement, therefore, and in cyclical 'coming-to-be,' that the 'absolutely necessary' is to be found" (*de gen. et corr.*, II.2, 338a).[13]

Florovsky concludes that: "Greek philosophy was always concerned rather with the 'first principles' than with the 'last things'.... [In the Greek conception], no increase in 'being' is conceivable.... The true reality is always 'behind' ["from eternity"], never 'ahead.'"[14]

As Father Florovsky's clear statements aver, Christian thought and Hellenism part ways with regard to the eschatological and historical nature of human experience and the cosmos. Even for Aristotle, who moved away from some of the accepted categories of earlier Hellenistic thought, history was still not history as such, but a disclosure of a pre-existing fullness. His ἐντελέχεια, or teleology, while linear in form, is still rooted in the notion of fixed, eternal, and pre-existing forms. Teleological development is simply a "disclosure" in individual development of an end. History, whether personal

---

12. Ibid., 3:33–34.
13. Ibid., 4:68–69.
14. Ibid.

or universal, therefore, never leads to the creation and development of new and unique forms or modes of existence; it is not directive in its nature. Aristotelian and Hellenistic thought in general could not tolerate the idea that a thing could become more perfect in kind by acquiring some characteristic that was not implicit in its nature from the beginning.[15] The eternal cosmos, in its essential principles or λόγοι, exists from the very inception, or ἀρχή, of existence in a state of full perfection. Any sense of "regaining" one's lost original nature (as in the Neo-Platonic ἐπιστροφή) is, therefore, still always an historically "unproductive" act. One simply returns to the primordial state, and both personal and universal history have only a provisionary significance; history adds nothing to the essence of a being.

In the Greek patristic scheme of things, history is significant, since it records a productive sequence of events both in the personal and universal sense. It is a productive unfolding in time and space of something creative: a move toward the ἔσχατον and the restoration of the fallen universe—a restoration which embodies perfection and which moves creation from glory to glory, from lost perfection to "greater perfection." If we understand this Christian notion of time and space, then we come to see the wrongness of attributions of Platonic world-views, by some Western (and Westernized Orthodox) scholars, to such renowned Greek Fathers as St. Gregory of Nyssa and St. Dionysios the Areopagite. The Greek Fathers speak of movement *into* eternity in a manner which gives meaning to historical existence, since the virtues, spiritual character, and "perfection" are "acquired" in embodied existence and in time and space. Indeed, the very flesh indissolubly linked to the human soul during the course of embodied existence is "translated" into eternity and participates in Divinity. It is not shed but transformed. Though not everything in temporal empirical existence is so transformed—but only that which has a referent in the divine and eternal realm—there is obviously a very fundamental divergence between the Greek patristic understanding of the importance of historical existence and that of the Greek ancients.

Let us now emphasize that the Christian idea of "productive" free will is a direct outgrowth of the stress which the Greek Fathers place on the entry of historical, empirical bodies into eternity. By exercising choice, the human being accomplishes a spiritual task *within history*. Though this task is ultimately perfected in the ἔσχατον, it is actualized by free action in time and space. The ancient Greek view of the cosmos is *a*-productive, as it were.

---

15. See also Mascall, *Openness of Being*, 246.

The Sculptor and His Stone

For the Hellenistic philosophers, though the universe is in motion, this motion is inefficacious, since it effects no alteration in the essences or ideas of things.[16] Empirical "reality" is defined only with reference to these essences of things and constitutes what is essentially a "closed" ontology. Their ontological scheme is inconsistent with the dynamic patristic idea that creatures are not only created out of nothing, but that they are also created in a state of relative spiritual immaturity. History describes the process of *attaining* to perfection: a productive passing of time in which the human will and person have critical meaning.

Father Florovsky has also placed great emphasis in his writings on another essential area of concern which highlights the differences between the Hellenistic philosophers and the Greek Fathers: *human personhood*.[17] Here, especially, we see that Hellenistic philosophical terms and categories are radically transformed in their patristic usage. *In fact, the Greek patristic concept of personality is a uniquely Christian contribution to the history of thought.* As Florovsky notes, in their understanding of the relationship between the human soul and the body, the Greek Fathers were actually closer to Aristotle than to Plato.[18] *Prima facie,* this appears strange, since, strictly speaking, Aristotelian anthropology and cosmology make no claims for life after death: nothing human passes beyond the grave, and man's singular being does not survive death. Nonetheless, Father Florovsky argues that Aristotle understood the unity of human existence, of the body and soul, at an intuitive level. Aristotle understood better than any of the Greek philosophers the empirical wholeness of human existence, and thus empirical existence and the human personality took on an importance for him that could not be detached from the eternal elements of the soul. And so, he discounted the idea of a transmigration of souls to other bodies, in that he could not free himself from a compelling respect for the unity of these two elements of the human person. He never came to attribute permanence or an immortal dimension to the person, but the foundations for such an attribution are everywhere to be found in his thought.

The Greek Fathers, according to Florovsky, drew on Aristotle's notion of the mortal unity of body and soul and effected a synthesis, of sorts, from

---

16. Compare Zizioulas, *Being*, 71–72.

17. In particular, see his chapter, "The Patristic Age and Eschatology," *Collected Works*, 4:63–78.

18. Ibid., 75.

this and the impersonal[19] and eternal νοῦς of Plato.[20] The patristic witness affirms the integrity and eternal dimension of empirical, embodied, and uniquely individual human existence and, at the same time, pays homage to the noetic qualities of existence that Plato reserved only for the soul. There is a direct continuity of the person from the mundane to the spiritual realm, not only by virtue of the resurrection of the body, but because individual personality, formed and shaped in time and space, survives in its uniqueness outside time and space. In essence, this patristic synthesis is a rejection of body-soul dualism, since the life of the material body and its sensible faculties acquire an ultimate significance, or at least possess a referent in the eternal or divine realm. In their transformation of Platonic and Aristotelian precepts, the Greek Fathers were able to convey with loyalty the unique Christian idea of the person, without indeed tainting that teaching with the foibles of Hellenistic dualism.

John Zizioulas, following Father Florovsky's observations about the synthesis of the Platonic and Aristotelian concepts by which the Greek Fathers formulated a Christian statement of personhood, makes some interesting comments about the implications of this synthesis for a Christian ontology. His arguments also provide an opportunity to see the crucial differences which separate Greek patristic and Hellenistic thought at the most fundamental of levels. Zizioulas observes that Aristotle's notion of man as a psychosomatic entity void of an eternal or permanent quality renders impossible the conceptual union of the "person" (πρόσωπον) with the "substance" (οὐσία) of man. Thus Aristotelian man has no true ontology. For Plato, the soul can be united with another physical body; through reincarnation, it can assume another "individuality" and thus ensure a kind of human, but not unique, personal continuity. Greek philosophical thought, then, is unable to endow human individuality with unique permanence and, therefore, with a true ontology of the *person*. This is partly because, for the Hellenistic sages, being in the final analysis is an eternally existing unity (in spite of the multiplicity of existent things),[21] and every differentiation within the course of embodied human existence is nothing more than a falling away from the unity of true being.[22] Individual human personhood compromises ontologi-

---

19. The doctrine of μετεμψύχωσις denies the personal continuity of the soul in Platonism.

20. Florovsky, *Collected Works*, 4:77.

21. Zizioulas, *Being*, 29.

22. Plotinos tries to solve this dilemma by offering positive "reasons" for this falling

cal unity. Hellenistic notions of the universe lead to a kind of "ontological monism," from which not even God—merely the first of the hierarchy of intelligible beings—can escape.[23] Moreover, Zizioulas notes, from the standpoint of Hellenistic ontology, humans are never free to add or contribute anything significant to "being" or existence. True being, in its essential sense, exists already from the *arche* of existence. In the words of Plutarch, "no particular thing, not even the least, can be otherwise than according to common nature and reason (*logos*)."[24] For the Greeks, Zizioulas concludes, existence is therefore determined by a pre-existing necessity.

It is also important to note that the term πρόσωπον, or "person," originally denoted in Greek theatre the mask worn by an actor as he played various roles. In Hellenistic philosophy the term continued to convey the idea of a temporary "role" assumed or played by an individual in his temporal life. It is not used to describe the true "hypostasis" of an individual, and ultimately *remains without ontological content*.[25] To the classical Greeks, Zizioulas contends, personhood was no more than an *adjunct* to concrete ontological being.[26] Of course the Greek ancients had intuitions about individual personality;[27] this one cannot deny. The point is that these intuitions were never so strong as to prompt the Hellenistic philosophers to find, in temporal existence, real significance—anything beyond the temporary and illusory world of the "mask"; and again, therefore, to find in the individual personality traits suggestive of a genuine ontology.[28]

In patristic thought, personhood has ontological authenticity because in synergy, in conjunction with the will of God, the human is responsible for his or her own destiny. The soul is not *inherently* immortal, but only so with regard to its συγγένεια with the divine realm. The soul possesses Divinity "thetically," that is, in a *thetic* participation, a participation by free will, in God. God has, of course, given eternal life to humankind as an act

---

away, but he ultimately attributes only a derived "goodness" to these "reasons," which fall short of the ideal "good."

23. Zizioulas, *Being*, 29.

24. Ibid., 32. Interestingly enough, Professor Zizioulas believes that Plutarch linked the *logos* with nature and fate, another element in Hellenistic ontology that the Greek Fathers would have rejected *prima facie*.

25. Ibid., 31–33.

26. Ibid., 34.

27. Compare G. C. Stead, "Individual Personality in Origen and the Cappadocian Fathers," in *Origeniana*. See esp. his remarks on Proclos.

28. Zizioulas, *Being*, 35.

of His own will and energies. But there is also a higher level of existence, in which the person comes to virtuous well-being and full communion with God. It is this level of participation that the creature must acquire within the course of embodied historical existence and by an exercise of the will. Thus a personal encounter with God in temporal existence, in an historical context, and in an "existential" way, one might say, brings the human person (and, as we have noted above, both personal and universal history) into the eternal realm, endowing him, in this synergistic interaction, with its energetic character, a character inaccessible to the human person in Hellenistic thought.[29]

In the Greek Fathers, the historical existence of the person, the individual human person as a psychosomatic whole of complementary elements of soul and body, is linked to the eternal human essence, the individual *logos*, or genuine identity. Human empirical existence is given an ontological foundation in the patristic identification of ὑπόστασις with πρόσωπον and with its translation or movement into eternal existence. Even the very course of the productive acquisition of virtue by which the personality attains to genuine ontology is, for the Greek Fathers, a participation (μετουσία), or "sharing," in divine existence, and therefore possesses an eternal dimension itself.

Certainly our discussion, along many dimensions, of man and the cosmos in Hellenistic and Greek patristic thought leaves little doubt that the Greek Fathers cannot be accused by any justifiable criterion of contamination, as the doctrinaire Christian thinkers would characterize it, by the dualism and cosmological and anthropological limitations which rendered history, the body, human existence, and temporal experience *ontologically* insignificant for the Greek ancients. Rather, a careful and objective examination of the larger paradigms and presuppositions which underlie these two approaches to reality, as it were, reveals that the Greek Fathers—if we may express this without pejorative implication—"contaminated" Hellenistic philosophy by borrowing its insights into ontological truth, its terminology, and to some extent its philosophical methodology and adapting them to the revelations of Christian truth: "baptizing" them and transforming them. Only the most superficial or polemical observers, even from such a cursory treatment as our present one, can argue that the Greek Fathers were anything but seekers after old bottles for new wine, readily and acutely conscious that, lest the new wine be spoiled in these old vessels, they had

---

29. Ibid., 39.

to cleanse and purify them of certain residues from former content. Such is a proper and intellectually honest image of the Greek Fathers as they undertook to use, transform, and remold Hellenistic thought.

Bibliography

Armstrong, A. H., ed. *The Cambridge History of Later Greek and Early Medieval Philosophy*. Cambridge: Cambridge University Press, 1967.

Bouyer, Louis. Review of *The Origins of the Christian Mystical Tradition*, by Andrew Louth. *Sobornost* 4.1 (1982) 70–74.

Crouzel, Henri, Gennaro Lomiento, and Josep Rius-Camps, eds. *Origeniana: Premier Colloque International des Études Origéniennes*. Bari: Istituto di Letteratura Cristiana Antica, Università di Bari, 1975.

Dörrie, H. "Was Ist 'Spätantiker Platonismus'? Überlegungen zur Grenzziehung zwischen Platonismus und Christentum." *Theologische Rundschau* N.F. 36 (1971) 285–302.

Florovsky, Georges. *The Collected Works of Georges Florovsky*. Edited by Richard S. Haugh. 5 vols. Belmont, MA: Nordland, 1972–1979.

———. *The Collected Works of Georges Florovsky*. Edited by Richard S. Haugh. 14 vols. Vaduz, Liechtenstein: Büchervertriebsanstalt, 1987–89.

Gregory of Nyssa, St. *The Life of Moses*. Translated by Abraham J. Malherbe and Everett Ferguson. New York: Paulist, 1978.

Mascall, E. L. *The Openness of Being*. London: Darton, Longman and Todd, 1971.

Romanides, John S. "Original Sin according to St. Paul." *St. Vladimir's Seminary Quarterly* 4.1–2 (1955–56) 5–28.

Tsirpanlis, Constantine. "Aspects of Maximian Theology of Politics, History, and the Kingdom of God." *The Patristic and Byzantine Review* 1.1 (1982) 1–21.

Zizioulas, John D. *Being As Communion*. Crestwood, NY: St. Vladimir's Seminary Press, 1985.

CHAPTER 2

Body, Soul, and Spirit in the Greek Ancients and in the Greek Fathers and Their Theological Legacy in Eastern Orthodox Christianity

The Most Reverend Chrysostomos

> "[I]f we understand ourselves to be organic creatures, then no part can be fully disaggregated..., and all elements of the self are interlocked."
>
> CAROLYN T. BROWN[1]

IN THE PAST THREE or four decades, philosophy, psychology, and medicine in the West have consciously embraced the idea that the body and the mind, or the body and soul, are inseparable parts of the whole human person. Holistic ideas have become part of the social discourse. Whether as a consequence of this trend or as part of whatever it is that ultimately sparked it, there is a renewed interest in spirituality, in the religions of the East (where the mind-body, or soul-body, dualism that has long reigned in Western thinking holds little sway), and in philosophies and ways of thought that address the person as a whole and aim at the restoration of that wholeness. However, an holistic view of the human being is nothing unique to Western intellectual thought, even if the rise of rationalism and the decline in spiritual concerns that followed the Renaissance and, more strikingly, the Enlightenment have tended to separate matters of the mind from those of the body and, most certainly, of the spirit. The Greek

---

1. Brown, *Footprints of the Soul*, 53.

ancients, to whom we attribute the rudimentary elements of our Western intellectual tradition, not only consistently called for an immediate engagement between philosophy and the study of the physical body,[2] but firmly believed that the human being was made up of body and soul. This was a fundamental feature of their world-view, shaping their anthropology and their highest social and political ideals: man the rational animal, engaged in fulfilling his physical and material needs, yet accommodating, in that effort, the lofty and more noble qualities and virtues of the soul.

As Constantine Cavarnos observes, this bipartite vision of man is one of the basic elements of the philosophy of life set forth by Pythagoras, who believed that the source of human illness was a state of disharmony between the body and the soul and that wellness lay in the "process of banishing disharmony and restoring harmony in the body and the psyche."[3] Plato, too, Cavarnos says, embraced this universal teaching of the ancients about the connection between body and soul, telling us—in positing a hierarchy in that relationship—that "in the last analysis, the condition of the body is a result of the condition of the psyche."[4] He points out that certain pathological mental conditions, in which an individual is "distraught" or "incapable of exercising reason," have, according to Plato, as their "proximate cause a bad bodily state." This state, nonetheless, derives from matters of the soul and is the result of "wrong education and a wrong mode of life."[5] In Aristotle, as well, we find clear evidence of the classical Greek belief in man as a composite of body and soul,[6] in which, as Cavarnos confirms (quoting Aristotle's *Politics*), "it is natural for the body to be governed by the soul."[7] All in all, then, in addition to believing that the human being is

---

2. Professor Constantine Cavarnos cites, for example, Plutarch's "emphatic rejection of the view that the subjects of *philosophy (philosophía)* and *medical science (iatriké)* are 'separate.'" See Cavarnos, *Plutarch's Advice*, 15–16.

3. Cavarnos, *Pythagoras*, 24.

4. Cavarnos, *Fine Arts*, 14.

5. Ibid., 29. At this juncture, it should also be said that there have been a few psychoanalysts who, though certainly rare exceptions, even early on in the development of the psychoanalytic movement held to a holistic view of the human being that included spiritual elements. One such example was the Venetian psychiatrist Robert Assagioli (1888–1974), a student of Freud and the father of so-called "psychosynthesis." His psychosynthetic system envisioned a "higher Self" that served to bring about harmony in the whole human being—mind, body, and spirit. See a synopsis of his ideas in *Psychosynthesis*.

6. Cavarnos, *Aristotle's Theory*, 15–16.

7. Ibid., 23.

made up of body and soul and that the soul dominates the body, the Greek ancients also maintain that a proper and harmonious interaction between the body and soul is the source of human health and reflects a correct way of life; indeed, it is the stuff of that "wonder" that is man at his best and which Sophocles so eloquently praises in his *Antigone*: "Πολλὰ τὰ δεινὰ κοὐδὲν ἀνθρώπου δεινότερον πέλει (Wonders are many, and none is more wonderful than man)."[8]

The Anthropology of the Greek Fathers

The Judeo-Christian tradition (if I may be allowed that somewhat imprecise and often misused designation), with its undeniable influence on the development of Western intellectual trends, also emphasizes, of course, the nexus between the body, soul, and mind, as evidenced by—if nothing else—the fact that it was the very object of the countertrend of the rationalist tradition, which sought to separate the body from the mind and soul and, ultimately, to engender the Cartesian body-mind dualism, in its various forms, that has so long preoccupied Western philosophy. Within the Christian tradition, the writings of the Greek Fathers have always underscored the unity of body and soul with special emphasis. As Jean-Claude Larchet writes:

> [T]he Fathers strive constantly to defend a balance in understanding the constitution of the human being: the two substances which comprise him are distinct without being separated and united without being confused. "The soul is united to the body," St. Symeon the New Theologian writes, "in an unutterable and indiscernible manner, in a fusion without admixture or confusion."[9]

It is not by accident, of course, that the patristic language which Larchet cites—nomenclature typical of that used by the Greek Fathers—is reminiscent of the language of the Christological controversies, which resulted, in the mid-fifth century, in a schism between the so-called "Chalcedonian" and "Non-Chalcedonian" Christian communities that persists to this day. The issues raised, in the attempt to describe the Nature of God, and that led to the Synod of Chalcedon (451), mirror patristic concerns about the nature of man. While contemporary theologians often dismiss these

---

8. Sophocles, *Antigone*, 332–33.
9. Larchet, *Thérapeutique des Maladies Mentales*, 29.

controversies as meaningless academic arguments over "terminology" and inessentials, they were, in actuality, centered on complex, technical distinctions and refinements in language that touched on essential conceptual distinctions with immense soteriological importance. The vocabulary which the disputants used was designed to safeguard the integrity of the Christian understanding of God, the human being, and the image of God in man, in the light of the Incarnation.

The reduction of such vital concerns to supposed matters of terminology is no more intelligent or historically valid than the popular pseudo-intellectual and nescient penchant for portraying the Emperor Constantine as a non-believer who, out of political motivation, *dictated* to the assembly of Church Fathers the theological formulae that they sanctioned at the Nicene Synod in 325. According to the vapid popular myth of a Christianity created by imperial machination, rather than attempting to preserve the core of vital Christian experience in which Trinitarian and Christological doctrines were reified, "Roman [Hellenic] Orthodoxy," this phantom of a post-Nicene Christianity serving the ends of theocratic imperialism, "transformed a large portion of the Christian East into heretics."[10] This is not unlike another absurdity peddled by purveyors of pulp fiction passing as historical fact: the contention, proffered with anserine consequences, that the orthodox canon of Scripture adopted by the early Church deliberately obfuscated the genuine Christian tradition, rather than contain it and protect it (as it candidly purported to do) from extraneous influences. The fact is that, by closely defining the nature of the human soul, as we shall see, the Greek Fathers sought to preserve an understanding of human nature

---

10. See Reza Aslan, *No god but God*, 11. Referring to misapprehensions like those of Aslan, and reacting to what she sees as the literalism of Isaac Newton's approach to Trinitarian doctrine, Karen Armstrong makes some insightful statements about the actual *theological* principles underlying the "Roman Orthodoxy" of Constantinople: "The Greek Orthodox theologians of the fourth century," she argues, spoke of the Trinity "precisely as *mythos*, similar to that later created by the Jewish Kabbalists. As Gregory of Nyssa had explained, the three *hypostases* of Father, Son, and Spirit were not objective facts but simply 'terms that we use' to express the way in which the 'unnameable and unspeakable' divine nature (*ousia*) adapts itself to the limitations of our human minds. It made no sense outside the cultic context of prayer, contemplation, and liturgy" (Armstrong, *Battle for God*, 69). Though one may perhaps rightly entertain some reservations about her sometimes bold assumptions in the realm of comparative religion, and while the reader must be careful to understand the words "myth" and "fact" in the classical sense in which she uses them, Armstrong's focus on doctrine formed in response to religious experience ("prayer, contemplation, and liturgy") effectively leads us away from just the kind of theological and historical superficiality which I have criticized here.

that was implicit in and, as I said above, of immense importance to the unique soteriological scheme of the Christian East. By envisioning Christ as the Divine Ἀρχέτυπον, for the Orthodox believer, an imprecise definition or description of His Nature directly impinges on how one sees and grasps Christ's role in the sanctification and deification of the human being. In becoming man, Christ "assumed a complete human nature, made up of soul and body, and it is the human in his entirety, body and soul," who is "saved and divinized," according to Orthodox soteriology.[11]

Aside from maintaining that the body and soul are united integrally and that, as Larchet observes (paraphrasing St. Maximos the Confessor [d. 662]), "every action and every movement of the human being is at once an act of his soul and of his body"[12] (a coincidence of action and movement, as St. Maximos elsewhere states, which is ideally achieved by "one who brings the body into harmony with the soul [ὁ ἁρμωσάμενος τὸ σῶμα πρὸς τὴν ψυχήν]"[13]), the Greek Fathers also insist on the *exclusively* bipartite nature of man. That is, they reject the idea that the human being is comprised of three distinct elements—body, soul, and spirit (mind or intellect)—and insist that he is, as we have said, understood as a composite of body and soul alone. The tripartite concept of human composition can be found in two forms: in the rather crude and inchoate idea, so often expressed in contemporary thought, that the human being is made up of a body, a mind (or intellect), and a separate spiritual component, the soul; and at times, in the Christian East, in the teaching—officially condemned by the Orthodox

---

11. Larchet, *La Divinisation de l'Homme*, 640–41.

12. Ibid., 30.

13. St. Maximos the Confessor, "Peri Theologias kai tes Ensarkou Oikonomias tou Hyiou tou Theou, Pros Thalassion" (Regarding theology and the incarnate oeconomy of the Son of God, to Thalassios), in *Philokalia*, 2:90. This ideal spiritual goal of "harmony," I might observe, is what St. Gregory of Nyssa (d. ca. 385) considers the purpose of man's creation, "by conceiving man," as the historian John Cavarnos says, "as a link between the spiritual and sensible worlds." (See *St. Gregory of Nyssa and the Human Soul*, 23.) St. Gregory, of course, also believed in the integration of the soul and body as "man's true being" (ibid.), even if certain Western scholars, whom Dr. Cavarnos skillfully refutes, have attributed to his psychology (i.e., his understanding of the soul) certain Platonic elements inconsistent with Christian doctrine. In that respect, Gregory, in using Greek philosophical terms and imagery, Cavarnos contends, "gave new meaning to old concepts, ... choosing and appropriating for himself whatever portions of ... [the classical Greek philosophical corpus] ... seemed to him to possess the essential qualities of reason, beauty, and form, and assimilability into Christian teaching" (ibid., 18). The issue of the relationship between classical Hellenistic thought and Greek patristic wisdom is one to which we will return.

Church as heretical or inconsistent with the patristic consensus—that man is composed of body, soul, and a separate quality, the spirit, which is distinguishable from the soul. Those who argue in favor of this latter formulation frequently do so on the basis of their interpretation of certain scriptural and patristic passages that seem to support a tripartite understanding of human composition. Professor Constantine Cavarnos, quoting the Greek theologian Zikos Rossis (d. 1917), points out that, when properly understood, these scriptural and patristic sources

> in essence express one and the same teaching. For "spirit" does not constitute a *substance* distinct from the soul and hence is *not a third element of man,* but is a higher *power* of one and the same immaterial substance, that is, of the soul, or signifies the *grace* and gift of the Divine Spirit, which does not constitute an element of man, but only illuminates and sanctifies his soul.[14]

In like manner, one may dismiss more incondite efforts to trichotomize human composition by observing that, for the Greek Fathers, the things of the mind or intellect, including reason, are considered faculties of the soul, endowed with the qualities of the soul. This is affirmed by St. Anthony the Great (d. 356), who asserts that, "[w]ith regard to the body, man is mortal, while, with regard to the intellect (νοῦς) and reason (λόγος), he is immortal."[15] Thus, when they speak of body, soul, and spirit (or mind), Eastern Orthodox theologians inevitably do so with clear reference to, and in the context of, the dichotomous nature of the human being.

We should also note that in Orthodox anthropology, the integral union of the body and soul is, despite the clear concinnity of the two, marked by a *hierarchy* of interaction, in which the soul is *superior* to the body *in that interaction*. This is because the soul is immortal and immaterial, while, in man's fallen state, the body is material and mortal. This patristic teaching is one which popular contemporary Christian ideas of the body and soul fail to acknowledge. This is especially so in the West,

---

14. Cavarnos, *Modern Greek Thought*, 63–64. See Rossis, *Systema*, 397–98. Cavarnos also observes that those who point to scriptural references which seem to make a distinction between the soul (ψυχή) and spirit (πνεῦμα) fail to understand that the word "spirit" is also used in the New Testament "to denote life," to refer to the soul, or "occasionally ... to denote the highest faculty of the soul, the rational, usually spoken of in Scripture as 'mind.'" See Cavarnos, *Immortality*, 14–15.

15. St. Anthony the Great, "Paraineseis Peri Ethous Anthropon kai Chrestes Politeias" (Exhortations regarding the character of men and the virtuous way of life), in *Philokalia*, 1:19.

where the soul is often thought of as something which exists within the human body, distinct and separate from it and unmarked by any *essential interaction* with the body. The Greek Fathers teach, instead, that the soul not only "pervades (χωροῦσα)" the "entire body (ὅλου . . . τοῦ σώματος)," as St. Maximos the Confessor writes, but that every member of the body responds to the presence of the soul, though it is incorporeal.[16] We should also note that, following St. Paul (1 Cor 15:44), the Fathers very often make a distinction between the spiritual body and the physical body, or the σῶμα πνευματικόν and the σῶμα ψυχικόν (this latter term, literally the "psychic body," is a special term used by St. Paul to denote the physical body and does not suggest any connection with the spirit or soul, as some wrongly think). The spiritual body is the body which the human being will have in the afterlife, after the death of the physical body, when the soul and physical body are separated. It is a "resurrected" body that is both ethereal and delicate and untouched by the materiality, disease, corruption, and mortality of the fleshly body in the present life. With regard to the immortality of the soul itself, this is testified by both Scripture and the patristic witness. Thus Professor Constantine Cavarnos has written that "[t]he immortality of the soul is taught in the Old and the New Testaments, in the works of the Church Fathers and other ecclesiastical writers of the Orthodox Church, and in its iconography and hymnography."[17] Of the Old and New Testamental witness he says the following: "Although in neither the Old nor in the New Testament is it asserted, in so many words, that 'the soul of man is immortal,' its immortality is implicit in many things that are said in both."[18]

As we have observed, things of the intellect and reason have the immortal qualities of the soul. Dr. Cavarnos says that these powers, too, are mentioned in Scripture:

> [W]e find . . . the "heart" (*kardia*), "intellect" (*nous, dianoia*), "conscience" (*syneidesis*), and "will" (*thelema*). The activities that spring from these powers and are mentioned in Scripture are emotions, desires, dreams, cares, thoughts, reasoning, understanding, faith, attention, prayer, volition, self-control, remembering, and so on.[19]

---

16. St. Maximos the Confessor, "Peri Diaphoron Aporion" (Regarding various difficult texts [*Ambigua*]), in *Patrologia Graeca*, 91:1100AB.
17. Cavarnos, *Immortality*, 13.
18. Ibid., 18.
19. Ibid., 17–18.

These qualities, sometimes called the "powers of the soul (δυνάμεις τῆς ψυχῆς)," are divided into three categories: a kind of basic principle of life or *élan vital* that belongs to all created things (whether plant, animal, or human); the lower and basic psychological attributes and motivations of sensation, perception, desire, instinctual drives, etc., which humans have in common with animals; and reason (ἡ λογικὴ δύναμις), an attribute which pertains solely to man and which he can employ, unlike animals, to control the lower and more basic psychological attributes and motivations.[20] Cavarnos observes that the power of reason, according to the Greek Fathers,

> has two distinct aspects, the contemplative or intuitive, generally called *nous,* and discursive, most often denoted by the term *dianoia.* ... Reason is the highest faculty in man. It is the governor (*kybernētēs*) or master (*autokratōr*) of the whole man, free in its activity. It is the faculty not only of knowledge, but also of inner attention or observation and of contemplation. It can observe itself as well as what is distinct from itself. Its power of attention renders it the guardian of the whole man.[21]

Citing the teachings of St. Gregory Palamas (d. 1359), he further explains that one must distinguish "between the essence (*ousia*) of the rational faculty and its 'energy' or operation (*energeia*). The energy consists of thoughts, while the essence is the power that produces these." He goes on to say, with regard to the function of the rational faculty, that

> [t]he highest activity of the rational faculty is pure prayer. In its truly natural state, reason can intuitively apprehend higher truth. ... It is in its natural state when it is pure, free of bad or useless thoughts and feelings.[22]

Larchet says of the νοῦς, or noetic faculty, in particular, that it "represents the contemplative possibilities of man. It is fundamentally, for the Fathers, that by which man is brought to God, directed towards Him, and united with Him.... [I]t is, in effect, the image of God in man." Larchet pinpoints in the νοῦς the "indelible mark" of man's "true nature."[23]

---

20. These three "powers" of the soul are very clearly enumerated by St. Gregory of Nyssa in his "Peri Kataskeues Anthropou" (On the make-up of man), *Patrologia Graeca*, 44:237C.

21. Cavarnos, *Byzantine Thought and Art*, 51.

22. Ibid.

23. Larchet, *Thérapeutique des Maladies Mentales*, 37–38.

The Human Condition and Eastern Orthodox Cosmology

It becomes immediately apparent from what we have said about the contrast between the mortal body and the immortal soul, as well as from Larchet's pithy portrayal of the noetic faculty as a mark of true human nature, that the Greek Fathers, in describing the constitution of man, distinguish between an ideal state and the prevailing human condition. Just as its anthropology reflects the general teaching of the Judeo-Christian tradition regarding the nexus between the body and soul, so Orthodox cosmology, in concord with mainstream Christian thought, posits that the human being, in his present state, is fallen; i.e., that men and women have sullied the image of God with which they were created and lead lives that are at odds with the Divinity with which they were originally endowed by their Creator. Following the creation story in Genesis, the Greek Fathers describe man, in the prototype of Adam and Eve,[24] as having deviated from the aim and goal for which he was originally created—as a "failed god," to rephrase the ancient Greek vision of man as a "fallen god" *in illo tempore*, or some past age. It is to "missing the mark," or having taken a path of folly in the place of the road set out by the Creator, that they refer when they speak of human sin or sinfulness. (One can see both the Hebrew and Greek roots of this idea of sin in Proverbs 14:21. In the Greek *Septuaginta*, we read: "He that dishonors the needy [πένητας] sins [ἁμαρτάνει]."[25] The King James Version of the Hebrew text of the same passage says that one "sins [*chata*]"

---

24. The creation narrative in Genesis, according to Bishop Kallistos (Ware), while "concerned with certain *religious* truths, . . . [is] . . . not to be taken as literal history. Fifteen centuries before modern Biblical criticism, Greek Fathers were already interpreting the Creation and Paradise stories symbolically rather than literally" (Ware, *Orthodox Church*, 218, note 2). The Romanian theologian, Father Eugen Pentiuc, lends support to Bishop Kallistos's view when he argues that the Hebrew word "*adam*," as it is used in the creation narrative, "connotes 'humanity' as a totality, not a particular person or individual gender. The original *adam* was, then, a single human *collective*, an undifferentiated aggregate of the male and female individuals created by God." (See Pentiuc, *Jesus the Messiah*, 1 [emphasis mine].) These observations argue persuasively for a non-literal or symbolic interpretation of the Genesis creation story. This is not to say, of course, that there are not Orthodox who follow a literal interpretation of the Genesis account of the creation of man. Citing a number of patristic sources, though admittedly influenced by Protestant Evangelical commentaries on the subject, as well, a recent work by the late Father Seraphim Rose, *Genesis, Creation and Early Man*, proffers just such an interpretation.

25. *Septuagint*, 801.

thus, not against the needy, but against one's "neighbour [*rea*]." In the two readings, despite the variation in wording between "πένητας" and "*rea*," both the Greek "ἁμαρτάνει" and the Hebrew "*chata*" derive from roots that denote a missing of the mark or target: *sin as a deviation from some aim or standard*.) The original *Lapsus*, or universal Fall of man from the divine image and from pre-lapsarian Paradise through sin, had universal consequences, according to the Greek Fathers, for all human beings, who, though they do not share in the guilt of Adam and Eve, suffer from the consequences of the Fall. This suffering is beautifully expressed in several verses from the First Canticle of the Great Canon of St. Andrew of Crete, which is recited in Thursday Matins of the fifth week of the Orthodox Great Lent (the fast before the Feast of Pascha[26]):

> I have rivaled in transgression Adam the first-formed man, and I have found myself stripped naked of God, of the eternal kingdom and its joy, because of my sins.
>
> Woe to thee, miserable soul! How like thou art to the first Eve! For thou hast looked in wickedness and wast grievously wounded; thou hast touched the tree and rashly tasted the deceptive food.
>
> Instead of the visible Eve, I have the Eve of the mind: the passionate thought in my flesh, shewing me what seems sweet; yet whenever I taste from it, I find it bitter.
>
> Adam was justly banished from Eden because he disobeyed one commandment of Thee, O Saviour. What then shall I suffer, for I am always rejecting Thy words of life?
>
> By my own free choice I have incurred the guilt of Cain's murder. I have killed my conscience, bringing the flesh to life and making war upon the soul by my wicked actions.[27]

Not only has all of mankind in some way been implicated in the degradation of humanity, in the Greek patristic view, but as a result of the besmirching of the image of God in man, and as a consequence of this tragic change in the course of the human being's God-ordained spiritual

---

26. The proper term for the Orthodox Feast of the Resurrection of Christ, commonly called "Easter" in Western Christendom. "Pascha" is the Greek word for "Passover," and the Orthodox Church celebrates the Resurrection as a Christian Passover: "Πάσχα Κυρίου," or the "Passover of the Lord." The Orthodox Church still celebrates Pascha according to the fourth-century formula appointed by the First Oecumenical Synod in Nicea (i.e., on the first Sunday after the first full moon following the Vernal Equinox, and after the Jewish Passover), whereas Western Christians no longer follow this ancient dictum.

27. *Lenten Triodion*, 378–79.

and ontological evolution, the essence of life itself has been distorted. St. Gregory Palamas, in a homily on this subject, tells us that all of our "illnesses, infirmities, and other misfortunes," as well as "death," come "from our ancestral sin in Paradise (ἀπὸ τῆς ἐν τῷ παραδείσῳ . . . προγονικῆς ἡμῶν ἁμαρτίας)"; i.e., from the original disobedience of our Forebears, Adam and Eve, which resulted in our exile into a "corruptible world (ἐπίκηρον τοῦτον κόσμον)," to a "path" set by man's sin, resulting ultimately in the "final stop (ὁ τελευταῖος σταθμός)": death. This errant course, St. Gregory points out, was not one willed by God; rather, it was one which He tried to impede by establishing a commandment that, should it be transgressed, would lead to death, thus assuring human beings the freedom to prevent their own destruction through obedience. However, the same freedom of will that provided for man's progress in the divine path established by God also allowed him to choose the path of disobedience; and in deliberately abandoning God and His "life-giving counsel (ζωοποιὸν συμβουλήν)," humankind suffered tragic consequences.

The first of these consequences, according to Palamas, was the spiritual death of the soul: separated from God, the soul is now, "as Paul says [1 Tim 5:6], dead yet still alive (ζῶσα τέθνηκε)," and "its life worse than death (θανάτου χείρων αὐτῆς ἡ ζωή)," having been moved away from the good and finding itself driven by "self-reviling evil (αὐτοφθόνῳ κακίᾳ)." Thereupon, St. Gregory says, there followed the death of the body. These consequences did not come from God, he avers, but "by reason of divine abandonment, which is precisely what sin is (ἐκ τοῦ αἰτίου τῆς θείας ἐγκαταλείψεως, ὅπερ ἐστὶν ἡ ἁμαρτία)"; they follow on man's estrangement from God and the mark or target set for the human being by Him.[28] In falling to disobedience, man imitated the disobedience of Satan, "the spiritual serpent and source of evil (ὁ ἀρχέκακος ὄφις)," who first separated from God and who, St. Gregory tells us, is not dead, since death has "no essence," except through "the casting-off of true life (ἀποβολὴν τῆς ὄντως ζωῆς)." Bringing man to "partake in his own death (πρὸς κοινωνίαν τῆς οἰκείας νεκρώσεως)," Satan, "making himself a death-bestowing spirit (νεκροποιὸν ἑαυτὸν ποιεῖ πνεῦμα),"[29] ushered in, beyond the tragedy of spiritual death, man's fall to illness and, again, physical death. Thus, in the words of St. Gregory of Nyssa, man's

---

28. St. Gregory Palamas, "Homilia 31: Ekphonetheisa en Lite Teloumene Kata ten Proten tou Augoustou" (Homily 31, delivered at the litany on the first day of August), in *Gregoriou tou Palama: Hapanta*, 10:276–82.

29. Ibid., 292.

Fall clothed him in the "flesh" (St. Gregory Palamas, following Gregory of Nyssa, remarks that lapsed humans assumed "coats of skin [δερματίνους χιτῶνας]"³⁰), introducing him to sexuality, conception, birth, irrationality, and all of the debilities, foibles, and ills of fallen human nature.³¹

The Greek theologian Panayiotis Nellas writes that, because of the Fall, "the disruption which sin created in man brought with it the disruption of the cosmos." Since

> [i]n creating man in the image of the King of the ages, God made him, according to Nikitas Stithatos,³² "king of creation" and enabled him "to possess within himself the inward essences, the natures and the knowledges of all things." It was therefore unavoidable that the disruption of man should have brought about the disruption of the "essences" and the "natures" of beings, that is, the disruption also of creation.³³

Father John Romanides also emphasizes, in his study of sin in the cosmology, anthropology, and soteriology of the early Greek Fathers (originally submitted, in 1957, as his doctoral thesis at the University of Athens³⁴), the consequence of the *Lapsus* for the whole of creation: "The fall was not limited to the human race but extended to reasonless animals and reasonless nature."³⁵ St. Basil the Great (d. 379), in his "Peri tes tou Anthropou Kataskeues (On the make-up of man)," illustrates these devastating effects of the Fall on the whole of creation, including the animal world, by observing that the snake—the "frightful serpent (φρικτὸς ὄφις)" of fallen nature—was once an upright creature of "affable character (προσηνής)" and "tame (ἥμερος)."³⁶ In effect, the degradation of the human condition by the power of Satan is also reflected in the degradation of the cosmos by decay (illness) and deterioration (death); the Satanic bacterium of sin, which led to the

---

30. Ibid., 276.

31. See St. Gregory of Nyssa, "On the Making of Man," in *Select Library*, 5:407–8.

32. Niketas Stethatos, an eleventh-century Greek monk and theological writer (d. ca. 1085), was a disciple of St. Symeon the New Theologian (d. 1022).

33. Nellas, *Deification*, 85.

34. Romanides, *To Propatorikon Hamartema*.

35. Romanides, *Ancestral Sin*, 81. The original Greek text (see Romanides, *To Propatorikon Hamartema*, 72) reads, "'Η πτῶσις δὲν περιωρίσθη εἰς τὸ ἀνθρώπινον γένος, ἀλλὰ ἐπεξετάθη καὶ εἰς τὴν ἄλογον φύσιν," which might better be translated, in order to underscore the issues at hand, as follows: "The Fall was not limited to the human race but *spread* even to *dumb animals* and *inanimate nature*" (emphasis mine).

36. *Patrologia Graeca*, 30:68A.

abasement of the "king of creation," has infected the universe, compromising its structure and thwarting its purpose. The human being's coöperation with, and subjugation by, Satan and his powers are at the root of imperfection in all of creation:

> Despite the fact that marvelous order and harmony prevail in the cosmos, clearly demonstrating that all things are governed by God, nevertheless, there exists in it a kind of parasite that is manifested by death and consequently by disharmony in the societal relations of man. The evils that are produced by death are not from God.... As a result, this world which is in subjection to death and corruption cannot be considered natural, if by natural we mean the world as God intended it to be. In other words, the world is abnormal, but this is not because of its own nature but because a parasitic force exists in it at present.
>
> According to the later testimonies of Judaism and the earliest ones of Christianity, the devil and his demons are not only the cause of death, they are also agents of illness.... As created by God, the visible and invisible world is very good . . . because that is how God wanted it. This is precisely why death is the tragic outcome of man and the work of the devil.[37]

In this description of the collapse of man and the cosmos to the power of Satan by the human sin of turning from the divine path set out for men and women by God to that trail of tribulations which, in exercising free will, men and women embraced when they succumbed to the wiles of Satan, it is essential that we understand that mankind and the world were not made victims of divine wrath and have not been abandoned by God. Such ideas are foreign to the Greek patristic consensus; rather, that consensus holds that human beings were infected by sin and made slaves to a demonic power which challenges and works against Divine Providence. Humankind and the world were reduced, through the Fall, to dwelling in illness and imperfection (and this, again, by man's free choice); but they were still subject to God's Grace and were not wholly separated from Him. While they were *debased* to an abnormal, unhealthy state, man and the universe were not *deprived* of the potential for perfection and a return to normality. Moreover, before the Fall, as Bishop Kallistos writes, in the teachings of the Greek Fathers, "[h]umans . . . were perfect, not so much in an actual as in a potential sense." That is, "[e]ndowed with the image [of God] from the start"—namely, as "icons" of God and His "offspring"—, "they were called

---

37. Romanides, *Ancestral Sin*, 82–86.

to acquire the likeness [of God] by their own efforts (assisted of course by the grace of God)."[38] This striving for perfection, then, was not erased by sin; rather, in many ways it took on an even greater significance, once man had deviated from the path towards ensured perfection appointed for him by God. Not only are these points important to keep in mind, but they stand in sharp contrast to human sin and degradation as they are often understood in Western Christianity.

Bishop Kallistos further notes that

> [t]his image of Adam before the fall is somewhat different from that presented by Augustine[39] and generally accepted in the west since his time. According to Augustine, humans in Paradise were endowed from the start with all possible wisdom and knowledge: theirs was a realized, and in no sense potential perfection.[40]

Romanides expands on this point, contrasting the earliest theological traditions of the Greek Fathers with the theology of Augustine and later Western thinkers:

> The first theologians of the Church who dealt with the subject of the fall took the New Testament's teachings about perfection very seriously. The fall for them was not at all a juridical matter but rather the failure of man to attain to perfection and *theosis* (divinization) because he fell into the hands of him who has the power of death. Thus, salvation for them was the destruction of the power of Satan and the restoration of creation to its original destiny through the perfecting and *theosis* of man. . . . That destiny is the basis of the theology of the fall and of salvation.[41]

Sickness and death, the separation of the mortal body from the immortal soul at the time of death, and every other imperfection in man and the universe, then, are not, for the Greek Fathers, punishments brought down on man by a wrathful God;[42] they are, as the Eastern Christian tradition

38. Ware, *Orthodox Church*, 219.
39. St. Augustine, Bishop of Hippo (d. 430).
40. Ware, *Orthodox Church*, 220.
41. Romanides, *Ancestral Sin*, 112.

42. Though it is not within the scope of my discussion here to develop this idea at great length, I should note that a number of the early Greek Fathers argued that the Fall of man facilitated his divinization. As Romanides summarizes this argument, drawing on the theology of Sts. Theophilos of Antioch (d. ca. 183–185) and Irenaeus of Lyons (d. at the end of the second or beginning of the third century), "the destiny of man was for him not to remain in the state in which God made him [*sic*] since he was made to

emphasizes, the consequences of his having missed the mark, the stuff and substance of the "ancestral curse" (the circumstance of man's "unnatural" post-lapsarian nature) that befell him through the wiles of Satan, and a departure from his true nature—from the perfection, divinization, and participation in the divine for which he was originally created. Only by grasping these cosmological principles can one properly understand, in turn, the anthropology of the Greek Fathers and, as we shall see, the unique soteriology of the Orthodox Church and the "great divergence between the way in which the Orthodox East and Roman Catholics (as well as Protestants) see man and his relationship with God."[43]

Salvation and Restoration according to the Theological Consensus of the Greek Fathers

The teaching of the Greek Fathers on salvation cannot be understood without reference to the *apokatastasis* or "restoration" of man and the universe which it encompasses. Man is not saved, according to the soteriology of the Orthodox Church, by the mere atonement of mankind for some juridical infraction against the Will of God. Though an expiatory model of salvation can be found in some of the writings of the Greek Fathers, even in such cases, the aim of atonement is not a juridical compensation paid to God in recognition of man's sin—of reparation; rather, this model speaks of the restoration of man's oneness with God through the repentant redirection of human actions and intention, facilitated as this effort is by the loving Grace of God. This restoration captures the inclination of post-lapsarian man to return to the course set out for him by the Creator, turning from evil (which was brought about by man's deviation from God and goodness, under the influence of

---

become perfect and, thus, to be divinized. He was made needing to acquire perfection, not because he was made flawed in nature and morally deficient but because moral perfection is achieved only in total freedom" (ibid., 126). God, respecting man's freedom, allowed him to be lured away by Satan and to fall to the illness of the ancestral curse. But the consequences of the curse were not wrathful punishments by God; rather, man's Fall through his own free will served to allow God to facilitate the human path towards divinization and perfection. This understanding—which Romanides says that Eastern Christianity holds in common with Judaism and, as we mentioned earlier, was distorted by the Augustinian tradition (ibid., 123)—runs contrary, once more, to any idea of "original sin," the total depravation of human nature after the Fall, or some legalistic notion of man's need to justify his sin before a wrathful Creator.

43. Chrysostomos, *Ortodoxia de Est*, 44.

Satan) to the spiritual path that leads to deification[44] and the restoration of both human nature and the world to the original state of Paradise in Eden—indeed, to a state of future perfection that will, in fact, *exceed* the glory of Eden. As Vladimir Lossky describes man's pre-lapsarian state and his state after restoration, while "man was created perfect," this "does not mean that his first state is identical with his last. . . . [B]oth the cosmology and the anthropology of the Eastern Church are dynamic in character."[45]

Briefly, in presenting the idea of *apokatastasis* as a rudimentary element in the soteriology of the Eastern Fathers, I must say something about the misunderstanding of this term that can be found in many Western commentaries on the Greek Fathers and in some Orthodox writers. According to the idea of *apokatastasis*, as I said above, evil has no existence in and of itself but is, instead, a distortion or perversion of good inspired by Satanic influence. Moreover, man and the world are subject to restoration and perfection in the salvific efforts of God to free man from the ancestral curse. A clear exposition of the idea can be found in the writings of St. Gregory of Nyssa, who also argues, however, that in the restoration of all things, "there will be thanksgiving with one accord on the part of all creation," and that both the righteous and those who have been purified by the fire of Hell will find themselves in this joint act of rejoicing.[46] In so arguing, St. Gregory seems to be saying that both the virtuous and those cleansed by the fires of Hell will be restored to perfection. Thus, some authorities argue that he, along with the Orthodox who honor his theological sagacity, advocated the heresies of Origen (d. 254), who was condemned by the Church for a variety of unorthodox ideas, among them the doctrine of the pre-existence of souls,[47] or the assertion that all souls—including Satan and

---

44. Or, according to St. John of Damascus (d. ca. 749), "participation in the Divine Radiance (μετοχὴ τῆς θείας ἐλλάμψεως)." See his "Ekdosis Akribes tes Orthodoxou Pisteos" (Exact exposition of the orthodox faith), in *Patrologia Graeca*, 94:924A. It is interesting to note that one finds, in this passage, an adumbration of the Essence-Energies distinction of St. Gregory Palamas. St. John thus contrasts "Divine Radiance," or deification, with "the Divine Essence (τὴν θείαν οὐσίαν)" (ibid.).

45. Lossky, *Mystical Theology*, 126.

46. St. Gregory of Nyssa, "Logos Katechetikos ho Megas" (Great catechetical discourse), 26, in *Patrologia Graeca*, 45:69B.

47. The doctrine that the human soul exists prior to its attachment to the human body. This teaching is rejected by Orthodox Christianity on the grounds that it violates the integrity of the human being as a composite of body and soul, rendering the body inferior to the soul. Orthodox Christian doctrine, in concord with the Old Testamental record, attests that the body was created by God and that it is inherently good: "[Y]our

his minions—will eventually return to God, and the teaching that Hell, or alienation from God by a rejection of His will and deliberate acts of evil without repentance, is not an eternal state.[48]

In actuality, though he was profoundly influenced by Origen (as was his contemporary St. Gregory the Theologian [d. 389]), St. Gregory of Nyssa did not believe in the pre-existence of souls and was certainly not, as one of the first Orthodox divines to examine his writings on the restoration of man and the universe, St. Barsanouphios (d. *ca.* 540), implies (in the words of Father Florovsky), an "uncritical disciple" of Origen.[49] From a careful and critical reading of St. Gregory, one can in no way conclude that he argues against the necessity of repentance and forgiveness for the attainment of salvation; nor, to be sure, does he seem to think that everyone will ask for and receive forgiveness. Rather, he stresses that, in the face of the forgiving love of God, everyone will be given the *opportunity* to accept and follow the

---

body is the temple of the Holy Spirit, which ye have from God (οὗ ἔχετε ἀπὸ Θεοῦ)" (1 Cor 6:19). So it is also that, according to the teachings of the Orthodox Church, with the General Resurrection of the dead, at the end of time, the body will be resurrected and reunited to the soul.

48. As a number of Orthodox writers have pointed out, in its doctrine of *apokatastasis* the Orthodox Church has never endorsed the supposition that all human beings will eventually be saved, regardless of their spiritual state. From a psychological standpoint, alone, it is obvious that such a deterministic idea would thwart the human striving for perfection. Hence, Protopresbyter George Metallinos, Professor of Theology at the University of Athens, in his comments on the pastoral theology of St. Nicodemos the Hagiorite (d. 1809), tells us that images of the wrath of God and eternal punishment, and emphasis on acts of penitence and repentance, "more than anything else," help to maintain "the penitent in a state of constant vigilance" (Metallinos, "*Exomologetarion*," 16). Father Metallinos contends that it is in an effort to make the human being "aware of the essence of sin and its devastating power" that Nicodemos and other Church Fathers employ starkly punitive imagery and language, focusing our attention on the human "capacity for divine sonship" and perfection (ibid., 21). If sin (or, for that matter, spiritual struggle) had no ultimate consequence, save that of the indiscriminate restoration of all things, human action and spiritual striving would not only lack any ultimate meaning, but, as Metallinos argues, religious imagery would come to lack any motivational power.

49. Florovsky, *Eastern Fathers*, 219. It should be noted that, despite Father Florovsky's assessment of St. Barsanouphios's comments on St. Gregory of Nyssa's views on this matter, the former nowhere suggests that the latter is a heretic. Barsanouphios concludes his considered observations with the following non-condemnatory remark: "Do not suppose that even the holy ones were able to grasp truly (γνησίως) all of the profundities of God" (St. Barsanouphios, "Didaskalia peri ton Origenous, Evagriou, kai Didymou Phronematon" (Instruction on the opinions of Origen, Evagrios, and Didymos), in *Patrologia Graeca*, 86 [A]:901B).

Will of God. Father Florovsky also points out that St. Maximos the Confessor, who undertook to study and defend the theology of St. Gregory,

> interpreted ... [St. Gregory's] ... doctrine of the universal restoration as the turn of every soul to the contemplation of God, which is the realization of the "totality of the faculties of the soul." ... Maximus [also] distinguished between ἐπίγνωσις, the knowledge of Divine truth, and μέθεξις, participation in the Divinity, which requires a definite movement of the will.[50]

Florovsky admits that St. Gregory does not, in fact, *clearly* make a "distinction between the consciousness of Good and the inclination of the will towards it," as does St. Maximos. But St. Maximos, in his interpretation of St. Gregory's theology, as Florovsky observes in another place, insists that "God will be everything, and in everything," but that this "deification ... must be accepted and experienced in freedom and love."[51] Here we have a definition of *apokatastasis* which, in its carefully defined expression, confirms the orthodoxy of St. Gregory of Nyssa's doctrine of restoration and certainly contains none of the overt heresies held by Origen. We also have a lucid statement about the fundamental element of Orthodox soteriology on which I would like to build: that salvation entails the restoration of man to his pre-lapsarian state, his eventual attainment to a greater state of perfection than that which he had in the Paradise of Eden, and his deification, as the crown of divine creation, along with the world and universe around him.

If the soteriology of the Greek Fathers rests conceptually on a restorative model of man and the world, a *sui generis* quality of that model that cannot be overstated is its Christocentricity. The entire soteriological scheme of the Orthodox Church is formed around the Person of Christ, "in Whom we all dwell and find our true identities," being, as He is, the "source" of the restored man,[52] the *novus homo,* and the source of the transformed world—a "New World" and a "New Earth"—"in which he dwells."[53] As we observed earlier, Christ represents the Ἀρχέτυπον, the Divine Archetype, of the human being as he is restored to his proper and God-ordained path to perfection and divinization (deification). Speaking of Christ as the

---

50. Florovsky, *Eastern Fathers,* 219. See St. Maximos the Confessor, "Peuseis, kai Apokriseis kai Eroteseis" (Questions, inquiries, and responses), 13, in *Patrologia Graeca,* 90:796A–C.

51. Florovsky, *Byzantine Fathers,* 245.

52. Chrysostomos and Thornton, *Love,* 49.

53. Chrysostomos et al., *Contemporary Eastern Orthodox Thought,* 15.

Archetype of restored man, St. Gregory the Theologian, for example, writes in a stirring Paschal oration: "[Today] I am glorified with Him . . . , today I am quickened with Him, . . . let us honor our Archetype."[54] Similarly, St. John of Damascus, speaking of the deification of man, refers to the divine image in man as it is "mingled" with Christ the "Archetype."[55] As Metropolitan Cyprian states, Christ is the "Archetype, . . . Who will grant Grace and deification."[56] Christ the Savior and Christ the Redeemer, the focus of the Orthodox Church's ineluctably Christocentric soteriological teachings, also brings to those teachings a truly anthropocentric element, expressed in an intimate relationship between man and the Divine Archetype of man restored, perfected, and deified through Christ, Who, taking on human nature, perfected it, revealing, in His Person, God made man: God Incarnate, the *Theanthropos*, the God-Man, both Perfect Man (τέλειος Ἄνθρωπος) *and* Perfect God (τέλειος Θεός).

The idea of Christ as the restored human, the new or second Adam, taking on the flesh of man, effecting a new creation, and setting human beings once more on the path towards deification and perfection, is beautifully expressed in one of the *Theotokia* (hymns to the Virgin Mary, appointed in the *Octoechos*, the service book containing hymns for the eight modes [tones] of the weekly liturgical cycle of the Orthodox Church) for Sunday Matins in the second mode: "Most blessed art thou, O Virgin Theotokos; for through Him Who was incarnate of thee . . . , Adam hath been restored (ἀνακέκληται, or, literally, 'recalled' [to new life])."[57] St. Gregory Palamas echoes this theme in the following passage from one of his sermons, in which he says that the Resurrection of Christ restored Adam to immortality:

> [W]e were taken by night and seized by the shadow of death, having fallen in sin and having lost the power of seeing, which was by the Grace of God ours and with which we perceived the light that grants true life. Night and death were poured upon our nature, not because the true light withdrew, but because we turned away, no longer having within our persons an inclination towards that light which bestows life. However, . . . the Giver of eternal light

---

54. St. Gregory the Theologian, "First Oration: On Easter and His Reluctance," in *Select Library*, 7:203.

55. St. John of Damascus, "Homilia in Transfigurationem Domini" (Homily on the transfiguration of the Lord), in *Patrologia Graeca*, 96:552C.

56. Cyprian, "To Archetypon Mas," 235.

57. *Parakletike*, 69.

and the Source of true life had mercy on us, not only coming down for our sake, becoming a man like us, but enduring the Cross and death for us . . . , resurrecting on the third day, showing once more that the light of eternal and immortal life in our nature was for it the light of resurrection.[58]

Vladimir Lossky draws direct lines between the image of Christ as the restored Adam and the deification of man and the universe: "Since this task of deification . . . given to man [by God] was not fulfilled by Adam, it is in the work of Christ, the second Adam, that we see what it was meant to be."[59]

Many Church Fathers, it should be noted, extend the image of Christ as the new, or second, Adam to the Virgin Mary, making the Mother of God, in this expanded imagery, a symbol of the new or second Eve in her restoration to the path towards perfection. In this way, they emphasize that the abrogation, by Christ's Incarnation and Resurrection, of the ancestral curse that fell upon Adam and Eve and their descendants is universal. Thus, St. Irenaeus of Lyons writes:

> [F]or Adam had necessarily to be restored in Christ, that mortality be absorbed in immortality, and Eve in Mary, that a virgin, become the advocate of a virgin, should undo and destroy virginal disobedience by virginal obedience.[60]

St. Maximos the Confessor further clarifies this image of Eve, by asserting that the souls of those who come to resemble God through deification participate in the bodily birthgiving of the Virgin Mary in a mystical way:

> Christ always desires to be born in a mystical way, becoming incarnate in those who attain salvation, and making the soul that gives birth to Him a Virgin Mother.[61]

This is an important clarification: whereas Christ, as the second Adam, *restored* humankind—men and women alike—by taking human form *as God*, the Virgin Mary *represents* the restoration and deification, by her birthgiving, of humankind (once more, *both* men and women) and is not considered, as one theological trend in the Roman Catholic Church would hold, in any sense a Co-Redemptrix with Christ or, like Christ (as the Roman

---

58. St. Gregory Palamas, "Homilia 23: Eis to Dekaton Heothinon Evangelion" (Homily 23: On the tenth matins gospel), in *Gregoriou tou Palama: Hapanta*, 10:74, 76.

59. Lossky, *Mystical Theology*, 110.

60. St. Irenaeus, *Proof*, 69.

61. *Philokalia: The Complete Text*, 2:294.

Catholic dogma of the Immaculate Conception affirms), to have been Perfect Man, free from sin at her birth. The celebrated twentieth-century Orthodox churchman, St. John of Shanghai and San Francisco, observes, in this regard, that

> [n]one of the ancient Holy Fathers say that God in miraculous fashion purified the Virgin Mary while yet in the womb; and many directly indicate that the Virgin Mary, just as all men, endured a battle with sinfulness, but was victorious over temptations and was saved by her divine Son.[62]

In short, the image of a new Eve in the person of the Virgin Mary is wholly Christocentric and does not for the Greek Fathers—even if they praise her as the pure vehicle of the Incarnation, immaculate, ever-virgin (ἀειπάρθενος), spotless and pure in her life and intentions, victorious over her battle with sin, a perfect image of deified man, "'Η Πλατυτέρα τῶν Οὐρανῶν" ("She who is more spacious than the heavens"), and an effective intercessor for her fellow humans—contain even a hint of co-redemptive Mariological doctrine.

In presenting Christ as the Archetype of the *novus homo* and of Adam and Eve restored to the divine course appointed by God, there is present everywhere in the writings of the early Greek Fathers an unmistakable soteriological leitmotif: that God—Christ—became man, so that man could achieve deification by Grace. Thus, St. Athanasios the Great (d. 373), tells us, in the characteristic wording of this universal patristic axiom, that Christ "ἐνηνθρώπησεν ἵνα ἡμεῖς θεοποιηθῶμεν (was made man, that we might be made God)."[63] The importance of this aphoristic statement cannot be overemphasized. It contains within it two essential elements in the deification of man: first, an affirmation of the restoration of man by his Creator, God Himself; and, second, the indispensable affirmation of the humanity of Christ, Who, while remaining God, at the same time had to become a true man. This delicate balance between Christ's Divinity and humanity is not a trifling matter.

With regard to the Divinity of Christ, the Fathers of the Church teach unequivocally that God is unknowable and beyond what is bodily or sensible. Thus, as one writer, drawing on the theological commentaries of St. John of Damascus, asserts,

---

62. Maximovitch, *Orthodox Veneration*, 38–39.

63. St. Athanasios the Great, "Logos Peri tes Enanthropeseos tou Logou" (Discourse on the incarnation of the word), in *Patrologia Graeca*, 25:192B.

in Holy Scripture "many things" are said "concerning God" which are more applicable to what is "corporeal"; but the Saints explain to us that these anthropomorphic expressions should not be taken literally or in their exact sense, but "symbolically": "Everything that is said of God as if He had a body is said symbolically, but has a higher meaning; for the Divine is simple and formless."[64]

The same writer also cites the following words by St. Gregory of Nyssa on the unknowable nature of God:

> The Divine Word above all forbids that the Divine be likened to any of the things known by men, since every idea deriving from some conceptual image according to our understanding, which is the product of conjecture about the Divine Nature, makes an idol of God and does not proclaim God.[65]

Indeed, in the apophatic tradition of the Orthodox Church, which approaches God not solely by assertions about what He is, but in terms of His unknowable Nature, or what He is not (for He encompasses being and non-being alike), "the divine essence remains in all respects beyond comprehension and participation (ἀσύλληπτος καὶ ἀμέτοχος). Only the uncreated divine energies are accessible (προσιταί)."[66] We have said more about the technical distinction between the Divine Essence and Energies of God elsewhere.[67] The point here is that,

> [t]o safeguard the doctrine of God's ultimate transcendence of human cognition, Orthodoxy makes a hierarchical distinction between "cataphatic" and "apophatic" theologies, which correspond in type to theological affirmations or denials, respectively. Cataphatically, God is an ultimate and eternal Being; on the higher and more "truthful" apophatic level, however, God is not in essence understandable by terms like ultimate, eternal, or Being. God is, in the apophatic sense, beyond levels of gradation and beyond the categories of time and space themselves, since these are but categories appropriate to mere human thinking.[68]

---

64. [Cyprian], "On the Ascension of Our Lord," 2. See St. John of Damascus, "Ekdosis," in *Patrologia Graeca*, 94:851AB.

65. Ibid. See St. Gregory of Nyssa, "Peri tou Biou Mo[y]seos" (Concerning the life of Moses), *Patrologia Graeca*, 44:377B.

66. Romanides, *To Propatorikon Hamartema*, 99.

67. See "Orthodox Psychotherapy: Hesychasm and the Cleansing of the Mind," chap. 3 of Chrysostomos, *Guide*, 67–97.

68. Chrysostomos et al., *Contemporary Eastern Orthodox Thought*, 3.

St. Gregory Palamas thus insists that the Essence of God "is not a subject for speech or thought or even contemplation, for it is far removed from all that exists and is more than unknowable, . . . incomprehensible and ineffable."[69] Or, as St. Dionysios the Areopagite says of God, He "is above all affirmation . . . [and] . . . , being in His simplicity freed from all things and beyond everything, is above all denial."[70] Vladimir Lossky further contends that the apophatic understanding of God

> teaches us to see above all a negative meaning in the dogmas of the Church: it forbids us to follow natural ways of thought and to form concepts which would usurp the place of spiritual realities. For Christianity is not a philosophical school for speculating about abstract concepts but is essentially a communion with the living God.[71]

As Bishop Auxentios has also observed, in one of our co-authored theological collections, it is not just an understanding of the Essence of God that rests on "negative" theology; the very "doctrine of the Holy Trinity," of God the Father, Son (Jesus Christ), and Holy Spirit, is also "apophatic at heart."[72] Understood in superficial terms, Trinitarian doctrine leads to inane speculation about putative polytheistic tendencies in Christianity (if not, indeed, in some of its heterodox expressions, a subtle but perceptible deviation from the carefully-defined monotheism of Orthodox Christian Trinitarianism). From within the apophatic tradition, and as an experience of the revelation of the True God—as a "theology of facts," to use the words of Father Georges Florovsky[73]—, the Trinity, too, defies mere conceptualization. Rather, it affirms that God in His Essence (and, in fact, in His Energies), is

> indivisibly divided or distinguished into three persons on the basis of origin. The Father is the unbegotten or ungenerated, the Son is begotten of the Father, and the Holy Spirit proceeds from the Father; yet, each of them bears the fullness of the divine nature. The

---

69. St. Gregory Palamas, "Peri Theotetos kai tou Kat' Auten Amethektou te kai Methektou" (Concerning non-participation and participation in the Godhead itself), in *Gregoriou tou Palama: Syngrammata*, 2:242.

70. St. Dionysios the Areopagite, "Peri Mystikes Theologias" (Concerning mystical theology), in *Patrologia Graeca*, 3:1048B.

71. Quoted in Chrysostomos et al., *Contemporary Eastern Orthodox Thought*, 4.

72. Ibid.

73. Florovsky, *Bible*, 120.

"how" of the Son's begottenness or of the Holy Spirit's procession is a mystery that is simply unavailable to human understanding.... The oneness of the Godhead is preserved by the monarchy of the Father, who is the sole source of [the] divine nature.[74] Yet, ... the divine nature resides wholly in each of the three persons.... There is perfect balance in Orthodox dogma between the threeness and the oneness of God.[75]

At the core of this apophatic understanding of the Triune God is the human experience of God, which, though it involves a "spiritual fact" and a true revelation of God, at the same time insures the utter unknowability of that from which such experience, such facts, and such revelation come forth.

Concerning the humanity of the divine Christ, the Greek Fathers sedulously point out that the *Theanthropos,* the God-Man Christ, while remaining Perfect God, one with the Unknowable Essence of God, was also Perfect Man, in every way genuinely human, though, by virtue of being God, untainted by the ancestral sin and thus free of the dominion of Satan. As Lossky expresses this quintessential patristic teaching, God had to become a *true man,* taking on "all that was really human, such as it was after the fall, excepting sin: He took on an individual nature liable to suffering and death." In so doing, He "has assumed also all the imperfections, all the limitations that proceed from sin."[76] The following is a simple but pithily accurate statement of the patristic teachings on the humanity of Christ,

---

74. This principle led to the rejection, by the Eastern Orthodox Church, of an addition to the Nicene Creed by the Western Church, as early as the fifth century, of the so-called *Filioque* Clause, or what its formulators considered a logical addendum to the Creed: that the Third Person (*Hypostasis*) of the Trinity proceeds from the Father and the Son (*Filioque*). From an Orthodox perspective, this addition seriously compromises the unitive monarchy of the Father, subordinating one Hypostasis of the single Trinity. Thomas Aquinas (d. 1274), drawing heavily on the writings of St. Augustine, gave strong support to the *Filioque* Clause in his teachings about the Trinity, in which he posits, among other things, that the Holy Spirit is the love which exists between the Father and the Son. This speculative theology has traditionally been rejected by the Christian East as well, not only on the grounds that love is a manifestation of the unitive monarchy of the Father and thus common to all Three Hypostases of the Triune God, but that the theology of Aquinas and the Latin Scholastics grew out of intellectual exercise and conjecture and not the apophatic theological tradition of spiritual experience and revelation. The theological ideas espoused by the Scholastics also lie outside the consensus of the Greek Fathers, as it is informed by the apophatic tradition.

75. Chrysostomos et al., *Contemporary Eastern Orthodox Thought,* 5–6.

76. Lossky, *Mystical Theology,* 142.

capturing, at the same time, the inseparable Divinity of Christ in His Theanthropic unity:

> He was true God and true Man, or, more specifically, the Person [*Hypostasis*] and nature of God the Son united with the nature of man from His Mother, a daughter of Adam and Eve. As [*sic*] St. Paul confirms His [Christ's] manhood, saying, "when the fullness of the time was come, God sent forth His Son, made of a woman, made under the law [Gal. 4:4]."
>
> St. Athanasios (296–373) comments, "Therefore what came forth from Mary, according to the divine Scriptures, was human and the Lord's body was real; real, I say, since it was the same as ours. For Mary is our sister, in that we are all sprung from Adam."
>
> The two natures would be united without confusion or loss of identity as God or man. The humanity of Jesus was the same as our own and, according to His Divinity, He was of One Essence with the Father and the Holy Spirit.[77]

The perfect divine and perfect human Natures of Christ, as Lossky further comments, are themselves expressed by the Church Fathers in apophatic terms. In contradistinction to Hellenistic thought, which "could not admit the union of two perfect principles," the Church Fathers understood the two Natures of Christ, "indivisibly and inseparably" united, to be a revealed "mystery" of the kind in which the three Hypostases of the Godhead exist in "one nature." In the apophatic spirit of their theologizing, they not only contained such a truth, but acknowledged that the "'how' of this union remains for us a mystery" that is ultimately "based on ... [an] ... incomprehensible distinction," in which "[t]he Divine Person, Christ, has in Him two principles which are different and united at the same time."[78]

The divine and human Natures of Christ come into focus in the Incarnation and the Resurrection. In the one instance, Christ entered life through a Virgin, the *Theotokos* ("Bearer of God"), was conceived without seed, and came forth from her womb without violating her physical virginity.[79] In the other instance, He was crucified, suffered, died, and was

---

77. [Mariam], *Life of the Virgin Mary*, 181.

78. Lossky, *Mystical Theology*, 142–4.

79. The idea that the Virgin Mary not only gave seedless birth to Christ, but that she remained physically inviolate in birthgiving, is an ancient and established teaching of the Orthodox Church, even though, in recent times, some writers have questioned it. For example, Father Thomas Hopko, in his *Winter Pascha*, asserts that, beyond doctrinal affirmations that Christ was born supernaturally to a virgin, "there is," in the Orthodox Church, "no teaching of any other sort of miracle in regard to His birth; certainly no

buried, while at the same time His death was life-bestowing, transforming both the living and the dead *and* earth and Hades by His Resurrection and victory over death. As was befitting God, Christ was born preternaturally and miraculously rose from the dead; as was befitting man, Christ took human form and was born in a human body, just as He genuinely suffered on the Cross and died. While this focus is of theological import, of course, its anthropological and soteriological significance is immense. By His Incarnation and Resurrection, in which He assumed and deified human flesh, Christ restored man; freed him from the ancestral curse of the pangs of physical birthgiving and (giving assurance that the body and soul would be reunited, after their temporary separation before the full renewal of creation at the end of time and the General Resurrection) the ignominy of bodily death; and provided for human participation in the Divine Energies through His own restorative and transforming participation in the life of the fallen human.

The Incarnation and Resurrection are not simply miraculous events that confirm the Divinity of Christ; they are ontological events that affirm the restoration of human nature. Christ "assumed human nature, gave it its existence, and deified it."[80] It was in recognition of this ontological dimension of the Incarnation and Resurrection of Christ that the Oecumenical Synods that were convoked in the early centuries of Christianity were so assiduous in their efforts to define the theological, Christological, and soteriological precepts of the Church. These were not, for these Synods, matters of semantics or—again, as popular historical and theological prate would have it—the products of a would-be attempt to "create," for allegedly political and social gain, a new religion from the rudimentary moral teachings of various messianic Jewish sects. The Synods spoke to events that were central to human restoration and transformation and to the reshaping of the world and the universe. They centered on mega-events that spoke to the convergence of the past, present, and future in the *eternal now* of revealed truth.

---

idea that He came forth from His mother without opening her womb" (p. 175). As I have pointed out in a review of his book, the one hymnographic reference used by those who support Father Hopko's assertion, does not, when properly translated, actually support his view. In fact, it stands side-by-side with numerous other hymnographic references that clearly and without question attest to the preservation of the *Theotokos*'s physical virginity at the birth of Christ. I also point out that, contrary to his counterclaim, numerous Church Fathers and writers, from Justin Martyr to St. John of Damascus, uphold this teaching. See Chrysostomos, Review of *Winter Pascha*.

80. Lossky, *Mystical Theology*, 142.

The language of the Oecumenical Synods, therefore, is the language of existentialism—striving to protect the lofty profundities of human union with God from the very superficies that are attributed to them by those who reduce Christianity to mere religion and subject it to simple-minded thoughts about human motivation and political and social determinism. The Church Fathers, and especially those who sought to express the teachings of the Orthodox Church about the *Theanthropos,* as Vladimir Lossky concurs, "never lost sight of the question concerning our union with God." That was the primary thrust of the "usual arguments which they bring up against unorthodox doctrines," since "the fullness of our union" with God, human salvation, and "our deification . . . become impossible,"[81] if one succumbs to the theology and Christology of those who deviated from the experiential theological revelation of the patristic consensus ("heretics," in the patristic lexicon, or those alienated from the genuine spiritual experience of Christianity and suffering from the pathology of mere religious belief).[82]

It is perhaps worth noting that Christ was born in the humblest circumstances and without the trappings of earthly royalty that some of the messianic traditions of sectarian Judaism anticipated. To the extent that, disabused of a literal messianic royalty because of the ignobility of these

---

81. Ibid., 154.

82. Interestingly, as Father John Romanides points out, the idea of primacy in Orthodox ecclesiology is also inextricably bound up with the Church's primary task of uniting the faithful to God and assuring "that they may be one, as we are" (John 17:11–12). As Romanides asserts, the contemporary ecumenical interpretation of this phrase "is not part of the [Orthodox] Patristic tradition." He maintains that "Christ prays here that His disciples and their disciples may in this life become one in the vision of His Glory (which He has by nature from the Father)." This deifying vision "was part of the Old and New Testament Church's becoming the Body of Christ." Hence, the experience of deification "is the real core of Church history" and the criterion of ecclesial authenticity, and Christ's prayer is "certainly not a prayer for the union of churches." That it should be applied to "churches which have not the slightest understanding of glorification (*theosis*)," he remarks with some irony, "is very interesting, to say the least." Ecclesiastical primacy, in the purest Orthodox patristic tradition, centers on fidelity to those teachings, doctrines, and observances which lead to holiness and "the cure of the human personality" through union with God "via the purification and illumination of the heart and glorification (*theosis*)." (See Romanides, "Orthodox and Vatican Agreement.") In another place, Father Romanides even argues that "the abolition of Satan's power" and man's consequent deification and union with God form "the connecting link that gives unity to the Gospels," chastising "contemporary critics of the New Testament" for their preoccupation with the "inner unity of the Synoptic Gospels" at the cost of the core of the message which they relate in different depths and with divergent catechetical and pastoral aims. (Romanides, *Ancestral Sin,* 71–72.)

circumstances, we pass beyond the image of "Royal messianism" to that of "Ontological messianism,"[83] we come to an understanding that, in the messianic tradition, too, there is a certain conceptual duality. On the one hand, Christians see Christ as the fulfillment of God's covenant with the Hebrew people in their earthly sojourn, extending this Royal messianism to the messianic catholicity of a "New Israel" (that is, an Israel that includes the non-Jew[84]); on the other hand, the Church Fathers tell us that Christ is the fulfillment of an ontological promise to man, contained within His archetypical revelation of human perfection. Christ was not just the historical Messiah of the Hebrew Covenant, according to patristic teaching. His Incarnation was, to quote St. Nicodemos the Hagiorite, part of the Divine Oeconomy, "both foreknown and foreordained" by God the Father "prior to the foreknowledge and foreordination of all ... creatures, both noetic and sensible," which were themselves "both foreknown and foreordained" by the Father "to be created for the sake of the great Mystery of the Incarnation of His Beloved Son." The mystery of the Incarnate Oeconomy, then, is the "foreordained divine purpose of the origin of existing things."[85] It is "the final end of all things, higher than which there is nothing, ... [entailing] ... perfection, deification, glory, and blessedness for Angels, for mankind, and for the whole of creation, ... the union of the Creator and His creation, and the glory of the unoriginate Father, ... glorified by His Son and Word, Who clothed Himself in human nature."[86] We see here both the Royal Messiah of human expectation and the Ontological Messiah of Divine Oeconomy.

The human condition, as it is expressed in the anthropology and cosmology of the Greek Fathers, leads one directly to the soteriological scheme which we have set forth in the Person of Christ as the Archetype of restored man, the Redeemer and Savior of the first Adam, and the Messiah Who, in

---

83. This is a distinction that I have borrowed, in part, from Father Eugen Pentiuc, though he uses it in a way that moves far beyond my point here. (See Pentiuc, *Jesus the Messiah*, xiii.)

84. St. Gregory Palamas underscores this messianic inclusiveness in his comments on the two blind men mentioned in Matt 9:27, who followed Christ, saying, "Thou Son of David, have mercy on us." They signify, he tells us, "the two [human] races, that of the Jews and that of the Gentiles (τὸν ἐξ ἐθνῶν)," who were enlightened and thereby recognized Christ as "both God and man." St. Gregory Palamas, "Homilia 30: Hypothesin Echousa Tous Kata ton Euangelisten Matthaion En Oikia Anablepsantas Typhlous" (Homily 30: On the blind men who regained their sight in a house, according to the Evangelist Matthew), in *Gregoriou tou Palama: Hapanta*, 10:262–64.

85. St. Nicodemos the Hagiorite, *Hermeneia*, 165–66.

86. Ibid., 166, note 1.

His ontological dimensions, is the Creator, the Almighty, and the Ineffable One Who unites the Creator and His creation. The "normal" or "natural" human being is one who, by union with God, restores the perfect connection between the body and soul, lost through the Fall. As Bishop Kallistos affirms, "since the human person is a single unified whole, the image of God embraces the entire person, body as well as soul."[87] The restoration of the image of God in human beings, as well as their attainment of likeness to God, is therefore directly associated with this connection. "[N]ot only the soul, but also the body of man shares" in this deification, as Lossky also says, "being created, as they are, in the image of God."[88] "Living . . . with temperance (ἐν μετριοπαθείᾳ)" and "traversing in ease the period of the present life," the restored man is "delivered" from "the tribulations of both soul and body" by "Christ Himself, the Physician and God of our souls and of our bodies," as St. Gregory Palamas tells us.[89]

The normal, or natural and "healthy," state of the human being is also characterized by the Greek Fathers as one of mental deification, which, in turn, is considered a *sine qua non* for salvation. Hence, St. Nicodemos the Hagiorite categorically states that, "[i]f your own mind is not deified (θεωθῇ) by the Holy Spirit, it is impossible for you to be saved (νὰ σωθῇς)."[90] This notion of mental deification, of course, assumes a perfect harmony between body and soul, which share in salvation and immortality, and in the enlightenment of the νοῦς, or the spiritual faculty of the mind. Once again, in his natural state, "man is a single totality of soul and body" and it is thus that his deification is accomplished.[91] To a great extent, because of their emphasis on the "eschatological now (τὸ ἐσχατολογικὸν νῦν)," or the notion that the Incarnation and Resurrection of Christ restored human nature and the universe ontologically, the Greek Fathers hold that this process of deification begins here and now. Through the cleansing of the mind and body, men and women are lifted into a state of deification, such that they live partly, even in the present life, in the future glory of human perfection. In his affirmation, we see the great debt of the Greek patristic notion of the oneness of body, soul, and spirit to the wisdom of the Greek ancients, but at the same time come to understand the immense chasm that separates

---

87. Ware, *Orthodox Church*, 220.
88. Lossky, *Mystical Theology*, 116.
89. St. Gregory Palamas, "Homilia 31," 302.
90. St. Nicodemos the Hagiorite, *Nea Klimax*, 247.
91. Romanides, *To Propatorikon Hamartema*, 125.

the ontological ramifications of the soteriological scheme of Orthodox Christian theology from the cosmological and ontological *schemata* of the Hellenistic philosophers.

Bibliography

Armstrong, Karen. *The Battle for God: A History of Fundamentalism*. New York: Random House, 2001.

Aslan, Reza. *No god but God: The Origins, Evolution, and Future of Islam*. New York: Random House, 2005.

Assagioli, Robert. *Psychosynthesis: A Manual of Principles and Techniques*. New York: Hobbs, Dorman, 1965.

Brown, Carolyn T. *Footprints of the Soul: Uniting Spirit with Action in the World*, in *Dreaming the American Dream: Reflections on the Inner Life and Spirit of Democracy*. Edited by Mark Nepo. San Francisco: Jossey-Bass (a Wiley Imprint), 2005.

Cavarnos, Constantine. *Aristotle's Theory of the Fine Arts: With Special Reference to Their Value in Education and Therapy*. Belmont, MA: Institute for Byzantine and Modern Greek Studies, 2001.

———. *Byzantine Thought and Art: A Collection of Essays*. 3rd printing. Belmont, MA: Institute for Byzantine and Modern Greek Studies, 1980.

———. *Fine Arts as Therapy: Plato's Teaching Organized and Discussed*. Belmont, MA: Institute for Byzantine and Modern Greek Studies, 1998.

———. *Immortality of the Soul*. Belmont, MA: Institute for Byzantine and Modern Greek Studies, 1993.

———. *Modern Greek Thought*. Belmont, MA: Institute for Byzantine and Modern Greek Studies, 1969.

———. *Plutarch's Advice on Keeping Well*. Belmont, MA: Institute for Byzantine and Modern Greek Studies, 2001.

———. *Pythagoras on the Fine Arts as Therapy*. Belmont, MA: Institute for Byzantine and Modern Greek Studies, 1994.

Cavarnos, John. *St. Gregory of Nyssa and the Human Soul: Its Nature, Origin, Relation to the Body, Faculties, and Destiny*. Edited and revised by Constantine Cavarnos. Belmont, MA: Institute for Byzantine and Modern Greek Studies, 2000.

Chrestou, Panagiotes, ed. *Gregoriou tou Palama: Hapanta ta Erga*. 11 vols. Thessalonike: Paterikai Ekdoseis "Gregorios ho Palamas," 1981–94.

———. *Gregoriou tou Palama: Syngrammata*. Vol. 2. Thessalonike: Royal Research Society, 1966.

Chrysostomos, Archbishop. *A Guide to Orthodox Psychotherapy: The Science, Theology, and Spiritual Practice Behind It and Its Clinical Applications*. Lanham, MD: University Press of America, 2006.

———. *Ortodoxia de Est și Creștinismul de Vest* (The Orthodox East and the Christian West). Translated by Deacon Father George Balaban and Raluca Balaban. Bucharest, Romania: Editura Universitara "Ion Mincu," 2003.

———. Review of *The Winter Pascha: Readings for the Christmas-Epiphany Season*, by Thomas Hopko, *Orthodox Tradition* 9.2&3 (1992) 7, 22.

Chrysostomos, Archimandrite [Archbishop], Hieromonk Auxentios, and Hierodeacon Akakios. *Contemporary Eastern Orthodox Thought: The Traditionalist Voice.* Belmont, MA: Nordland, 1982.
Chrysostomos, Bishop [Archbishop], and Reverend James Thornton. *Love.* Themes in Orthodox Patristic Psychology 4. Brookline, MA: Holy Cross Orthodox Press, 1990.
Cyprian (Agiokyprianites), Archimandrite. "On the Ascension of Our Lord." *Orthodox Tradition* 19.2 (2002) 2–4.
Cyprian of Oropos and Fili, Metropolitan. "To Archetypon Mas kai He Diaphylaxis Apo Ta Eidola." *Hagios Kyprianos,* 14.329 (2005) 233–35.
Florovsky, Georges. *Bible, Church, Tradition: An Eastern Orthodox View.* The Collected Works of Georges Florovsky 1. 2nd printing. Belmont, MA: Nordland, 1972.
———. *The Byzantine Fathers of the Sixth to Eighth Century.* The Collected Works of Georges Florovsky 9. Vaduz, Liechtenstein: Büchervertriebsanstalt, 1987.
———. *The Eastern Fathers of the Fourth Century.* The Collected Works of Georges Florovsky 7. Vaduz, Liechtenstein: Büchervertriebsanstalt, 1987.
The Holy Bible: Containing the Old and New Testaments, Translated Out of the Original Tongues and With the Former Translations Diligently Compared and Revised (Authorized King James Version). New York: World Publishing, n.d.
Hopko, Father Thomas. *The Winter Pascha: Readings for the Christmas-Epiphany Season.* Crestwood, NY: St. Vladimir's Seminary Press, 1984.
Irenaeus, St. *Proof of the Apostolic Preaching.* Translated by Joseph P. Smith, S.J. New York and Ramsey, NJ: Newman, 1952.
Larchet, Jean-Claude, *La Divinisation de l'Homme Selon Saint Maxime le Confesseur* (The divinization of man according to St. Maximos the Confessor). Paris: Cerf, 1996.
———. *Thérapeutique des Maladies Mentales: L' Expérience de l'Orient Chrétien des Premiers Siècles.* Paris: Cerf, 1992.
The Lenten Triodion. Translated by Mother Mary and Archimandite Kallistos Ware. London and Boston: Faber and Faber, 1978.
Lossky, Vladimir. *The Mystical Theology of the Eastern Church.* Crestwood, NY: St. Vladimir's Seminary Press, 1976.
Mariam, Mother. *The Life of the Virgin Mary, the Theotokos.* Buena Vista, CO: Holy Apostles Convent, 1989.
Maximovitch, Blessed Archbishop John. *The Orthodox Veneration of the Mother of God.* Translated by Fr. Seraphim Rose. Platina, CA: St. Herman of Alaska Brotherhood, 1987.
Metallinos, Protopresbyter George. "The *Exomologetarion* of St. Nicodemos the Hagiorite." *Orthodox Tradition* 19.1 (2002) 14–31.
Migne, J.-P., ed. *Patrologiae Cursus Completus, Series Graeca.* 161 vols. Paris: 1857–66.
Nellas, Panayiotis. *Deification in Christ: Orthodox Perspectives on the Nature of the Human Person.* Translated by Norman Russell. Crestwood, NY: St. Vladimir's Seminary Press, 1987.
Nicodemos the Hagiorite, St. *Hermeneia eis tas Hepta Katholikas Epistolas.* Venice: 1806.
———. *Nea Klimax.* Thessalonike: B. Regopoulou, 1976.
Parakletike. Rev. ed. Athens: Phos, 1987.
Pentiuc, Eugen J. *Jesus the Messiah in the Hebrew Bible.* Mahwah, NJ: Paulist, 2006.
Philokalia: The Complete Text. Translated and edited by G. E. H. Palmer, Philip Sherrard, Kallistos Ware et al. 4 vols. London and Boston: Faber and Faber, 1979–95.
Philokalia ton Hieron Neptikon. 5 vols. 1957–63. Reprint. Athens: Aster, 1974–77.

Romanides, John S. *The Ancestral Sin: A Comparative Study of the Sin of Our Ancestors Adam and Eve according to the Paradigms and Doctrines of the First- and Second-Century Church and the Augustinian Formulation of Original Sin.* Translated by George S. Gabriel. Ridgewood, NJ: Zephyr, 2002.

———. "Orthodox and Vatican Agreement: Balamand, Lebanon, June 1993," *Theologia* 64.4 (1993) 570–80.

———. *To Propatorikon Hamartema: Etoi Symbolai eis Ereunan ton Proypotheseon tes Didaskalias peri Propatorikou Hamartematos en te Mechri tou Hag. Eirenaiou Archaia Ekklesia en Antibole Pros ten Katholou Kateuthynsin tes Orthodoxou kai tes Dytikes Mechri Thoma tou Akinatou Theologias* (Ancestral sin: Namely, contributions to the study of presuppositions concerning the doctrine of ancestral sin in the ancient church to the time of St. Irenaeus vis-à-vis the general direction of Orthodox and Western theology to the time of Thomas Aquinas). Athens: University of Athens, 1957.

Rose, Father Seraphim. *Genesis, Creation and Early Man: The Orthodox Christian Vision.* Platina, CA: St. Herman of Alaska Brotherhood, 2000.

Rossis, Zikos. *Systema Dogmatikes tes Orthodoxou Katholikes Ekklesias.* Athens: 1893.

The Septuagint with Apocrypha: Greek and English. Translated by Sir Lancelot C. L. Brenton. 3rd printing. Peabody, MA: Hendrickson, 1990.

Schaff, Philip, and Henry Wace, eds. *A Select Library of the Nicene and Post-Nicene Fathers of the Christian Church,* Second Series. 14 vols. Grand Rapids: Eerdmans, 1978.

Sophocles. *Sophoclis Fabulae.* Edited by A. C. Pearson. Oxford: Clarendon, 1924.

Ware, Timothy. *The Orthodox Church.* 2nd ed. London and New York: Penguin, 1993.

CHAPTER 3

The Greek Fathers and Secular Knowledge

The Most Reverend Chrysostomos and Archimandrite Patapios

THE PROBLEM OF ANTI-INTELLECTUALISM in Christianity is an ancient one and one that still sullies some aspects of its self-presentation. This is true not only of sectarian thinking but it also lingers, at least in the Eastern Church, in hermeneutical traditions that draw from the foundational theological witness of the Greek Fathers. In the name of patristic authority, which is the underpinning of Eastern Orthodox theological thought, we often find anti-intellectual arguments that lie outside the patristic consensus and thus serve to perpetuate the mistaken notion that the Greek Fathers were hostile to secular learning, and especially to the Hellenistic wisdom tradition from which they drew much of their language and imagery, as well as many classical paradigms—albeit restructuring them in the process—in putting forth a Christian cosmology and anthropology. We often find patristic quotations, designed to address specific issues in a specific historical or pastoral context, lifted out of that context and used to support a notion or precept foreign to the ethos of the Greek Fathers. Similarly, incautious or even incurious with regard to the unity and integrity of the *consensio Patrum,* there are those who boldly proffer the purely personal opinions, *theologoumena,* and casual observations of various Fathers as though they had the weight of universal authority. The damage occasioned by such improvidence is immense, harming at times the very repute of Christian thinking and theology.

As a result of this misuse and misinterpretation of the patristic witness, there prevails, and especially in Western scholarly tradition, a strong bias against the early Church Fathers in general as having held secular learning in low esteem. It is frequently thought that the formidable intellectual traditions of Eastern Orthodoxy are somehow anti-intellectual, if not preliterate. Indeed, with astonishment we have even seen claims that the Church Fathers ushered in the demise of the ancient institutions of higher learning, during the first centuries of Christianity, or that no one has ever seen a Saint, as a statement widely and variously disseminated and attributed to an Orthodox nun has it, "leaving a library or lecture hall." Many of these assertions are supported, again, by misused patristic quotations, thus leaving a reader unacquainted with the vaster patristic witness and the historical, pastoral, and consensual context in which such citations must be read, with the unfortunate impression, again, that the Greek Fathers spurn worldly knowledge and approbate, cultivate, and advocate anti-intellectualism. It behooves us to address this misconception directly.

The blossoming of Christianity in the Hellenic world and the Byzantine Empire was accompanied, not by a trend towards the rejection of secular knowledge, but by an open, if eclectic, adaptation of classical studies and the sciences for the formation of the Christian person. Nonetheless, many anti-religious historians attribute to Eastern Christianity especially, if not its demise, at least a hostile attitude towards education, inevitably adducing (and substantially misusing and overstating) the famous maxim of the second-century ecclesiastical writer Tertullian: "We want no curious disputation, after possessing Christ Jesus."[1] This attribution is simply an unjustified myth, one reinforced by historiographical prejudices towards the Byzantine East so egregious as to be downright embarrassing.[2] In response to it, and to those who invoke it as a kind of testament to Christianity's putative anti-intellectualism, we might point out that the oldest state-supported medieval university in the world was established in Constantinople by the Emperor Theodosios II in 425 AD. The Byzantines also established major universities in Alexandria, Beirut, Athens, Nicaea, and Thessalonike, where many Christian professors and, as we shall subsequently see, famous Saints

---

1. Tertullian, "The Prescription Against Heretics," 7, in *Ante-Nicene Fathers*, 3:246.

2. It has often been argued, for example, that Emperor Justinian closed the Athenian School of Philosophy. There is no evidence, in fact, to support this accusation. Asterios Gerostergios observes that the school actually closed because of limited resources and, of course, because its faculty was not sympathetic to Christianity. Many scholars fled to Persia, though, again, *not* because the Emperor *had dissolved* the Philosophical School. See Gerostergios, *Justinian*, 72–73.

studied and taught. Suffice it to quote what Argentine philologist and Classicist, Saúl A. Tovar, has written about the University of Constantinople:

> I am amazed when I read works concerning European education and the establishment of the first universities of the West, and find that they do not even mention the name of the University of Constantinople. It seems that the writers of these works do not know that Constantinople is a European city—a city that lies on the continent of Europe—but think that it is in Asia. Or else, they are deliberately, through some prejudice, keeping silent about the university there.... The University of Constantinople was established in 330 AD, whereas the universities of Europe were established nine centuries later.[3]

With regard to the fame of these schools, the university in Alexandria was celebrated for its school of medicine, while Beirut and Constantinople were distinguished centers for legal study.[4]

Many important Christian figures studied and taught at Byzantine universities throughout the Empire's history; they are numerous, indeed. St. Athanasios (d. 373) attended the university in Alexandria, which was called the Catechetical School and which had a full academic curriculum, as did St. Gregory the Theologian (d. 389/390). Clement of Alexandria (d. *ca.* 215) and Origen (d. *ca.* 254) were both students there and, later, headed the school. Clement also gave Christian instruction to its students. St. Basil the Great (d. 379) followed courses at the university for a short time, as well. Basil the Great, St. John Chrysostomos (d. 407), and St. Gregory the Theologian also studied at the University of Athens, the latter after having studied in Alexandria. St. Photios the Great (d. *ca.* 895), one of the more eminent Fathers of the Church, was a learned scholar (a professor of philosophy) at the University of Constantinople. When he was originally called to the episcopacy (having gone from a layman through the ranks of the priesthood—from monk to bishop—in the short span of six days), Photios greatly lamented the loss of his intellectual vocation and the "sweet

---

3. Quoted in Cavarnos, *Cultural and Educational Continuity*, 16–17. While there is historical evidence that professors were appointed by the Emperor Theodosios II to teach with state stipends at the University of Constantinople, there are less reliable data to support the view that the Emperor Constantine established a school at the date suggested by Dr. Tovar. However, there is also no reason, on account of the lack of explicit evidence, to consider this date wholly untenable.

4. Georgina Buckler, "Byzantine Education," in Baynes and Moss, *Byzantium*, 216.

and tranquil" scholarly way of life.⁵ Indeed, after his first exile, in 869, he returned to the University of Constantinople (the Higher School of Naura) and, *as a clergyman*, continued his teaching activities.⁶ What we have said of the first eight centuries of Christianity was true throughout the history of Byzantium (St. Gregory Palamas [d. 1359], for example, is presumed to have studied at the university in Constantinople). With the advent of Slavic Orthodoxy, many of its great theologians and Saints, mirroring the educational customs of the early Church, also studied and taught in theological academies of university status (St. Philaret of Moscow [d. 1867] is one example), and several significant theological figures in the Eastern Church in the modern age were scholars and teachers. St. Nectarios of Aegina (d. 1920), a graduate of the University of Athens, was Rector of the Rizareios Ecclesiastical School. St. Justin Popovich (d. 1979) studied at Oxford and the University of Athens and was, *as a clergyman*, Professor of Dogmatics in the faculty of theology at the University of Belgrade. St. Nikolai of Ohrid and Zhicha (d. 1956) held two university doctorates (one from Oxford) and taught philosophy, logic, history, and foreign languages at the theological faculty of the university in Belgrade. St. John of Shanghai and San Francisco (d. 1966), who also studied law, taught at the theological seminary at Bitol (now in the Republic of Macedonia). In many of these instances, then, we can argue that a number of Eastern Saints, consistent with the legacy of the Greek Fathers, have been seen, as clergymen, "leaving a library or lecture hall."

It is, of course, quite possible to find in the writings of these Church Fathers a number of very blunt and even acerbic statements about pagan philosophy and science, secular knowledge, and the pursuit of knowledge for the sake of knowledge. St. Gregory of Nyssa, for example, is unequivocal in his condemnation of secular knowledge per se: "Secular education, in very truth, is infertile, always in labor, and never giving life to its offspring."⁷ The Church Fathers considered Christianity to be the "science of sciences" and the unique and singular path to human restoration through the therapeutic application of its precepts and the mysteries of the Church. And to those who rejected or distorted the Church's teachings (heretics), they have, over the centuries, directed clear condemnation for offering a "stone" instead of "bread." However, this condemnation is quite distinct from

---

5. See his second letter to Pope Nicholas I, in *Patrologia Graeca*, 102:597.
6. Gerostergios, *St. Photios*, 69.
7. St. Gregory of Nyssa, *De Vita Moysis*, II, 36.

their admonitions about secular knowledge falsely elevated to something that it is not; i.e., to a stature that exceeds its *proper place* in facilitating the human ascent to knowledge beyond the mind to the heart, or beyond reason to noetic enlightenment.[8] Not only were the Fathers quite clearly not troglodytic anti-intellectuals, but, placing secular knowledge in proper perspective, they experienced the positive and productive awe that it can evoke and the inspiration which it can provide even to non-believers, when they approach it with humility and an openness to the spiritual knowledge to which natural knowledge can lead. A striking example of this awe towards the sciences and human knowledge of the world around us is found in the writings of St. Ignaty Brianchaninov: "The world presented nothing enticing for me. My mind was entirely immersed in the sciences, and at the same time I was burning with the desire to discover . . . the true faith . . . ." It was in his study of the sciences and the awe which they evoked in him that—despite, *or perhaps because of,* their inadequacy—Ignaty came to "the boundaries of human knowledge," which prompted his ascent to spiritual knowledge.[9] These sentiments are a cogent testimony to the fact that the Church Fathers have as much to say about the positive value of secular knowledge as they do about the dangers that they saw in it when it was improperly understood or made a fruitless end in and of itself. A few

---

8. The patristic scholar, Gregory Telepneff, has made some excellent observations on this subject that we consider worthy of repetition here:

"I am always amazed that these anti-intellectual types seem to misunderstand the nexus between worldly knowledge and theological knowledge. The latter is surely a matter of noetic illumination; but such illumination is not granted 'magically,' as it were. . . . The lives of the great Church Fathers demonstrate that they were assiduous in their efforts at educating themselves, even if only in their monasteries or by their superiors. There is no doubt that many Saints experienced the higher levels of the spiritual life by direct communion with God. But those Church Fathers who were also well-educated and intellectually brilliant Saints had the special gift of adequately conveying this experience in their [scholarly theological] writings.

"The confusion in our times—like that during the decades of struggle against Arianism, Nestorianism, Iconoclasm, *et al.*—is proof enough that we must also understand Church teachings intellectually, in the pursuit of apologetic ends. The dogmas of the Church require no small intellectual effort toward their understanding and assimilation—needless to say, within the context of prayer, fasting, piety, humility, obedience, etc., which are, among other things, epistemological principles in patristic thought. The Greek Fathers understood and respected secular learning as a tool for learning and for living theology. And St. Gregory of Nyssa chided those who, missing this point, mocked pagan and secular knowledge. (Father Gregory Telepneff to Archbishop Chrysostomos, June 24, 2004 [electronic transmission]; document in authors' hands.)

9. Brianchaninov, *Collected Works*, vol. 1.

representative quotations from the Fathers will further reinforce this point, one which anti-intellectual believers (who frequently include individuals with significant educational credentials[10]) too often ignore:

> I think that it is admitted by all intelligent men that education is our first good, and not only this noble form of it that is ours, which disregards fanciness or vainglory in speech, and cleaves to salvation alone and to beauty in the objects of thought, *but even that secular culture which many Christians injudiciously spit upon as treacherous and dangerous, and as putting us far from God.* . . . So, from secular literature we have taken heuristic and theoretical principles, whereas we have rejected whatever in it is demonic, erroneous, or leads to the pit of perdition. Indeed, even from secular literature we have derived benefit with regard to reverence for God, by ascertaining what is superior from what is inferior and by rendering what is in them weak a strength for our own aim. *We must not then dishonor education because some are pleased to do so, but rather consider such people to be boorish and uneducated, desiring all others to be as they themselves are, in order that this commonness within them might be concealed, and [thus] escape reproach for their lack of education [emphasis ours].*[11]

> [In the] . . . struggle before us, . . . [w]e must associate with poets and writers of prose and orators and with all men from whom there is any prospect of benefit with regard to the care of the soul.[12]

> If there is some affinity between Christian and pagan teachings, knowledge of this would be useful for us; but even if there is no affinity, yet to compare them and to understand the difference between them serves in no small way to assure us of what is superior. . . . It is said that Moses, that great man, who has the greatest name among all men for his wisdom, first trained his mind in Egyptian

---

10. It is often the tendency of the educated, when placed in an anti-intellectual setting, to become almost rabidly anti-intellectual themselves. This is in part, of course, related to issues of psychological provenance. However, it is also the natural tendency of any educated person, whether of a religious bent or not, to see the folly of knowledge for the mere sake of knowledge. This is because true education eventually creates in an individual a thirst for higher knowledge; hence, the inadequacy of mere intellectual exercises can provoke strong condemnation of sterile learning. Such is not unusual in the academic world.

11. St. Gregory the Theologian, "Oration 43," in *Patrologia Graeca*, 36:508–9.

12. St. Basil the Great, "Exhortation to Young Men About How They May Derive Profit from Greek Letters" (in Greek), in Wilson, ed., *St. Basil*, 21. (The translation is our own, with emendations from the text in Cavarnos, *New Library*, 2:62–63.)

learning, and then approached the theory of being. In a similar way to Moses, and closer to our age, it is said that the wise Daniel in Babylon first learned Chaldean wisdom, and then undertook to learn the things of God.[13]

Manners are wanted, not talking; character, not cleverness; deed, not words.... Stimulate not his tongue but cleanse his soul. *I do not say this to prevent you from teaching him these things [secular subjects], but to prevent you from attending to them exclusively.*[14]

The acquisition of education [παιδεία] becomes for one who has grown old the strongest staff of life, and it transports without pain one who is in the bloom of youth to the beauty of virtue.[15]

What we have said about secular knowledge and learning and the importance of counter-balancing the intellectual activities, gifts, and proclivities of the Greek Fathers, as well as their attestation to the contributions of worldly erudition to spiritual knowledge, against their sometimes seemingly choleric opposition to the vain elevation of intellectual pursuits is perfectly illustrated in the life and works of St. Gregory Palamas, a late-Byzantine Greek Father whom some have wrongly tried to transform into an anti-intellectual. In his writings (and especially his short treatise, "Essay on the Sacred Hesychasts"), Palamas speaks of two kinds of wisdom: worldly and spiritual.[16] While he places the latter above the former, he attributes to each form of knowledge the dignity of the appellation "wisdom." St. Gregory was himself a man of astounding intellect and brilliance and a gifted diplomat and administrator with a classical education and particular abilities in philosophy. This is evidenced in an anecdote from his life. In the presence of the Emperor, the young St. Gregory was discussing Aristotle's writings on logic. The Great Logothete of the Byzantine Court, Theodore Metochites, turned to the Emperor and said of the Saint, "if Aristotle himself had been present to listen to this young man, he would, I believe, have praised him beyond measure. For the time being, I say that it is those with such a soul and of such nature as his who should be pursuing knowledge,

---

13. Ibid., 21–22.

14. St. John Chrysostomos, "Homily 21 on Ephesians," in *Patrologia Graeca*, 62:152.

15. St. Photios the Great, "Letter 37," quoted in White, *Patriarch Photios*, 176. See the original in *Patrologia Graeca*, 102:952.

16. St. Gregory Palamas, "Hyper ton Hieros Hesychazonton," in *Philokalia*, 4:121–31.

and especially the omnifarious philosophical writings of Aristotle."[17] Once again, in the tradition of the Fathers before and after him, he certainly taught that secular wisdom, when embraced as something *superior* to spiritual revelation, or cast as something inimical to spiritual hunger and learning, could lead one astray and foster "demonic delusion" (a state of religious deception). It is primarily in his disputes with Barlaam the Calabrian, his Scholastic adversary, and the "Latinophrones" ("Latin-minded") scholars who championed the Calabrian's ideas that Gregory invokes this demonic image of secular knowledge. After all, it was Barlaam himself who portrayed theology drawn from philosophy as superior to the theological revelation given to the divines, a contention that perfectly illustrated, for Palamas, the Calabrian's misunderstanding of noetic or spiritual wisdom and the fact that the Apostles, at their enlightenment, attained to a knowledge above knowledge, which encompassed both a "vision of God" and insight into worldly wisdom (as illustrated by their reported ability to speak in foreign languages—tongues—that they had heretofore not known). In addressing this and other of Barlaam's theological deviations, Gregory was very clearly not acting in the spirit of misology.

The church historian Jaroslav Pelikan makes a number of very insightful and helpful comments about the general attitude towards education among the Greek Fathers and religious figures, and particularly the fourth-century Cappadocian theologians, Basil the Great, his younger brother, Gregory of Nyssa, and Gregory of Constantinople (the Theologian). He notes that "[t]he display of Classical learning that figured so often in the apologetics of the Cappadocians was of a piece with their high estimate of scholarship in general." Naturally, they used secular knowledge, not as having spiritual content in and of itself, but rhetorically "for purposes of illustration" and logically "for purposes of demonstration."[18] But they nonetheless showed an immense appreciation for reasoning as a tool and for its inherent usefulness in the revelation and discovery of what they saw as Christian truth: "Purely empirical observation did not suffice for arriving at ... conclusions of natural theology, but empiricism was not adequate even for valid scientific study, as [Saint] Basil argued: 'We must not measure the moon with the eye [alone], but with reasoning. Reasoning, for the discovery of truth, is much surer than the eye.'"[19] Pelikan then elaborates on the

---

17. See St. Philotheos, *Bios*, 52.
18. Pelikan, *Christianity*, 29.
19. Ibid., 101.

special significance of the science of mathematics in the theology of these paradigmatic theologians of the Greek tradition, citing the scholarly nun, St. Makrina, sister of Basil the Great and Gregory of Nyssa: "[T]he Cappadocians acknowledged that in their application of mathematics to natural theology they had as predecessors the ancient Pythagoreans. The apologetic value of geometry, according to Macrina, lay in its capacity to 'lead us step by step through visible delineations to truths lying out of sight.'"[20] Pelikan's general assertion and Makrina's specific words reinforce and clarify the fact that science and reason were not, for the Cappadocians and the early Greek theological tradition, ends in themselves, but apologetic devices and paths to a higher vision—a spiritual Truth, if you will—beyond normal seeing. As such, however, they bring into focus our argument against the putative opposition of the Greek Fathers and the foundational theological voices of Eastern Christianity to secular learning and education: "It was . . . clear that orthodox theology as a scientific discipline required a high level of education in the Classical as well as in the Christian tradition, and therefore the Cappadocians as orthodox Christian theologians repeatedly addressed themselves to the philosophy of education."[21]

It is often assumed that, even if the Church's theological tradition is not anti-intellectual, monastics in particular, who first blossomed in the deserts of the East after the Peace of the Church (the Edict of Milan) in 313 and who retreated from the "world," are called to disdain worldly knowledge. In response to this misnomer, it should be noted that many of the greatest theologians of the early Church, including those whom we have just cited, were monastics. Secondly, the monastic rejects, in his or her dedication to the spiritual life, what he or she sees as the passions, hypocrisy, pretense, and vainglory of the world, and *not* those innocent things and intellectual interests of the secular world that are edifying and even enjoyable. Moreover, there are different levels of, and callings in, monasticism; thus, the strict ascetic may live a life apart from many things in the world, while another monastic may live "in" the world but not "of it," combining the rigors of monasticism with an active life having clearly secular dimensions. And finally, many monastics, both in the Eastern and Western Christian traditions, receive a broad education in human behavior, social issues, history, and even the rudiments of science, by the very nature of a way of life that deliberately attempts to reach into the depths of human

20. Ibid.
21. Ibid., 175.

psychology and the soul. St. Kosmas Aitolos (d. 1779), a Hieromonk and another inheritor, in modern times, of the ethos of the Greeks, during the last century of domination of the Greek world by the Ottoman Empire, established schools throughout Greece. He highly regarded the value of education, both for society and for the Church, and in fact for monastic institutions themselves. His words are enlightening: "It is better, my brother, for you to have a Greek school in your village rather than fountains and rivers, for when your child becomes educated he is then a human being. The school opens churches; the school opens monasteries."[22] Characteristically, the Saint further affirms that the establishment and perpetuation of the Christian religion were accomplished not "by ignorant saints, but by wise and educated saints."[23] This affirmation is reflected in a contemporary scholar's comments about similar attitudes in the writings of an earlier monastic figure of great renown in the late Byzantine Empire, prior to the fall of Constantinople, Nicholas Cabasilas: "Cabasilas could contend that the saints themselves were incomplete personalities if they had not received sufficient instruction in this world."[24]

Elaborating on what we have said about a proper view of secular learning and education in the monastic setting in particular, it must be emphasized that education in the "monastic university," if we may use that expression, follows the patristic admonition that all learning should serve to form the soul. At the same time, monastic education contains within it a spiritual mystery that we would be remiss not to acknowledge. In the diligent pursuit of spiritual wisdom, there are many monastics who, though lacking even basic formal education in the world, come, through their spiritual discipline, to acquire knowledge of a secular kind. This is, of course, partly because, as we noted above, the spiritual life reaches into the depths of human psychology and the soul, touching on the same matters that any scholar, scientist, or intellectual sets out to explore. But it is also because a monastic sedulous in the study of the philosophy of philosophies, as the pursuit of spiritual wisdom is often styled, is said to be taught directly by divine enlightenment, becoming θεοδίδακτος, or "God-taught." The sagacity which he or she thus acquires is not only spiritual, but, according to the epistemology of the Greek Fathers, in restoring the proper harmony between the mind and the noetic faculty, the monk or nun comes to a natural

---

22. Vaporis, *Father Kosmas*, 77.
23. Ibid., 145.
24. Buckler, "Byzantine Education," 214.

knowledge of so-called "worldly" things. Such accomplished monastics may not, perhaps, hold forth with precision in areas of technical secular knowledge, but they will unflaggingly show that conceptual and theoretical breadth which is essential to an understanding of such. In short, logic and reason, as wholly natural attributes to the human being, are restored, in the view of the Greek Fathers, in one who pursues and succeeds in acquiring spiritual wisdom. This is why the true Saint, whether formally educated or not, is not a foreigner to libraries or learning, but an inexorable advocate of the ultimate unity of knowledge and wisdom, the latter encompassing the former and the former either a precursor to or a product of the latter. In the ethos of the early Church and the consensus of the Greek Fathers, therefore, an anti-intellectual Saint or monastic—or an anti-intellectual Christianity—is an impossibility. This is because enlightenment is not, for the Greek patristic tradition, some esoteric trait, but a sign of human and divine synergy.

Let us conclude by making two important observations. First, it is not just in the words of the Greek Fathers that we find guidance with regard to the Church's attitude towards, and understanding of, secular knowledge; it is also in their legacy in inspiring the ideal reaction of the Christian community to the world around it and the intellectual trends that dominate in a specific age. Given the vicissitudes of history, there are times when prevailing intellectual trends deviate significantly from the established principles of Christianity. In these instances, Christianity of necessity places itself at odds with the intellectual *Zeitgeist*. But in so doing, it acts out of a pastoral responsibility for the protection of the flock against what it sees as manifestly dangerous influences of a specific sort on what it holds to be true. It need not abandon, even in its dogmatic and doctrinal isolation from what it perceives as threatening, the general ethos of the Faith, which, as we have demonstrated, encourages the Christian to avail himself of what is good in secular and worldly knowledge. This point we see illustrated in the persons of Sts. Anthony the Great and Athanasios the Great, two celebrated Greek Fathers. As we learn from his life, the former was, though a formally unlettered man and a monastic desert-dweller, "not rough like a man of the mountain," but "graceful and polite," "lettered by the spiritual mind," from which, as he once affirmed, letters ultimately proceed.[25] The latter was formally lettered and likewise spiritually enlightened. Their common struggle against Arianism, which had triumphed in their age and which threatened

---

25. *Patrologia Graeca*, 26:945.

the patristic consensus as they saw it, reflects the early Christian attitude towards learning. The unlettered monk and the learned Patriarch, showing unreserved respect for one another, one learning from the other, made no distinction between "worldly knowledge" and "spiritual knowledge," but found common ground in their battle against an opposing party. Their strategy neither denigrated in some anti-intellectual way the theological learning of the Patriarch nor denigrated the noetic learning of the desert monk. In a common cause they brought two forms of knowledge together in an effective defense of their theological beliefs.

Second, and finally, from a pastoral standpoint, anti-intellectualism is a divisive thing, introducing unnecessary strife into the Church. As we repeatedly averred above, the Fathers of the Church, when they speak negatively of secular learning, do so to dissuade the Faithful from making worldly knowledge an end in and of itself. They act thusly, however, not in a spirit of anti-intellectualism, but from concern for the soul. They have the *same pastoral ends* in mind when they speak praisingly of intellectual awe and wonder, hoping that these will lead to the next step in personal growth: moving from the intellectual to the spiritual. In this perfect balance, treading the path of moderation that they inherited from the Classical Greeks ($\mu\eta\delta\grave{\epsilon}\nu$ $\check{\alpha}\gamma\alpha\nu$), they avoid the danger of setting the mind against the spirit or Christianity against learning. They fix us on a *oneness of mind* that wholly thwarts strife and that makes the learned and unlearned wise together.[26]

Bibliography

Baynes, N. H., and H. St. L. B. Moss, eds. *Byzantium: An Introduction to East Roman Civilization*. Oxford: Clarendon, 1948.

Brianchaninov, Bishop Ignaty. *Collected Works* (in Russian) 1. Jordanville, NY: Holy Trinity Monastery, 1957.

Cavarnos, Constantine. *Cultural and Educational Continuity of Greece: From Antiquity to the Present*. Belmont, MA: Institute for Byzantine and Modern Greek Studies, 1995.

———. *New Library*, vol. 2. Belmont, MA: Institute for Byzantine and Modern Greek Studies, 1992.

Gerostergios, Asterios. *Justinian the Great: The Emperor and Saint*. Belmont, MA: Institute for Byzantine and Modern Greek Studies, 1982.

———. *St. Photios the Great*. Belmont, MA: Institute for Byzantine and Modern Greek Studies, 1980.

Gregory of Nyssa. *De Vita Moysis*. Edited by Herbert Musurillo. In Werner Jaeger and Herman Langerbeck, eds., *Gregorii Nysseni Opera* 7.1. Leiden: Brill, 1964.

Migne, J.-P., ed. *Patrologiae Cursus Completus, Series Graeca*. 161 vols. Paris: 1857–66.

26. Compare 1 Pet 3:8.

Pelikan, Jaroslav. *Christianity and Classical Culture: The Metamorphosis of Natural Theology in the Christian Encounter with Hellenism.* New Haven: Yale University Press, 1993.

Philokalia ton Hieron Neptikon. 5 vols. 1957–63. Reprint. Athens: Aster, 1974–77.

Philotheos Kokkinos, St. *Bios Gregoriou Palama.* Hellenes Pateres tes Ekklesias 70. Thessalonike: Paterikai Ekdoseis "Gregorios ho Palamas," 1984.

Roberts, Alexander and James Donaldson, eds. *The Ante-Nicene Fathers.* 10 vols. Grand Rapids: Eerdmans, 1978.

Vaporis, Nomikos Michael. *Father Kosmas, Apostle of the Poor.* Brookline, MA: Holy Cross Orthodox Press, 1977.

White, Despina. *Patriarch Photios of Constantinople.* Brookline, MA: Holy Cross Orthodox Press, 1981.

Wilson, N. G., ed. *St. Basil on the Value of Greek Literature.* London: Duckworth, 1975.

CHAPTER 4

The Transformation of Hellenistic Philosophical Nomenclature in the Greek Patristic Tradition

*The Most Reverend Chrysostomos
and Archimandrite Patapios*

WE ARE QUITE ACCUSTOMED to the different ways in which words are used in various disciplines. When philosophers or theologians speak of ontology, for example, we recognize that the ontic and noumenal focus of their cosmologies determines how they define this concept. This focus is quite different than that of the linguist and philologist or, indeed, of the biologist, whose *empirical* cosmologies, as it were, transform the way in which they use this word. Such distinctions in the use of words and designations are the stuff of the nomenclatures that make up not only academic disciplines but intellectual traditions, too. Thus, we can speak of philosophical, theological, or biological nomenclatures, for instance, as well as the nomenclature of the classical era, the Middle Ages, or the modern era. We can even speak of a terminology peculiar to the poet or to the artist, as opposed to the specific vocabulary of the scientist. Somehow, we work with these differences in language, designation, and vocabulary with reasonable ease and minimum confusion. However, when our distinctions are made incautiously, or when nomenclature is improvidently applied, what we take for granted becomes at times unwittingly problematic. This danger is especially evident in history and philosophy. It is not unusual, today, to find global discussions in which even reasonably accomplished scholars use certain terms as though they were transhistorical and universally applicable, despite the fact that they have, in one historical period, far different meanings than they do in another.

Transformation of Hellenistic Philosophical Nomenclature

Let us, by example, look at the concept of "liberty." In the putatively luciferous age of Voltaire (d. 1778), this word conveyed a sense of personal empowerment. In the supposedly darker age of St. Augustine (d. 430), the term was used to describe one's personal freedom to make limited choices. Unless a scholar is careful to understand, again, the historical and philosophical context in which such words are used, he or she can wrongly establish what seem to be apodictic connections between systems of thought that are, in fact, sometimes oppositional. It is precisely in this way that most Western Christian scholars (and, indeed, some Eastern scholars influenced by Western thought) have traditionally argued, from an irrefragably superficial juxtaposition of the philosophical language of classical Hellenistic philosophy and the theological nomenclature of the Greek Fathers, that Eastern Orthodox theology was, in its formative stages in the primitive Church, deeply influenced by and conceptually formed around Hellenistic (Platonic, Neo-Platonic, and Gnostic) philosophical ideas—and, in particular, with regard to the world, the composition of the human being, and the ultimate fate of man. Here we have a paradigmatic case of similarities in γλῶσσαι and ὀνοματολογίαι inspiring wholly unfounded assumptions about semblances in the respective cosmologies, anthropologies, and soteriologies of the classical Hellenistic philosophers and the sages, divines, and Fathers of the Eastern Orthodox (or Byzantine) patristic tradition.

The familiarity of Western Christians and scholars of religion with the traditions of the Christian East and the Greek Fathers, as one of us has written elsewhere, ranges from "excellent to deplorable"[1]—significantly skewed, we must admit, towards the "deplorable." From as far back as the eighteenth and nineteenth centuries, Western scholars, theologians, historians, and philosophers alike have tended, as we noted above, to associate the teachings of the Eastern Christian tradition with Platonic, Neo-Platonic, and Gnostic thought. Some scholars have literally equated these traditions. Thus, the early twentieth-century scholar Edward Caird forthrightly stated that "the most important school of German theology" in his times held "that the great controversies of the early Church about the Trinity and the Incarnation were . . . about subtleties introduced by Greek philosophy into the Christian religion."[2] Among Eastern Orthodox scholars who have adopted this erroneous adequation are such figures as Maxim Tareev (d. 1934), who held the chair in moral philosophy at the Moscow Theologi-

---

1. Chrysostomos, *Guide*, 61.
2. Caird, *Evolution*, 359.

cal Academy and whom Father Georges Florovsky (d. 1979), one of the preeminent Orthodox theologians of the twentieth century, quotes—with some dismay, we should note—as saying that the Greek patristic tradition "is pure gnosticism."[3]

Nor do many scholars, in a similar instance of establishing careless parallels, distinguish Orthodoxy from Roman Catholicism. Writing in a volume on religious diversity in psychotherapy, one writer typically argues that "Eastern Orthodoxy is similar to Roman Catholicism in its theology .... The dominant difference is that rather than being fully united, the Eastern Orthodox Church is managed within national boundaries." He adds that "there is . . . [also] . . . less focus on doctrine than in the west and more on spirituality."[4] In the first place, however impolitic it may be to say so in an era as ecumenical as ours, there are profound and essential doctrinal and theological differences between the Eastern Orthodox and Roman Catholic Churches. These differences are probably, in fact, far more considerable than those that separate the latter from the mainline Protestant denominations. While these doctrinal dissimilarities are not our primary concern in the present paper, they will become immediately apparent in our discussion of Hesychasm and Scholasticism. They are, to be sure, intricately tied up with any serious attempt to portray with accuracy the confrontation between the spiritual practices and assumptions of the Hesychasts and the philosophical ruminations of the Scholastics. In the second place, the Orthodox Church is, of course, despite its system of localized administration (by autonomous and autocephalous synods of Bishops determined largely by ethnicity or nationality), closely united in its theological precepts and in a common confessional ethos that binds its various national groupings together. And thirdly, while it is true that there is an emphasis on "spirit" over "order" in the Christian East, this does not mean that doctrinal issues and rather meticulously formulated theological positions have a secondary place in Eastern Orthodoxy. The Eastern Church has always "been known for her great emphasis on precision," even in the terms used to "express the Faith."[5] The kinds of misapprehensions of the nature of Eastern Christianity that we have cited, which are widespread and common, distort both its history and

---

3. Florovsky, *Ways*, 300.

4. Roger R. Keller, "Religious Diversity in North America," in Richards and Bergin, *Handbook*, 35.

5. Cavarnos, *Orthodox Christian Terminology*, 61.

teachings. And they parallel, once more, the traducement which renders Greek patristic thought a subcategory of Hellenistic philosophy.

Returning to this central theme, it is of course true that, in formulating their apologetic statement of the unique and singular theology of the Orthodox East, the Greek Fathers knowingly and deliberately borrowed the nomenclature of, as well as certain cognitive structures from, Greek philosophy. In their somatology and epistemology, for example, they evidence the same concern for the somatic and noetic structure of man as the Hellenistic philosophers, discussing at length the human being as σῶμα and ψυχή (body and soul) or σῶμα and πνεῦμα (body and spirit). In concord with classical Greek philosophy, they also address the issue of the acquisition of spiritual knowledge and communion with the divine through the νοῦς, or a spiritual faculty that operates, in the human cognitive structure, alongside the dianoetic or intellectual faculty (διάνοια). But inflated conclusions about the significance of these kinds of terminological parallels ignore the fact that the Greek patristic tradition, in deliberately indigenizing the language of Greek philosophy, did so without adopting—and, indeed, without essential sympathy for—the anthropological, cosmological, and soteriological beliefs of the classical Greek world. As Father Gregory Telepneff and the senior author have noted, "the Greek Fathers, in 'borrowing' language, images, and ideas from the Greek philosophers, maintained, in this process, views that are wholly at odds with the cosmology and anthropology of the Greek ancients. One might even say that their debt was not so much that of a student to his mentor as that of a sculptor to his stone."[6]

In effect, the Greek patristic tradition "baptized" and "transformed" Hellenistic philosophical language to serve the precepts and tenets of Christianity. The purpose of the Greek Fathers, therefore, was not to construct a philosophy of Christianity, fitting it by some frantic Procrustean exercise into the framework of classical Greek philosophy; their stated task was to press the philosophical methods and vocabulary of the ancient Greeks—whom they at times characterized as pagans and bereft of true wisdom—into the service of Christian apologetics and theology. In the words of St. Gregory of Nyssa (d. *ca.* 394), Greek philosophy was as if "always in labor but never giving birth."[7] Hence, the worth of classical Greek philosophy and its nomenclature in expressing the experiential truths of Christian theology lay always in the ability of the Christian apologist to *bring the thought*

---

6. Chrysostomos, *God Made Man*, 20.
7. Ibid., 23.

of the ancients into fruition by way of the midwifery of Christian doctrine, thus exposing it to the light of a new world and a new experience.

With regard to scholars who refuse to take notice of this actual relationship between the Greek patristic tradition and the Hellenistic philosophers, we can, at a very basic level, respond to their primary charge against so-called Christian "Platonists": i.e., that the Greek Fathers embrace a dualistic cosmology. In fact, following the cosmology of Old Testamental Judaism, as Father Romanides avers, they rejected the whole body of Hellenistic dualistic teaching. The Hellenistic view of the cosmos "was wholly alien" to the Jews and equally so to ancient Christian doctrine.[8]

Elaborating on this point, Romanides writes that for the Jews, as for the Greek Fathers, "the world, visible and invisible, is the only real world created by God for man. Death, for the Jew [and the Orthodox Christian], is not phenomenological but real and tragic . . . . The present world and the future age are not two different worlds. Salvation, therefore, is not salvation from the world but from the present evil. Conversely, for the Greek philosophers, the natural way of salvation is the flight of the soul from the body and matter to the transcendent reality."[9] In a similar manner, the anthropology of the Greek Fathers was predicated on presuppositions wholly at odds with those of the Hellenistic philosophers, in spite of certain similarities, as we observed earlier, in how they speak of the constituent parts of the human body and the mind or spirit (that is, with regard to their somatology and epistemology). Romanides contends that the Greek patristic tradition is also at odds with the anthropology of the Platonists, who (along with the Neo-Platonists and Gnostics) would equate the "resurrection of the body" and its oneness with the soul—anthropological principles basic to the patristic tradition—"with the damnation of the soul, constituting its reimprisonment [in the body]."[10] Father Georges Florovsky further observes that the anthropology of the Greek Fathers was, in actuality, closer to that of Aristotle than to that of Plato,[11] "since Aristotle understood the unity of human existence, of the body and soul, at an intuitive level. . . . [E]mpirical existence and the human personality," for him, "took on an importance that could not be detached from the eternal elements of the soul."[12] Such

8. Romanides, *To Propatorikon Hamartema*, 41.
9. Ibid., 41–42.
10. Ibid., 42.
11. Florovsky, *Aspects*, 75.
12. See Chrysostomos, *God Made Man*, 37.

a concept of human personhood cannot be reconciled with Platonic and Neo-Platonic, not to mention Gnostic, anthropology.

It is in their understanding of human restoration, or salvation, that the Greek Fathers deviate most markedly, despite their use of Hellenic philosophical terms, from the presuppositions of classical Greek thought. It is true that some early Christian writers—Origen (d. 254) chief among them—did adopt, in their thinking on human restoration, the classical Greek idea of ἀποκατάστασις (restoration), including such ideas as the pre-existence of souls; however, they were condemned as "heretics" for deviating from the *consensio Patrum,* or the consensus of the experiential spirituality which is the underpinning of Eastern Orthodox theological doctrine. The Greek philosophers, in striving to return man to a Golden Age of the human condition *in illo tempore,* saw restoration as a process of separation from the illusion of this world and a return to some previous state of god-like status lost in the trap of materialism. By contrast, the Greek Fathers teach that the human being attains to genuine ontology by his participation (μετουσία) and sharing in divine existence, taking on an eternal dimension for the self while, at the same time, transforming and restructuring the physical universe and the material world, which have been reconciled by the Incarnation, or the joining of eternity with time and space by the union of God with humankind. This idea is expressed in an oft-quoted aphorism of the Greek Fathers: *God became man, in order to restore man to Divinity*—an idea perfectly reflected in a verse from the magnificent hymnography of the Orthodox Church, the *Doxastikon* at the Praises of Annunciation Matins: "'Ἄνθρωπος γίνεται Θεός, ἵνα Θεὸν τὸν Ἀδὰμ ἀπεργάσηται" (God becomes man, that He might make Adam [i.e., the fallen human] God).[13] Inarguably, then, the Greek patristic understanding of man (and most importantly of salvation) diverges essentially and categorically from that of classical Greek philosophy. This conclusion is, we might add, given significant support by I. P. Sheldon-Williams, in his classic investigation of the relationship between Hellenistic and Christian thought.[14]

In the Hesychastic Controversy of the fourteenth century, we see a clear articulation of the dissimilarities between the theology of the Greek Fathers and the Hellenistic philosophers that we have discussed. It was in this period that the Hesychasts so precisely defined the theological vocabulary and the anthropological, cosmological, and soteriological principles of

---

13. Patapios and Chrysostomos, *Manna,* 11.
14. Sheldon-Williams, in Armstrong, ed., *Cambridge History,* 426.

Orthodox Christianity, as Eastern and Western Christianity came into an essential and enduring conflict over these principles. This period followed long years of captivity—almost six decades—in the Christian East, when the Fourth Crusade conquered Constantinople and imposed Latin rule over much of the Byzantine Empire.[15] This confrontation is frequently characterized as a collision of Eastern Orthodox Platonic theological thought with the Aristotelian thinking of the medieval Latin scholastics. In fact, it was, more technically, a theological conflict between the Greek patristic tradition, which had expressed the Christian message in a new language adapted to that message from Greek classical philosophy (Platonic and Aristotelian alike), and a Western rationalistic revamping of Christian theology in the Thomistic tradition of applying the categories of Aristotelian Hellenistic philosophy to Christian doctrine. It is an oddity of intellectual history that this great clash between the Orthodox East and the Scholastic West, in the very age of the rise of Papal monarchy, should be viewed by Western scholars as a conflict between the putatively Platonic Hellenistic philosophical ideas of the Greek Fathers and the rationalism of the West. It is, rather, a meeting of an overarching Christian theological consensus in the undivided Christian world, that lasted well into the early Middle Ages, and a Christian rationalism formed, in the West, in the crucible of Aristotelianism—ironically enough, a school of Hellenistic philosophy.

The Hesychastic Controversy centered on two figures: St. Gregory Palamas (d.1359), representing the Hesychasts, whose center of influence was the monastic republic of Mt. Athos in Northern Greece (the Holy Mountain) and "whose teachings . . . constitute a *perfect manifestation* of the fullness of [Orthodox] Christian cosmology, anthropology, and theology";[16] and Barlaam the Calabrian (d.1350), a Greco-Italian monk who made his way into the Byzantine world *circa* 1330. St. Gregory Palamas was the scion of a Greek aristocratic family and was reared in the imperial court. As a young man, he distinguished himself as a scholar. A story is told of the Great Logothete of the Byzantine court, Theodore Metochites, that, when he heard the Saint, as a young student, discuss the logic of Aristotle in the presence of the Emperor, he commented: "If Aristotle himself had been present to listen to this young man, he would, I believe, have praised him beyond measure. For the time being, I say that it is those with such a soul and of such nature as his who should be pursuing knowledge, and especially the

---

15. Chrysostomos, *Orthodox and Roman Catholic Relations*, 93.
16. Chrysostomos, "In Honor," 15.

omnifarious philosophical writings of Aristotle."[17] (Aside from providing some insight into the early life and intellectual prowess of the Saint, this story also underscores our contention that the conflict between Hesychasm and Scholasticism cannot be dismissed as a simple struggle between Platonism and Aristotelianism; the "father" of putatively Platonic Hesychasm was, it appears, an expert in Aristotle!) Barlaam, by contrast, was educated and trained in the West, his personal history and roots somewhat clouded by the lack of clear historical documentation and claims for his intellectual eminence poorly supported in his exchanges with Palamas. At any rate, St. Gregory and the Hesychasts were the continuators of the Greek patristic tradition and Barlaam, to whatever level of excellence, championed the Latin Scholastic tradition. As for Barlaam's appearance in the Orthodox world, despite his claims that he went East because of his sympathies for, and attraction to, the Greek tradition, after his imperial condemnation at the final resolution of his long conflict with St. Gregory, he returned to the West and was made a Bishop in the Roman Catholic Church.[18] This has led some to believe that his *real purpose* in going to Constantinople was to work to effect a union between the East and West by challenging the theological impediments to rapprochement posed by the Hesychasts.[19]

The Hesychastic tradition, in keeping with a tradition that dates back to the monastics of the North African deserts in the first few Christian centuries, teaches a system by which the mind and body, cleansed by spiritual exercise, come into communion with God.[20] In concord with the soteriological principles that we cited above, this system takes its substance from the affirmation that Christ became a human being so that, by Grace, human beings might restore the image of God within them, which was sullied by the disobedience of Adam and Eve and passed on as an "ancestral curse" to all mankind. In the words of St. Athanasios the Great (d. 373), "Αὐτὸς ... ἐνηνθρώπησεν ἵνα ἡμεῖς θεοποιηθῶμεν" ("He [the Word of God, or Christ] ... became man so that we might be made God").[21] Indeed, the whole Hesychastic tradition, as evidenced by a statement of St. Nikodemos the Hagiorite (a monk of Mt. Athos, d.1809), teaches that "to be saved

---

17. St. Philotheos, *Bios*, 5.
18. Romanides, "Notes," 193.
19. Theokletos, *Ho Hagios Gregorios*, 44–45.
20. Chrysostomos, "Towards a Spiritual Psychology."
21. *Patrologia Graeca*, 25:192B.

(*sothenai*) and to be deified (*theothenai*) are the same thing."[22] According to the Hesychasts, the body and the soul are saved together, since they ideally exist in perfect harmony, the body, when freed from passions and sinful inclinations, ruled over by the νοῦς, "that highest part of the soul, the psyche, the eye of the soul,"[23] or, to be a bit more precise, the essential aspect of the mind or the very imprint of God in man. As Jean-Claude Larchet says of the νοῦς, or noetic faculty, it "represents the contemplative possibilities of man. It is fundamentally, for the Fathers, that by which man is brought to God, directed towards Him, and united with Him . . . . [I]t is . . . the image of God in man." Larchet pinpoints in the νοῦς the "indelible mark" of man's "true nature."[24]

The method of spiritual transformation which the Hesychasts followed—based, again, on ancient tradition—brought into focus, as we noted earlier, the distinct understanding of the world, the body and the mind (or the body and the spirit), and human deification that marks the teachings of the Greek Fathers. Hesychasm (ἡσυχασμός) derives from the Greek word for silence (ἡσυχία) and is, as the Greek theologian Metropolitan Hierotheos (Vlachos) says, "the practice of stillness in the presence of God"; and "those who practice it," he further states, "are called hesychasts."[25] Central to Hesychastic practice is the concentration of the eyes on the center of the body (the solar plexus) and the control of one's breathing, in conjunction with the recitation of the so-called "Jesus Prayer" ("Lord Jesus Christ, Son of God, have mercy on me, a sinner"), or "prayer of the heart." Combined with fasting and purity of life, this practice is said to lead to the vision of Uncreated Light, or the Energies of God. It is in that Light that the human being is deified and brought into union with the Energies of God, transforming both the body and the soul. In this salvific process, the mind enters into the heart, the repository of spiritual Grace, where it is purified. The discursive intellect, as the thoughts, emotions, and passions are cleansed, then comes into harmony with the νοῦς, and the human being—again, both in body and in mind—experiences deification or *theosis*. "As man is transformed by Grace," as one writer puts it, "he is literally divinized,"[26] participating in

---

22. Cavarnos, *St. Nicodemos*, 15.

23. Tony R. Young, "Psychotherapy with Eastern Orthodox Christians," in Richards and Bergin, eds., *Handbook* 102.

24. Larchet, *Thérapeutique des Maladies Mentales*, 37–38.

25. Hierotheos, *St. Gregory*, 394.

26. Hieromonk [Bishop] Auxentios, "Notes on the Nature of God, the Cosmos, and

the Energies of God while, at the same time, God remains, in His Essence, unknowable, ineffable, and wholly beyond human ken.[27] It is thus that the individual is "saved."

Proceeding from his Scholastic understanding of theology, Barlaam pilloried the Hesychasts for "navel-gazing (ὀμφαλοσκοπία)" and derided their physical spiritual exercises—which St. Gregory Palamas argued were mere bodily aids in achieving freedom from external distraction, in seeking communion with God—as attempts to capture a physical vision of God.[28] In his intellectual calumny against Palamas and the Hesychasts, Barlaam went so far as to accuse them of claiming to behold the unknown "Essence of God" in their vision of Uncreated Light. On this basis, he went on to say that they were guilty of the fourth-century heresy of Messalianism, which held that the Persons of the Trinity were visible to the human eye. About their teaching on salvation and *theosis,* Barlaam had nothing but the most opprobrious slanders to heap on the Hesychasts. This is undoubtedly partly because, from his background in Scholasticism, his soteriological convictions were formulated on the Thomistic notion of salvation as something centered on the expiation of human guilt for original sin and not on the medical model of the Greek Fathers, which envisioned salvation as the re-activation of the divine image in man through Baptism (φωτισμός, or enlightenment, as it was known in the early Church), his restoration to spiritual "health" through *theosis,* and his consequent liberation from the "ancestral curse."[29] Barlaam also accused the Hesychasts of theological innovation and of resorting to Greek paganism, a charge which was the direct result of his inability, significantly enough (given the theme of our essay), to understand the way in which the Hesychasts, in line with the Greek *consensio Patrum,* had recast the language of Hellenistic philosophy to fit the theology of Christianity as it was preserved in the doctrinal traditions of the Orthodox Church.

It becomes abundantly clear, therefore, that in their confrontation with Barlaam's Western Scholasticism, the Hesychasts brought into vivid focus the unique way in which the Greek Fathers employed the terms and categories of Hellenistic philosophy. Once again, this confrontation, in the fourteenth century, between Thomistic thought and a consensus

---

Novus Homo," in Chrysostomos et al., *Contemporary Eastern Orthodox Thought,* 15.

27. Chrysostomos, *Guide,* 78–84.

28. Hierotheos, *Orthodox Psychotherapy,* 293.

29. Chrysostomos, *Guide,* 83–85.

of theological thought which—in spite of the fact that its provenance was largely Eastern—in many ways constituted a doctrinal hegemony before the Great Schism, helped to define the basic anthropological, cosmological, and soteriological differences which to this day separate the Christian West from the Christian East. As we noted earlier, these differences are significant enough that, in many ways, they constitute—contrary to facile assertions to the contrary—a chasm which is far wider than that which separates Roman Catholicism from Protestantism, as some of the Protestant Reformers actually understood. More importantly, the confrontation of Eastern and Western theology in the fourteenth century puts to rest the simplistic idea that the Greek Fathers were influenced by Platonism and other Hellenistic philosophical traditions and thus found themselves separated from the course of theological thought as it developed in the West. This assumption is simply untrue. Indisputably of equal worthlessness is the charge that the Christian East, Platonic in its theological formulations, came into conflict, during the Hesychastic controversy, with the Aristotelian foundations of Western Scholasticism. It would be far more accurate to say, in fact, that, to the extent that Latin Scholasticism was Aristotelian in its foundations—and this is, admittedly, both an exaggeration of the Aristotelian influence on Aquinas and his followers and an imprecise characterization of Scholastic philosophical dialectics—it was the effect of Hellenistic philosophical thought on *Western Christianity* that drew *it* away from the theological consensus of the undivided Christian Church. That consensus the Greek Fathers received, expressed, and preserved in the "new language" of Christianity, cast as it was in the old terminology of Hellenistic philosophy pressed into the service of a view of the world, man, and human restoration wholly alien to the intellectual tradition from which it was drawn.

Discussion

We would like, in concluding these remarks about how language must be understand in the context of its deliberate application—as in the case of the Greek Fathers and their "baptism" of Hellenistic philosophical language for its use in their theological formulations—to draw attention to the curious and far-reaching distortions that can result from examining a school of thought or an intellectual tradition out of the context that we have said must be established in each instance. Many of the popular myths about

Christianity as a contrived politico-religious system subservient to the body politic and bent on controlling man and society are entwined with misapprehensions about the influence of Greek philosophy on the Greek Fathers. Hence, there are those who view the whole of Eastern Christianity as a Christian "version" (or "distortion") of Hellenistic philosophy, created at the Synod of Nicea by the Emperor Constantine, in the early fourth century, in order to impose on his Empire a "divine Christ" Who would lend His ethereal authority to the worldly Emperor. Such poppycock has long enjoyed credence and is still embraced by more myopic Western church historians; and it has, of late, gained a following among critics who would attribute to Christianity, as a whole, this sort of Machiavellian historical heritage. A corollary of this idea is that of a "shadow" Gnostic Christianity that was supposedly suppressed by the Constantinian recognition of the Church: a Christianity that generally denied the Divinity of Christ, had its own Gospels, preached a form of triumphal feminism, and embraced such (actually Platonic) novelties as the pre-existence of souls and reincarnation. These ideas have recently gained new attention because of the popularity of such fictional works as *The Da Vinci Code*, written by a private secondary school English teacher turned writer,[30] or *The Holy Blood and The Holy Grail*, a wholly fictional book often touted as an "historical work," written by a conspiracy theorist holding a degree in psychology, an academic with postgraduate degrees in comparative literature, and an actor and screenwriter (né Henry Soskin) who writes under the pseudonym of Henry Lincoln.[31] These works try to invoke variant Gospels and arcane historical sources to lend an aura of historical authenticity to what is simply pulp fiction, penned by artful writers and peddled as scholarship.

We have argued in this essay that the Greek Fathers and the early Church were in some areas inimical to Hellenistic philosophy; as such, they of course rejected Gnostic beliefs. Thus, contrary to the nonsense spawned by poor scholarship, Nicene Christianity was nothing innovative or at odds with prevailing Christian beliefs. The Nicene Synod was not, in fact, convened to suppress the Gnostic or pagan Greek views of those who impugned or challenged the Divinity of Christ, but to consider disputes that had arisen over the *nature* of Christ's Divinity vis-à-vis His humanity. Gnostics, who are sometimes portrayed, in the popular presentation

---

30. Brown, *Da Vinci Code*.

31. Baigent et al., *Holy Blood, Holy Grail*. (Published in Great Britain as *The Holy Blood and The Holy Grail*.)

of Christianity in works of the kind that we mentioned above, as the keepers of a more genuine Christianity than that of Nicea, actually saw Christ through the prism of Docetism (from the Greek word δοκέω, to "seem" or "appear") and considered Him to be "pure spirit." It was their claim that He was *not a human being* and that His humanity and His body, as well as His suffering on the Cross and His death, were illusions. The Emperor Constantine, moreover, was not a theologian, did not dictate the decisions of the Synod of Nicea, and did not create a Christianity tailored to his political needs. With regard to some hidden feminist agendum in early Christianity, we might recall that the very idea of the equality of men and women (not to mention Jew and Gentile or master and slave) put forth by St. Paul ("There is neither Jew nor Greek, there is neither bond nor free, there is neither male nor female: for all are one in Jesus Christ")[32] was itself a revolutionary teaching. Strident feminism was unknown in this period of history and cannot be validly cited, on the basis of extant historical evidence, as having played any role whatever in the development of primitive Christianity.

Additionally, there is absolutely no support in the canonical Gospels accepted by the early Church for any of the accusations against Nicene Christianity spawned by these foregoing distortions, paralleling, as they do, unwarranted assumptions about an exaggerated relationship between Hellenistic philosophy and Christian doctrine. Though many biblical scholars date the canonical Gospels to the second century and thus place them on equal historical footing with such later uncanonical and dubious texts as the so-called Gnostic Gospels, the Christian East has always held that the Gospels and the Epistles date to a much earlier period (the Apostolic Age) and thus reflect the true beliefs of early Christians. This view is supported by various Western scholars, as well. Anglican Bishop John A. T. Robinson, in a work in which he set out to dispute what he actually finally averred, concluded some decades ago that the New Testament in its entirety was written before AD 70, when Jerusalem fell.[33] Similarly, Jean Carmignac, a Dead Sea Scrolls scholar and expert in Greek and Hebrew, argues on the basis of brilliant linguistic analyses, for the same dating of the Gospels.[34]

Whatever the claims and fancies of those turning to the witness of the Gnostic Gospels, one can with some justification, and with the weight of the witness of the Eastern Church behind him, posit that they are later

---

32. Gal 3:28–29.
33. Robinson, *Redating the New Testament*, 336–58 esp.
34. Carmignac, *Birth of the Synoptics*.

products of the second century and not artifacts of the early Church. In the final analysis, the teachings of the Greek Fathers and the pronouncements of the Oecumenical Synods which expressed and defended the spiritual experiences of the primitive Church are unique unto themselves; stand in contrast to the philosophy of the Greek ancients, in whose language the Fathers often expressed their theology; and place our assumptions about the *consensio Patrum*, if not the entire experience of undivided Christendom, in its proper philosophical and philological context.

Bibliography

Armstrong, A. H., ed. *The Cambridge History of Later Greek and Early Medieval Philosophy*. Cambridge: Cambridge University Press, 1967.
Baigent, M., R. Leigh, and H. Lincoln. *Holy Blood, Holy Grail*. New York: Delacorte, 2005.
Brown, Dan. *The Da Vinci Code*. New York: Doubleday, 2004.
Caird, Edward. *The Evolution of Theology in the Greek Philosophers*, vol. 2. Glasgow: MacLehose, 1904.
Carmignac, Jean. *The Birth of the Synoptics*. Translated by Father M. J. Wren. Chicago: Franciscan Herald, 1987.
Cavarnos, Constantine. *Orthodox Christian Terminology*. Belmont, MA: Institute for Byzantine and Modern Greek Studies, 1994.
———. *St. Nicodemos the Hagiorite*. Modern Orthodox Saints 3. Belmont, MA: Institute for Byzantine and Modern Greek Studies, 1979.
Chrysostomos, Archbishop. *God Made Man and Man Made God*. Belmont, MA: Institute for Byzantine and Modern Greek Studies, 2010.
———. *A Guide to Orthodox Psychotherapy: The Science, Theology, and Spiritual Practice Behind It and Its Clinical Applications*. Lanham, MD: University Press of America, 2006.
———. "In Honor of St. Gregory Palamas." *Orthodox Tradition* 17.4 (2000) 14–21.
———. *Orthodox and Roman Catholic Relations: From the Fourth Crusade to the Hesychastic Controversy*. Etna, CA: Center for Traditionalist Orthodox Studies, 2001.
———. "Towards a Spiritual Psychology: A Synthesis of the Desert Fathers." *Pastoral Psychology* 37 (1989) 255–73.
Chrysostomos, Archimandrite [Archbishop], Hieromonk Auxentios, and Hierodeacon Akakios. *Contemporary Eastern Orthodox Thought: The Traditionalist Voice*. Belmont, MA: Nordland, 1982.
Florovsky, Georges. *Aspects of Church History*. Belmont, MA: Nordland, 1975.
———. *Ways of Russian Theology: Part Two*. Vaduz, Liechtenstein: Büchervertriebsanstalt, 1987.
Hierotheos of Nafpaktos, Metropolitan. *Orthodox Psychotherapy: The Science of the Fathers*. Translated by Esther Williams. Levadia, Greece: Birth of the Theotokos Monastery, 1994.
———. *St. Gregory Palamas as a Hagiorite*. Translated by Esther Williams. Levadia, Greece: Birth of the Theotokos Monastery, 1997.

Larchet, Jean-Claude. *Thérapeutique des Maladies Mentales: L' Expérience de l'Orient Chrétien des Premiers Siècles*. Paris: Cerf, 1992.

Migne, J.-P., ed. *Patrologiae Cursus Completus, Series Graeca*. 161 vols. Paris: 1857–66.

Patapios, Hieromonk, and Archbishop Chrysostomos. *Manna from Athos: The Issue of Frequent Communion on the Holy Mountain in the Late Eighteenth and Early Nineteenth Centuries*. Byzantine and Neohellenic Studies 2. Oxford: Lang, 2006.

Philotheos Kokkinos, St. *Bios Gregoriou Palama*. Hellenes Pateres tes Ekklesias 70. Thessalonike: Paterikai Ekdoseis "Gregorios ho Palamas," 1984.

Richards, P. Scott, and Allen E. Bergin, eds. *Handbook of Psychotherapy and Religious Diversity*. Washington, DC: American Psychological Association, 2002.

Robinson, John A. T. *Redating the New Testament*. London: SCM, 1976.

Romanides, John S. "Notes on the Palamite Controversy and Related Topics: Part I." *The Greek Orthodox Theological Review* 6.2 (1960–1961) 186–205.

———. *To Propatorikon Hamartema: Etoi Symbolai eis Ereunan ton Proypotheseon tes Didaskalias peri Propatorikou Hamartematos en te Mechri tou Hag. Eirenaiou Archaia Ekklesia en Antibole Pros ten Katholou Kateuthynsin tes Orthodoxou kai tes Dytikes Mechri Thoma tou Akinatou Theologias* (Ancestral Sin: Namely, Contributions to the Study of Presuppositions Concerning the Doctrine of Ancestral Sin in the Ancient Church to the Time of St. Irenaeus Vis-à-Vis the General Direction of Orthodox and Western Theology to the Time of Thomas Aquinas). Athens: University of Athens, 1957.

Theokletos [Dionysiates], Monk. *Ho Hagios Gregorios ho Palamas: Ho Bios kai he Theologia Tou 1296–1359*. Thessalonike: P. Ginnoules, K. Tsolerides, G. Dedouses, 1984.

CHAPTER 5

The Notion of Rhetoric in the Eastern Orthodox Patristic Tradition

Bishop Auxentios

RHETORIC IS NOT SOMETHING disassociated from the Greek Fathers. It would not be an exaggeration to say that the vast majority of patristic scholars, East and West, look to these Fathers as a paradigm of theological discourse set forth in image, language, and form reminiscent of the most beautiful in classical rhetoric. Saint Gregory the Theologian (d. 390), for example, has been universally hailed in the Church as a master of classical rhetoric. But if style and form and impression and expression are integral to the transmission and communication of truth in Western theological and spiritual thought; indeed, if they form that two-part construct of spirit and message so vital to the traditional Reformed notion of preaching as the very revelation and actualization of the Word of God—a notion which has reached far beyond the Reformed tradition in present-day homiletics; such, to be sure, is still not an apt statement about rhetoric as it is understood in traditional Eastern Christian thought. This point must be made. From an Eastern Orthodox perspective, from that perspective formed in and by the Greek patristic ethos, rhetoric is an adornment, as it were, to the truth, albeit one intimately and immediately linked to the truth. Just as truth, for the Greek Fathers, is expressed in their rhetoric, so, too, they reserved for such rhetoric, for this special medium of expression, the message of truth. If rhetoric and the truth form a single thing, it is not so much that one is contained in the other, but that rhetoric most appropriately complements the truth.

If we are to understand the subtly unique nature of rhetoric as it is received in Greek patristic thought, then we must understand this uniqueness, in turn, within the context of the singularly unique truth to which it is suited. If rhetoric is an adornment, as we have said, its particular character and beauty can be understood only by clearly understanding the truth which it adorns and which, in turn, gives to it a distinct flavor and effectiveness. To the extent that rhetoric has a power of its own, that power constantly and inevitably returns to the truth from which it derives by adornment. Let us, then, look at the statement of theological truth put forth by the Greek Fathers and the crucial role which that statement plays in analyzing and understanding rhetoric in that tradition and in distinguishing it from rhetoric as it might be understood in other theological and intellectual systems.

How is it that the search for truth is set forth in the corpus of traditional Orthodox theological writings and discourses? In his now classic study, *Bible, Church, Tradition: An Eastern Orthodox View*, the late Protopresbyter Georges Florovsky proffers a trenchant treatment of the problematic relationship between Scripture and Tradition in the early Church. In it lies a classical statement about theological truth from the Eastern patristic view. He observes that the essential hermeneutic concern of the early Fathers was not the search for an image or principle of authority—in the sense of an institution or a dogma—but rather the establishment of a *criterion* upon which to determine Christian truth: an operational principle to guide one in the science of authentic and authoritative interpretation that we today call hermeneutics. Indeed, in the early Church both the orthodox and heretical parties were in accord in affirming that what is true is authoritative. One might say that, for the early Fathers, these two terms were virtually synonymous. Orthodox and heretics in the early Church were, for the most part, also in agreement with regard to the necessity of putting forth any appeal to truth in a strictly scriptural context. Thus, Scripture constituted for the primitive Christian community the most perfect expression of the truth. The disagreements which separated the orthodox and heretical parties centered on how this appeal was to be made: How does one rightly determine the meaning of the words contained in Scripture? And here, in contradistinction to the heretics—for whom there reigned multifarious determinants—the Orthodox were in full agreement. "Tradition," in the words of Father Florovsky, "was the only means to ascertain and to disclose the true meaning of Scripture."[1] He expands on this pithy formula as follows:

---

1. Florovsky, *Collected Works*, 1:74–75.

> [T]radition was in the Early Church, first of all, an hermeneutical principle and method. Scripture could be rightly and fully assessed and understood only in the light and in the context of the living Apostolic Tradition, which was an integral factor of Christian existence. It was so, of course, not because Tradition could add anything to what has been manifested in the Scripture, but because it provided that living context, the comprehensive perspective, in which only the true "intention" and the total "design" of the Holy Writ, of Divine Revelation itself, could be detected and grasped.[2]

In further speaking of truth as a product of proper scriptural interpretation drawn from authentic Tradition, Father Florovsky undertakes a careful examination of the various terms employed by the Orthodox in their appeals to Tradition: Saint Vincent of Lérins's "ecclesiastical understanding," Tertullian's "rule of faith," Saint Athanasios the Great's "scope of faith," Saint Basil the Great's "unwritten mysteries of the Church" and "intention of the Scripture," and Saint Augustine of Hippo's "catholic preaching."[3] His conclusion is that, in the early Church, an appeal to Tradition, or, as it is later more commonly called, an appeal to the witness of the Fathers, was neither a selective appeal—an appeal to a particular Father whose words confirmed what one wanted to say—nor an appeal to antiquity—grounded, as such an appeal usually is, on the erroneous premise that what is older is always more genuine (for, indeed, there are heresies older than the formulations by which they were subsequently refuted). Rather, the appeal to the Fathers was to a certain commonality of mind and thought, the patristic φρόνημα, the *consensus Patrum*. And the unique characteristic of this consensus was its spiritual—its ecclesiastical—dimension. The consensus of the Fathers was not contained in majority opinion, though the majority might hold to it; rather, it was rooted in, belonged to, and proceeded from the spiritual authority of the Church, the Pillar and Foundation of Truth.[4] "This consensus was much more than just an empirical agreement of individuals. The true and authentic consensus was that which reflected the mind of the Catholic and Universal Church—τὸ ἐκκλησιαστικὸν φρόνημα ['the ecclesiastical mind' or 'the mind of the Church']."[5]

---

2. Ibid., 79.
3. Ibid., 73–79.
4. Compare 1 Tim 3:15.
5. Florovsky, *Collected Works*, 1:105.

The *consensus Patrum* (the mind [φρόνημα] of the Fathers), the mind of the Church, and, indeed, the mind of Christ—all of these are synonymous for Father Florovsky. To some extent, they refer to yet another and essential criterion of truth recognized by the early Church and championed by the Greek Fathers: one which rests in the transformation and renewal of the human mind. This renewal is one to which all Christians are called. The response of the *novus homo*, a man or woman restored in Christ, to the imperative call of this vocation lies at the very core of Eastern Orthodox spirituality: "And be not conformed to this world: but be ye transformed by the renewing of your mind, that ye may prove what is that good, and acceptable, and perfect, will of God."[6] This vocation is, as much as anything else, the vehicle for an epistemological and hermeneutic principle: the beginning of a spiritual ascent and renewal of the mind in which we come to know and understand the criterion of Truth.[7]

But in another and more universal sense, the renewal of human consciousness, the single believer's participation in the mind of the Fathers, itself focuses on the Christian community, on Christ, and, as such, stands on the Pillar and Foundation, even the Source, of Truth. The logic here is somewhat tautological in nature, though in no way compromised by the pejorative connotations attached to the tautological; rather, it is the logic appropriate to that which in singularity is one with what single elements in consort form together. For He Who quickens His Body, the Church, is the source of Truth and the Supreme Authority. To the extent that we have the mind of Christ, that we attain, through spiritual transformation, to a oneness with Him, we apprehend and understand the Truth, according to the Greek Fathers. In the transformed individual resides that mind which makes all individuals one and which gives to the one that universal knowledge dwelling in all and derived from the One. Thus, we know the truth by possessing it and possess it by our knowledge. To help unravel this circularity, let us look a little closer at the Orthodox conception of dogmatic truth and its relation to the renewal of the human mind.

Father John Romanides, a contemporary Greek theologian and a student of Father Florovsky, is one of the more prominent figures in the so–called "patristic renewal" of the Orthodox Church, an intellectual movement that began some decades ago both in Eastern European and the Western Orthodox theological circles. He has been an active voice

---

6. Rom 12:2.
7. Compare 1 Cor 2:15–16.

in efforts, at least in the theological arena, to return Orthodox thought to its traditional roots and to remove from it many of the Western ideas and theological conceptualizations that have compromised and distorted its witness. In several of his works, he has maintained that the dogmatic contentions of the early Church arose from a confrontation between an empirical (what he considers the properly Orthodox) and a speculative (potentially or manifestly heretical) view of the science of theology. The former view (theological method, if you will), he argues, is founded and formulated on a therapeutic asceticism (a curative restoration of the human being through spiritual and bodily ascesis; *viz.*, among other things, intense love for God, the cultivation of selfless love, mental prayer, fasting, and warfare with the fallen world). It uses the nomenclature of its day, both Hebraic and Hellenic, to formulate its observations and to guide others to a verification of its formulae by replication.

Father Romanides remarks that, "in the Orthodox Patristic tradition, genuine spiritual experience is the foundation of dogmatic formulations which, in turn, are necessary guides for leading [one] to glorification . . . . The experience of glorification of the prophets, apostles, and saints are [*sic*] expressed in linguistic forms, whose purpose is to act as a guide to the same experience of glorification by their successors."[8] In contrast to this, the purveyors of the speculative tradition were not convinced of the necessity of grounding theological formulae in empirical fact. Rather, this school was generally optimistic about the intrinsic ability of the mind, independent of empirical experience, to reason and formulate on the loftiest of matters pertaining to the divine. The highly refined philosophical vocabulary of the Greek language and, more importantly, the basic presuppositions of the philosophies that shaped that language were the tools of this speculative school. Father Romanides contends that this approach, divorced as it was from any notion of empirical verification and trusting in the mind's innate reasoning abilities, was destined to repeat the "errors of the ancients." The "dogmas" of these speculative heretics, while perhaps pleasing in their logic and consistency, were essentially counterfeits, he argues, that misled the Faithful and gave them "stones instead of bread."[9]

Father Romanides characterizes the foregoing distinction between the empirical and speculative theological methods with a remarkable analogy, likening those who were Orthodox in their understanding to contemporary

---

8. Romanides, *Franks*, 39.
9. Compare Matt 7:9; Luke 11:11.

practitioners of the hard sciences. His analogy also clarifies the patristic understanding of human language (thus, we should emphasize, touching tangentially on matters rhetorical), vis-à-vis the spiritual, and the importance of the traditional hermeneutic that accompanies that language.

> The Fathers did not understand theology as a theoretical or speculative science, but as a positive [*i.e.,* positivistic] science in all respects....
>
> Scientific manuals are inspired by the observations of specialists. For example, the astronomer records what he observes by means of the instruments at his disposal. Because of his training in the use of... [these]... instruments, he is inspired by the heavenly bodies, and sees things invisible to the naked eye.... Books about science can never replace scientific observations. These writings are not the observations themselves, but [are] about these observations....
>
> [Moreover]..., the writings of scientists are accompanied by a tradition of interpretation, heeded by successor scientists, who, by training and experience, know what their colleagues mean by the language used, and how to repeat the observations described.[10]

And here follows the completion of the analogy:

> The same is true of the Orthodox understanding of the Bible and the writings of the Fathers. Neither the Bible nor the writings of the Fathers are revelation or the word of God. They are *about* revelation and *about* the Word of God [*emphasis mine*].
>
> ... Only those who have the same experience of glorification as their prophetic, apostolic, and patristic predecessors can understand what the Biblical and Patristic writings are saying about glorification and the spiritual stages leading to it. Those who have reached glorification know how they were guided there, as well as how to guide others, and they are the guarantors of the transmission of this same tradition.[11]

The general points that Father Romanides is making are simple enough. Firstly, he contends that Holy Scripture and the writings of the Fathers are essentially testimony *about* God's revelation to man. This revelation, itself, is primarily comprised of the vision of the Uncreated Glory of God, whether it be in the Old Testament Prophetic visions of the Logos

---

10. Romanides, *Franks*, 40–41.
11. Ibid.

appearing as the Angel of God, the Angel of Great Counsel, the Lord of Glory, or the Lord God of Sabaoth; or, after the Incarnation and Pentecost, through the Human Nature of God the Word incarnate. Secondly, he claims that the *utterances* made by those who have received this vision *are not to be mistaken* for the revelations themselves. From the standpoint of these visions (revelations) themselves, such words are necessarily imperfect—though from our standpoint they may carry the force of infallible dogma or correct doctrine.

Finally, the revelation of God—the vision of God—is not a unique historical event, not something confined to scriptural revelation or even the Incarnation or *Parousia*; it is, rather, something assigned to each person, to be experienced by every human being, first in this life and then in the other. Therefore, the recorded testimonies of those who, throughout the course of history, have had this vision—the Prophets, Apostles, and Fathers and Mothers of the Church—are meant as guidebooks. And these books are most properly and correctly employed by those who, in each succeeding generation, have passed through (or at least are undergoing) the stages of purification and illumination that lead to glorification, or the vision of God. Such men and women, in turn, can wield these books, by their own discretion and with their counsel, to guide others through the same processes and to the same experiences. This mastership of spirituality was the original criterion for election to ordination and license to preach.

We must touch on a few final elements in our treatment of the unique notion of truth found in Eastern Orthodox theology and spiritual practice. First, the Greek Fathers everywhere insist on the ultimate unknowability of God. This is a touchstone, one might say, of the consensual theology. "Eastern theology," Father Florovsky notes, has "been always committed to the belief that God [is] absolutely 'incomprehensible'—ἀκατάληπτος—and unknowable in His nature or essence . . . . 'One insults God who seeks to apprehend his essential being,' says Chrysostom . . . . The 'essence of God' is absolutely inaccessible to man, says St. Basil (*Adv. Eunomium* 1.14)."[12]

As well, there is, in Eastern patristic thinking, a fundamental division between the Uncreated and the created realms, the Uncreated pertaining to the Holy Trinity and the created to all else—from Angelic beings to lifeless matter. Now, human language is among those things included in the category of the created and is wholly incapable of describing or conveying the Uncreated. This observation has obvious importance for the subject of

12. Florovsky, *Collected Works*, 1:115–16.

rhetoric, since it speaks to the notion of communication, though in a fundamentally theological way. It behooves us, here, to quote Father Romanides's reference to the thought of Saint Gregory of Nyssa on this matter, since the latter's observations have become authoritative for the Orthodox patristic Tradition. As such, they will reinforce our subsequent specific commentary on rhetoric in the Eastern patristic Tradition.

> St. Gregory . . . insists that all words and languages are products of human accommodations to the necessities of communication on the human level, and all concepts either conveyed by words or simply contemplated can never extricate themselves from their creaturely qualities. Knowledge of God, therefore, cannot be conceptual. God cannot be reached by contemplation. God is not like anything man experiences either intellectually or by sensation. Knowledge of God can be had only from those who have been the objects of this revelation, which is above all rational and sentient categories. It is a knowledge which can be indicated but not conveyed by human language or concepts.[13]

Lastly, as we have observed, through the process of purification, illumination, and ultimately glorification, it is possible for us to become "partakers of the divine Nature."[14] This participation, according to Orthodox theology, does not compromise the unknowability of God, since the Greek Fathers make a clear and firm distinction between the Divine Essence and Divine Energies of God. The Divine Essence of God is totally unknowable. The transcendent God, as Essence, is forever transcendent and beyond human knowledge. The Divine Energies, however, correspond to God's creative, vivifying, and ruling powers, and, being communicable, account for man's glorification. But even these communicable aspects of God, because they are Uncreated, are also inconceivable; they can be communicated, or passed on, but they are beyond human conceptualization. Let us recall the words of Saint Gregory the Theologian:

> What is this that has happened to me? . . . I was running to lay hold on God, and thus I went up into the Mount, and drew aside the curtain of the Cloud, and entered away from matter and material things, and as far as I could I withdrew within myself. And then when I looked up, I scarce saw the back parts of God; although I was sheltered by the Rock, the Word that was made flesh for

---

13. Romanides, "Highlights," 177.
14. 2 Pet 1:4.

us. And when I looked a little closer, I saw, not the First and unmingled Nature, known to Itself—to the Trinity, I mean; not That which abideth within the first veil, and is hidden by the Cherubim; but only that Nature, which at last even reaches to us. And that is, as far as I can learn, the Majesty, or as holy David calls it, the Glory which is manifested among the creatures, which It has produced and governs . . . .

Therefore we must begin again thus. It is difficult to conceive God but to define Him in words is an impossibility, as one of the Greek teachers of Divinity taught, not unskillfully, as it appears to me . . . . But in my opinion it is impossible to express Him, and yet more impossible to conceive Him.[15]

It was his mystical experience that first prompted Saint Gregory to theologize. In fact, in his "First Theological Oration" he maintains that to theologize "is permitted only to those who have passed examinations and have reached *theoria* ["mystical vision"—often badly translated as "contemplation" or "meditation"], and who have been previously purified in soul and body, or at least are being purified."[16] Yet he immediately qualifies his observation by noting that such experience is not within the domain of human language and concepts: "It is impossible to express Him, and yet more impossible to conceive Him." "In this way"—that is, on the foundation of personal spiritual experience and mindful of the limitations of human thought—Saint Gregory says, "shalt thou discourse of God."[17]

Let us now weigh some of the implications of the unique theological schema of the Eastern Fathers for an Orthodox rhetoric. In the first place, the spiritual stature of a minister or church teacher; advancement through the stages of purification, illumination, and glorification; empirical, rather than merely conceptual or theoretical knowledge of the goal of Christian life, the vision of God; or progress along these paths—these constitute the fundamental criteria for Orthodox Christian preaching. In the words of Saint John Chrysostomos: ". . . I pass over all those qualities and . . . superfluous embellishments of pagan writers. I take no account of diction or style. Let a man's diction be beggarly and his verbal composition simple and artless, but do not let him be inexpert in the knowledge and

---

15. St. Gregory Nazianzen, "The Second Theological Oration," in *Select Orations*, 289–90.

16. Quoted in Romanides, *Franks,* 49.

17. St. Gregory Nazianzen, "Second Theological Oration," 289.

careful statement of doctrine."[18] Indeed, as we earlier noted in a remarkable quote from Father John Romanides, "[I]n the Orthodox patristic tradition, genuine spiritual experience is the foundation of dogmatic formulations which, in turn, are necessary guides for leading to glorification."[19] By the same token, the proclamation of the Word of God, the virtual explication of dogma and doctrine, rests squarely, in the Orthodox spiritual Tradition, on the same "genuine spiritual experience." As one Orthodox writer has noted, true preachers of the word are found "where there is theory pregnant with true experience," warning us, in the words of the Desert Fathers, that those who employ beautiful words to describe things which they have not themselves experienced are like "a tree which has beautiful leaves but does not bear fruit."[20]

In terms of classical rhetorical categories, it is ethos, the formation of the preacher, to which Orthodox homiletics is primarily subject. And this formation is founded upon an asceticism therapeutically applied to the preacher's whole being; an ascesis that in turn affords him or her an empirical knowledge of the subject matter, the *logos* (and, indeed, the *Logos*). Orthodox rhetoric can best be likened, therefore, to the third of the three ancient rhetorical traditions: the technical, sophistic, and philosophical. Plato (or Socrates) placed great emphasis on a rhetor's need for intimate knowledge of the truth of things, as opposed to knowledge based on deductions from logical probabilities. It is this image of true rhetorical art that best fits that of the Eastern Orthodox Church. As Plato writes, "Until someone knows the truth of each thing about which he speaks or writes . . . , not until then will it be possible for speech to exist in an artistic form . . . ."[21] This quotation might easily be attributed to an Eastern Orthodox commentator on homiletics or the rhetoric attendant to it.

For the Eastern patristic Tradition, then, Plato was right on the mark in his statement about the fundamentals of effective rhetoric or preaching. The Greek Fathers, however, placed much less trust in the perceptual apparatus of the human being than Plato. Whereas the classical Greek ideal of the rhetorician entails lofty demands on human capabilities, the Greek patristic Tradition rests its ideal on the transformed individual—on a person

18. St. John Chrysostom, *On the Priesthood*, 121–22.

19. Romanides, *Franks*, 39.

20. Chrysostomos and Auxentios, "Saint Gregory Palamas on the Hesychasts," in *Contemporary Traditionalist Orthodox Thought*, 62.

21. Quoted in Kennedy, *Classical Rhetoric*, 59.

purified of the foibles that render this philosophical ideal, however lofty and elevated, unattainable. Moreover, the transmission of the very method by which human nature is lifted up to the traits of the ideal rhetorician is part and parcel of what Orthodox rhetoric is. This transmission, this tradition or handing-down (παράδοσις) of the rhetorical ideal, is for the Orthodox Fathers a living process, giving birth and form to human words and images; the philosophical rhetorical ideal, in this sense, is no tradition at all, but is at best stillborn.

In the second place, we can make some remarks in regard to "invention," the process by which the rhetorician decides upon the subject of his discourse. Many rhetorical theories confidently commend Holy Scripture as a multi-faceted source of wisdom or inspiration for the preacher's art—an indispensable aid in homiletic invention. Saint Augustine, though he elsewhere expresses some reservations in this regard, succinctly expresses the same idea in the fourth book of his *On Christian Doctrine*: "For a man speaks more or less wisely to the extent that he has become more or less proficient in the Holy Scriptures."[22] For an Orthodox theory of invention, the order is backwards. Saint Augustine's words *should read*: "One speaks more or less scripturally to the extent that one is more or less proficient in wisdom."

Divine wisdom, indwelling the purified, illumined, and glorified human soul, is that which enables one properly to comprehend the message of Sacred Scripture and to employ it, or similar words, in guiding others to purification, illumination, and glorification—to divine wisdom, and, thereby, to an identical understanding of Scripture. In the East, centuries of struggle with heretics, most of them tremendously facile and "proficient" in the Scriptures, drove this point home. So did the preaching and Orthodox witness of a veritable choir of desert ascetics, many of whom, though actually unversed in literal or rhetorical knowledge of Holy Writ, rose to Prophetic stature and were thus able to transmit the genuine wisdom of the Christian Scriptures.

For the Christian East, the fruit of a spiritual life correctly cultivated and the copious wisdom proceeding from the transformed and God-bearing soul are the proper sources of and inspiration for the preacher's words. To the extent that a preacher relies on logical, conceptual, or linguistic analyses of the Scriptures or any other spiritual writings, he or she is all the more open to the subjective faults of "personal interpretation" and to possible error. At best, the speculative spirit of the unenlightened is a matter

---

22. St. Augustine, *On Christian Doctrine*, 122.

of the "blind leading the blind."[23] At worst, especially when it engenders philosophical speculation about God, this spirit gives birth to heresy, a fall "into the ditch."[24] Thus it is that the Christian East carefully heeds such scriptural warnings as that of Saint Peter about the Epistles of Saint Paul, "in which are some things hard to be understood, which they that are unlearned and unstable wrest, as they do also the other Scriptures, unto their own destruction."[25]

In the third place, the Orthodox understanding of rhetoric also places tremendous responsibility on the listener. Just as the preacher can only rightly speak to the extent that he has been—or is being—purified, illumined, and glorified, so the listener can only rightly receive these words to the extent that he or she has undergone or is undergoing the same process of transformation. "Purify yourselves," cries Saint John Chrysostomos over and over again in his introductory homily on Saint John's Gospel, warning that otherwise hours of listening are in vain. The theme is ubiquitous in patristic homilies.

What we have said regarding the Orthodox understanding of true Christian knowledge, as well as the role and limitations of human language and concepts in attaining that knowledge, profoundly affects the Eastern Orthodox view of the various prescriptive rhetorical traditions bequeathed to the Christian world by the ancients. Because Eastern Christians are so keenly aware of the limitations of words and concepts, especially with regard to the Uncreated realities which they know so well as the cornerstone of Christian experience, the Orthodox Church has never canonized a particular technical or prescriptive rhetoric. Rather, comments about rhetorical methods seem to be limited to warnings against excess. Classical rhetorical traditions did remain the foundation of primary education in Byzantium, and various Greek Fathers enjoyed such training, as their writings demonstrate. But for these Fathers, as for the Christian East in general, rhetorical elements of style and technique are wholly a matter of accident, not essence. Moreover, however lofty even the accidental rhetoric of the Eastern Greek Fathers, it has from the very beginning enjoyed a dignity secondary always to that of spiritual wisdom itself. Let us illustrate this with a story from the Egyptian desert:

---

23. Compare Matt 15:14.
24. Ibid.
25. 2 Pet 3:16.

The Notion of Rhetoric

Once Abba Arsenios revealed his thoughts to an Egyptian Elder and asked him about them. But a certain other Abba saw him and said to him: "Abba Arsenios, you have had so much education in Greek and Latin, yet you ask this man, so unlettered in worldly knowledge, about your thoughts?" Abba Arsenios said to him: "Indeed, I know Roman and Greek letters well; but I have not yet learned even the alphabet of this simple man."[26]

Bibliography

Augustine, St. *On Christian Doctrine*. Translated by D. W. Robertson Jr. New York: Macmillan, 1987.
Chrysostomos, Archbishop. *Ancient Fathers of the Desert*. Brookline, MA: Holy Cross Orthodox Press, 1980.
Chrysostomos of Etna, Archbishop, Bishop Auxentios of Photike, and Archimandrite Akakios. *Contemporary Traditionalist Orthodox Thought*. 2nd. ed. Etna, CA: Center for Traditionalist Orthodox Studies, 1998.
Florovsky, Georges. *Bible, Church, Tradition: An Eastern Orthodox View*. The Collected Works of Georges Florovsky 1. Edited by Richard S. Haugh. Vaduz: Büchervertriebsanstalt, 1987.
Gregory Nazianzen, St. *Select Orations of Saint Gregory Nazianzen*. Translated by Charles Gordon Browne and James Edward Swallow. A Select Library of Nicene and Post-Nicene Fathers, 2nd series 7. Edited by Philip Schaff and Henry Wace. Grand Rapids: Eerdmans, 1978.
John Chrysostom, St. *Six Books on the Priesthood*. Translated by Graham Neville. Crestwood, NY: St. Vladimir's Seminary Press, 1977.
Kennedy, George A. *Classical Rhetoric and its Christian and Secular Tradition from Ancient to Modern Times*. Chapel Hill, NC: University of North Carolina Press, 1980.
Romanides, John S. *Franks, Romans, Feudalism, and Doctrine: An Interplay between Theology and Society*. Brookline, MA: Holy Cross Orthodox Press, 1982.
———. "Highlights in the Debate Over Theodore of Mopsuestia's Christology and Some Suggestions for a Fresh Approach." *The Greek Orthodox Theological Review* 5.2 (Winter 1959–60) 140–85.

---

26. Chrysostomos, *Ancient Fathers*, 19.

CHAPTER 6

The Concept of Philosophy in the Hellenic Tradition

Constantine Cavarnos

THE WORD PHILOSOPHY AND the cognate term *philosopher* have been used in many senses in the long philosophical tradition of Greece, which began with Thales in the seventh century BC and has continued without interruption down to the present. I shall discuss sixteen of these meanings, proceeding in chronological order. My discussions will begin with the Greeks of Antiquity, continue with the Greeks of the early Christian and Byzantine periods, then with those of the centuries of Turkish Rule, and end with those of our time.

The Term "Philosophy" in Pre-Christian Times

1. Philosophy as Love of Wisdom

Pythagoras, who lived during the sixth century BC, is said to have been the first to call himself a "philosopher" (φιλόσοφος). The term "philosopher" is a compound one, derived from the words φίλος, which means "friend," "lover," and σοφία, which means "wisdom." Thus, a philosopher is "a lover of wisdom," and philosophy is "the love of wisdom."[1] According to Sosicrates, Pythagoras "compared life to the Great Games, where some went to compete for the prize, others went with wares to sell, but the best as

---

1. With regard to this sense of the term "philosophy," John Burnet has this to say: "It was in all probability Pythagoras that first gave the word philosophy the deeper meaning of science 'touched with emotion'" (*Greek Philosophy*, 1:215).

spectators, for similarly, in life, some grow up with servile natures, greedy for fame and gain, but the philosophers seek for truth (ἀλήθεια)."[2]

Closely related to the conception of philosophy as the love of wisdom is the belief of the ancient Greeks that no man is wise, in the sense that no man is actually in possession of the whole body of eternal truths. Hence, strictly, no man can justifiably call himself wise, no matter how learned he may be or how wise he may be regarded. At most, one can say that he is a *lover* of wisdom, a *seeker of wisdom,* and a possessor of it only in some small measure. We find this stated clearly and emphatically by Socrates in the *Apology* written by Plato. Socrates says here: "The truth is, O men of Athens, that God only is really wise . . . ; the wisdom of men is worth little or nothing."[3] In another dialogue of Plato, the *Phaedrus,* Socrates says this, speaking of such men as the famous poet Homer and the equally famous lawgiver Solon: "I think, Phaedrus, that the epithet 'wise' is too great, and befits God alone, but the name 'philosopher,' that is, 'lover of wisdom,' or something of the sort would be more fitting and modest for such a man."[4] In Plato we find the idea that the true philosopher aspires to become a possessor, as far as possible, of the *whole* of wisdom, to become, as he puts it in the *Republic,* a contemplator of "all time and all being (παντὸς μὲν χρόνου, πάσης δὲ οὐσίας)."[5]

2. Philosophy as Μελέτη Θανάτου

Another important conception of philosophy that we find in Plato's writings is that of philosophy as μελέτη θανάτου. This appears in the *Phaedo.*[6] The word μελέτη is used here in a threefold sense. In some statements that are made in the *Phaedo,* μελέτη means "study"; in others, "meditation"; and in still others, "practice." Philosophy is a "study" of death in that he who philosophizes seeks to understand the nature of death and its significance in human life. Such a study discloses that death is nothing but the absolute separation from one another of two distinct and very different things:

---

2. Sosicrates, *Succession of Philosophers,* quoted by Diogenes Laertius in *Lives* 2:327, 329. See also Plato, *Republic*: "Whom do you mean by the true philosophers?" "Those for whom the truth is the spectacle of which they are enamored" (V.475e).

3. *Apology,* 23a.

4. *Phaedrus,* 278c–d.

5. *Republic,* VI.486a; see also 486b; *Seventh Epistle,* 344a–b; and *Phaedrus,* 270c.

6. *Phaedo,* 64a–67e, 80e–81a.

the soul, which is invisible, incorporeal, and incorruptible, from the body, which is visible, earthy, and corruptible. Philosophy is μελέτη θανάτου in the sense of "meditation" on death, insofar as one focuses the mind on this phenomenon, dwells on it, both from the perspective of time and from that of eternity. Μελέτη θανάτου is also a "practice" of death, in that the true philosopher (ὁ ὡς ἀληθῶς φιλόσοφος) strives to "separate" his soul from his body, in the sense of freeing himself from bondage to it, using the body as an instrument for the attainment of spiritual ends, instead of being used by the body as its slave.

The "dying" which the philosopher practices consists in curbing the bodily desires for food, drink, and sensual gratification, stilling the senses of sight, hearing, and so on. It consists in turning the attention from the outer, material world apprehended by the physical senses, to the inner world of the soul, to the world of the mind and its ideal objects. It consists in turning away from the realm of flux, of perpetual change, in which the body is immersed, to the world of the truly real (τὰ ὄντως ὄντα), the realm of unchanging being, the spiritual, divine reality. Socrates and Plato believed that only through μελέτη θανάτου can the soul rise—as far as possible while still in the body—to philosophy in the sense of "the contemplation of all time and all being."

3. Philosophy as Self-examination and Cross-examination

In the Platonic dialogues, especially in the early ones, the term "philosophy" has a third important meaning, that of ἔλεγχος or ἐξέτασις, of critical examination of the contents of the soul, particularly its beliefs and opinions. The ἔλεγχος is applied both to oneself, and thus assumes the form of self-examination, and to others, where it is carried on through cross-examination—through questions and answers.

Socrates, who was the greatest master in history of ἔλεγχος in the form of cross-examination, says in the already mentioned *Apology*: "The unexamined life is not worth living."[7] This is one of the most remarkable statements ever made by a philosopher. In accordance with this conviction, Socrates's philosophizing assumed particularly the form of self-examination and of cross-examination. He called this activity "philosophizing," and regarded it as a duty divinely imposed upon him.[8]

7. *Apology*, 38a.
8. Ibid., 28e.

The ἔλεγχος was viewed by Socrates as the most effective means of opening the path to wisdom, because it removes the greatest obstacle to wisdom, namely, the conceit that one *already* possesses it. The removal of this conceit (οἴησις) results in intellectual humility, which is the starting point of progress towards wisdom. Socrates regarded intellectual conceit as the worst kind of ignorance: he called it ἀμαθία, stupidity. Ἀμαθία is ignorance which is unconscious of itself, regards itself as knowledge. The ἔλεγχος, both as self-examination and as being cross-examined by another, exposes this ignorance and makes one conscious of it. It thereby humbles one intellectually, making him realize what he in fact knows and what he does not know.[9]

4. Philosophy as Dialectic

A fourth sense of the term philosophy is "dialectic" (διαλεκτική). This is a form of philosophizing which Plato emphasizes in his Republic and in some other dialogues. In the *Republic*, Books VI and VII, dialectic is presented as the highest part of education, the highest art and kind of knowledge. It consists in the activity of the supreme power of the soul, νοῦς, intuitive reason, rising above the realm of sense-experience, above even scientific hypotheses, to the contemplation and exploration of the realm of archetypal ideas or forms (ἰδέαι, εἴδη). In dialectic, the rational faculty moves on "through ideas, to ideas, and ends with ideas."[10] It aspires to rise even above archetypal ideas to the contemplation of the absolute, supreme Good, which Plato calls the "Idea of Good." This has been identified by many interpreters of Plato with God. If we accept this interpretation, then dialectic in its highest reaches becomes theology, mystical theology. It becomes a contemplation, in some sense, of God.

5. Philosophy as the Way of the Best Life

Another, fifth conception of philosophy, is that it is the highest all-embracing way of life. This conception appears clearly in Plato's *Republic*. Here, in Book VI, Plato characterizes philosophy as "the best vocation" (τὸ

---

9. See my book *Plato's View of Man*, 21–23.
10. *Republic*, VI.511c.

βέλτιστον ἐπιτήδευμα).[11] The general idea of philosophy as a way of life goes back to Pythagoras, but it is in Plato's writings that it acquires clear, definite content.

In our discussion of the conception of philosophy as the "love of wisdom," we saw how Pythagoras is reputed to have distinguished three types of human character, resulting in three kinds of lives: those of the lovers of material gain, the lovers of honor, and the lovers of truth, the philosophers. We saw also that he regarded himself as belonging to the third category. His way of life was the philosophic. Plato praises Pythagoras in the *Republic* for having established "the Pythagoric way of life" (Πυθαγόρειος τρόπος τοῦ βίου).[12]

The nature of the philosophic way of life as conceived by Plato has to be gathered from what we have said about the other senses which the term "philosophy" has for him, and from his teaching about the virtues. The philosophic way embraces *the love of wisdom*, μελέτη θανάτου, the ἔλεγχος or ἐξέτασις, *dialectic*, and *the cultivation of the virtues*.[13]

6–10. Philosophy as Organized Knowledge in General, and Four Divisions of It

When we pass from Plato to his greatest pupil, Aristotle, we find that the term "philosophy" acquires some other meanings. One of these is that philosophy is the *whole of organized knowledge* (ἐπιστήμη). He breaks down this knowledge into two major divisions: "theoretical philosophy" (θεωρητικὴ φιλοσοφία) and "practical philosophy" (πρακτικὴ φιλοσοφία). Then he subdivides theoretical philosophy into "first philosophy" (πρώτη φιλοσοφία) or "theology" (θεολογία), "mathematical philosophy" (μαθηματικὴ φιλοσοφία), and "physical philosophy" (φυσικὴ φιλοσοφία).[14] "First philosophy" or "theology" is what is commonly called in modern times "metaphysics." The word "metaphysics" is one that was coined some time after the works of Aristotle were published by Andronikos of Rhodes. The earliest known use of the word "metaphysics" to refer to Aristotle's "first philosophy" occurs in Nicolaos of Damascus, a younger contemporary of Andronikos. This term was given to Aristotle's "first philosophy" because in

---

11. Ibid., 489c.

12. Ibid., X.600b.

13. See my book *Plato's View of Man*, 19–24.

14. *Metaphysics*, V.1026a. See also Aristotle, *Eudemian Ethics*, I.1214a9–15, 1216b10–18.

the corpus of Aristotle's published works it was placed by Andronikos *after* (μετά) the physical treatises (τὰ φυσικά). At times Aristotle gives to his first philosophy the name "theology." The reason for this is that it culminates in a theory of God, the "Unmoved Mover" of the whole universe.

"First philosophy" is defined by Aristotle as that branch of knowledge which studies "being as such, what it is and what its attributes are."[15] That is, first philosophy seeks to discover the most ultimate principles underlying reality.[16]

With regard to what Aristotle calls "physical philosophy," it should be explained that this includes, besides physics, the sciences of astronomy, biology, and psychology, as well as what we would call philosophy of Nature.

Although he subdivides "theoretical philosophy," Aristotle does not explicitly subdivide "practical philosophy." Later, students of Aristotle subdivided "practical philosophy" into "ethics," "economics," and "politics."

Thus, in Aristotle we find a sixth sense of the term "philosophy"—that of *organized knowledge in general* and these four additional ones: the distinction of two major divisions of such philosophy: (7) "theoretical philosophy" and (8) "practical philosophy"; (9) the most important division of theoretical philosophy: "first philosophy" or "theology," called in later times "metaphysics," and (10) "physical philosophy." The nature of these divisions will become clearer as we compare them later in this lecture with the meaning and content which they assume in the writings of the Greek Church Fathers.

The Term "Philosophy" in the Christian Period

1. Philosophy as the Love of Wisdom

The notion of philosophy as the "love of wisdom"—the first one that we have discussed—is accepted by Christian Greek thinkers from the earliest centuries to the present. But they assert—particularly those known as Church Fathers—that *true wisdom is God,* and hence philosophy is *love of God.* St. John Damascene, who flourished during the first half of the eighth century, gives six definitions of philosophy in his magnum opus, *Fount of Knowledge.*

---

15. *Metaphysics,* V.1029a29–32.
16. See Taylor, *Aristotle,* 49.

One of these definitions states: "Philosophy is love of wisdom (φιλία σοφίας). But true wisdom is God. Therefore love of God, this is true philosophy."[17]

This conception of philosophy did not originate with Damascene. It is implicit in the writings of Justin Martyr, who lived in the second century. Justin, a philosopher who embraced Christianity and became a great Apologist of it, identified true wisdom with the Divine Wisdom or Logos—that is, Christ.[18] In the fifth century, the great mystic Neilos the Ascetic, a disciple of St. John Chrysostom, gave vivid expression to this conception of philosophy when he wrote: "Many of the [ancient] Greeks and not a few of the Hebrews undertook to philosophize; but only Christ's disciples zealously sought after the true wisdom, for they alone had Wisdom itself [that is, the Divine Logos] as their Teacher, actually showing them the conduct proper for such a pursuit."[19] Another great mystic, Gregory of Sinai, who lived in the fourteenth century, shared this conception of philosophy. Thus, he says about the individual whom he calls a "divine philosopher" (θεῖος φιλόσοφος): "He is a divine philosopher who through active virtue and contemplation has attained direct union with God and has become a friend and lover of the first and creative and true wisdom more than of every other wisdom and knowledge."[20]

The passages from Neilos and Gregory, as well as countless others that could be quoted, not only make clear their identification of perfect wisdom with God, but also bring the intellectual activity of the philosopher into close relationship with his emotional center, with his capacity for love, and in fact into close relationship with the whole soul. This is consonant with the commandment to love God with all one's heart, with all one's soul, and with all one's mind.[21]

Philosophy thus conceived can be seen to be a pursuit that is possible to *all*: men and women, young and old, literate and illiterate. For to love God is a possibility open to all.

---

17. *Patrologia Graeca*, 94:533C, 669C–D.
18. See my book *Byzantine Thought and Art*, 17.
19. *Philokalia*, 1:190.
20. *Philokalia*, 4:58.
21. Matt 22:37.

The Concept of Philosophy

2. Philosophy as Μελέτη Θανάτου

The Platonic conception of philosophy as μελέτη θανάτου appears in the famous *Ladder of Divine Ascent* of St. John Climacos, in the *Fount of Knowledge* of St. John Damascene, and in many other patristic works. In the *Ladder* we read: "It is not possible . . . to pass the present day piously, unless one regards it as the last day of his life. And it is really astonishing that the Greeks, too, said something of this sort, for they define philosophy as μελέτη θανάτου."[22] By "Greeks" ("Ελληνες) here the author means Socrates and Plato. The latter, as we have seen, wrote the *Phaedo,* in which the conception of philosophy as μελέτη θανάτου is presented, and Socrates is credited with having given expression to it. Μελέτη θανάτου is viewed in the *Ladder* as meditation on death, as meditation on one's *own* death, with the idea that it is inevitable and may occur quite unexpectedly any day or hour. This meditation is regarded as having a powerful effect on our daily conduct, making us strive to live daily in the most impeccable manner. Thus, Climacos introduces in μελέτη θανάτου a very important perspective, not found in Plato's *Phaedo.* This perspective appears frequently in the writings of the Greek Church Fathers, both earlier and later ones, especially in the ascetic-mystical texts contained in the *Philokalia*. The latter emphasize the value of the practice of frequent "remembrance of death" (μνήμη θανάτου), of which they sometimes speak as μελέτη θανάτου. It should be noted that Climacos devotes a whole chapter to this subject, entitled "Concerning Remembrance of Death," and that his remark on μελέτη θανάτου which I quoted appears at the end of this discourse.

John Damascene includes μελέτη θανάτου among his six definitions of philosophy. He says,

> Philosophy is a meditation on death, whether this be voluntary or natural. For life is of two kinds, there being the natural life by which we live, and the voluntary one by which we cling lovingly to this present life. Death also is of two kinds: the one being natural, which is the separation of soul from body, whereas the other is the voluntary one by which we disdain this present life and aspire to that which is to come.[23]

By "voluntary death" he means the practice of "dying" in the sense taught in Plato's *Phaedo*. It involves, he says, disdaining this present life and aspiring

---

22. *Klimax*, Discourse 6, par. 26, 62.
23. *Patrologia Graeca*, 94:533B.

to that which is to come. He does not elaborate on this. He merely gives a definition, and definitions are brief. The point has to be understood in the light of the *Phaedo* and even more in that of the New Testament, particularly of some statements made by Paul the Apostle. Thus, Paul speaks of crucifying "the old man" in us, in order that sin in us "might be destroyed, that henceforth we should not serve sin."[24] By "the old man" he means all evil, wrong, vain thoughts and phantasies, all negative emotions and vices, all propensities to sin. Paul also says: "I live; yet not I, but Christ liveth in me."[25] By this he implies that already the "old man" in him has died, and as a result he now experiences the indwelling of God.

The concept of philosophy as μελέτη θανάτου appears in the Greek East in later times, too, even in our age. Photios the Great, one of the most renowned Byzantine philosopher-theologians, writing in his old age more than a century after John Damascene, says: "Now I philosophize on only one thing, death." One form such philosophizing should take, according to Photios, is "to see in the death of our neighbors our own death as in a mirror, and to use the demise of others for our own correction. . . . Let us correct ourselves by what we have seen and shared in suffering."[26]

Eugene Voulgaris (1716–1806) devotes two pages of his masterly *Treatise on Properly Confronting Death* to a discussion of the concept of philosophy as μελέτη θανάτου. His treatment of this topic is one of the most illuminating. Starting with the premise, upheld by Plato, that the human soul is spiritual in nature and immortal, Voulgaris says:

> The external sages, and especially Plato, have called philosophy Μελέτη Θανάτου, because philosophy not only teaches her devotees how they ought to *live*, ordering their actions and work according to right reason, but also how to *die* in a good and praiseworthy manner. And the whole power of the philosophic rule rests on this, that men train themselves zealously and diligently with regard to Death every day and every hour, in whatever they undertake or choose during their life, in order that they might put a seal of happiness upon their life, when the moment of their death will inescapably come. But how, in what manner is this truly philosophical preparatory training for death effected?

24. Rom 6:6.
25. Gal 2:20.
26. *Patrologia Graeca*, 101:684B; *Homilies of Photios*, 58. See also Niketas Stethatos (eleventh century): "Unseemly Thoughts are Bridled Through Self-Restraint and *Melete Thanatou*," in *Philokalia*, 3:322.

> In this manner: Today mortify one passion, tomorrow another. Today curb this desire, tomorrow that. Today subdue arrogance and conceit; tomorrow, anger and irritability; the following day, incontinence and lewdness, greed and the love of money, gluttony and intemperance, quarrelsomeness and disputatiousness, envy, malice, duplicity, guile, resentment, hatred, and likewise the other negative emotions. This is the real philosophy, the practice of death and meditation on death. It is, in a few words, separation from the passions, the extinction and mortification of vain desires and cravings. This practice little by little becomes a settled disposition of the soul. And it engenders in man courage and tranquility with regard to the thought of death.[27]

In our own time, I. N. Theodorakopoulos (1900–1981), who was Professor of Philosophy at the University of Athens, has spoken quite approvingly of Plato's conception of philosophy as μελέτη θανάτου in his book *Christian and Philosophical Studies,* and has shown its important relevance to the present situation. Theodorakopoulos says,

> Plato characterizes philosophy in the *Phaedo* as a meditation on death and a meditation on immortality. He disciplines the intellect, reason, but this discipline of reason is done in direct relation to the soul. Reason is an instrument that helps the soul become conscious of its immortality while still in time. Modern philosophy, on the contrary, especially the systems of the nineteenth century, separated thought from the soul to such an extent that thought became something cut off from the personality; and the soul was abandoned, neglected and forgotten.[28]

3. Philosophy as Ἔλεγχος

The use of ἔλεγχος, both in the sense of self-examination and in that of the examination of others through pointed questions and answers, is emphasized in the writings of the Greek Church Fathers, from the early centuries to modern times. However, they seldom apply the term "philosophy" to this activity. In the texts contained in the *Philokalia,* self-examination becomes part of a more encompassing practice, which includes inner attention (νῆψις, προσοχή) and confession (ἐξομολόγησις).

---

27. *Diatribe,* 149–50.
28. From my book *Modern Greek Philosophers,* 126.

In exercising inner attention, intuitive reason (νοῦς) watches and examines carefully the contents of the soul: thoughts, representations, phantasies, desires, emotions, and dispositions as they make their appearance. It accepts those that are good, pure, proper, but rejects those that are of the opposite kind. It also takes note of the promptings or censure of conscience. Hesychios calls this activity "mental philosophy" (νοητὴ φιλοσοφία),[29] "practical philosophy of the mind" (φιλοσοφία τοῦ νοῦ πρακτική),[30] and "intellectual philosophy" (διανοητικὴ φιλοσοφία).[31] He calls it thus because it is an activity which is carried on by intuitive reason and involves great knowledge and skill.[32] He also characterizes it as "a most beautiful virtue" (πάγκαλος ἀρετή),[33] because it is conducive to illumination. For "the more we exercise attention with the intellect, the more we are illumined, and in proportion as we do not exercise attention we lapse into darkness."[34] Hence, he remarks, guarding of the intellect may aptly be called "light-begetting," "light-giving."[35]

Regarding the examination of conscience, St. Photios says: "Each of us, setting up his conscience as his judge and examiner, let us consider which of our pledges we have kept and which we have neglected. And those we have kept—if in fact we have kept any—let us multiply, while those which we have betrayed let us retrieve."[36]

The other form of ἔλεγχος, the examination of the inner world of others, which Socrates made his chief occupation, has been left by the Christian Greeks to their spiritual father, one gifted and experienced in drawing out confessions.

4. Philosophy as Dialectic

The idea of philosophy as "dialectic" in the Platonic sense appears in the *Stromateis*, the "Miscellanies," of Clement of Alexandria. Clement praises Plato's dialectic, saying this among other noteworthy things:

29. *Philokalia*, 1:158.
30. Ibid., 161.
31. Ibid., 166.
32. Ibid., 159.
33. Ibid., 170.
34. Ibid., 161.
35. Ibid., 168.
36. *Homilies of Photios*, 68.

The Concept of Philosophy

> Dialectics, according to Plato, is, as he says in *The Statesman,* a science devoted to the discovery of the explanation of things.... The true dialectic, being philosophy mixed with truth, by examining things, ... gradually ascends in relation to the most excellent essence of all, and essays to go beyond to the God of the universe, professing not the knowledge of mortal affairs, but the science of things divine and heavenly.... This true dialectic is the science which analyzes the objects of thought, and shows abstractly and by itself the individual substratum of existences, or the power of dividing things into genera, which descends to their most special properties, and presents each individual object to be contemplated simply such as it is.[37]

Clement goes on to identify dialectic with theology and to relate it to Scripture. He says that Scripture desires to make us good dialecticians, and to this end it exhorts us to become skillful in "rejecting some things, but retaining what is good," aided in this by the Savior, "Who withdraws, by the divine word, the gloom of ignorance ... and bestows the best of gifts."[38]

The intellectual movement described by Plato and Clement and called "dialectic" is also spoken of by some later Christian writers of the Hellenic East—for instance, St. Theodore the Great Ascetic (fl. 660). Theodore does not refer to it, however, as dialectic or philosophy. This movement, according to him, takes place initially through the mind's use of sense-images. By means of these the intellect gains a mediate knowledge of the intelligible forms (νοερὰ εἴδη), not a direct one of them, so long as the soul is joined to the body. But in the case of those whose mind has been greatly purified, direct contemplation is possible through the action of divine grace. Such contemplation is called by him "supernal" (ὑπερφυής), because it cannot be attained by the human mind employing its own methods and powers, unassisted by divine grace.[39]

With many other Christian writers the term "dialectic" has come to denote the form which it took in Aristotle. This involves the methods of division of the genus into species, definition, analysis, and demonstration. An example is afforded by St. John of Damascus, who devotes one of the "Philosophical Chapters" of his *Fount of Knowledge* to dialectic in the Aristotelian sense. Generally, this dialectic was used by Christian writers to clarify some matter pertaining to the faith, or to refute some heresy or other

---

37. Bk. 1, chap. 28, in *Ante-Nicene Fathers,* 2:340.
38. Ibid., 340–41.
39. *Philokalia,* 1:326.

error. It is significant, in this connection, that Damascene's discussion of dialectic appears in the last of his "Philosophical Chapters," just before he turns to the treatment of "Heresies."[40]

5. Philosophy as the Way of the Best Life

In general, the schools of philosophy that came into existence after the death of Socrates, Plato, and Aristotle viewed philosophy chiefly as a way of life leading to the greatest possible happiness of the practicer in *this* life. Most of them did not concern themselves with the life beyond, either denying such a life or having very vague conceptions of it, such as not to constitute a motivating factor in conduct. Neo-Pythagoreanism and Neo-Platonism, which did believe in an afterlife, became fused with pagan worship and the mystery cults. They degenerated into demonology and superstition.

Gradually, particularly in the fourth century, Christian monasticism appeared on the scene. This way of life came to be viewed by Christians as the best way of life, especially in relation to man's destiny in eternity. And the term "philosophy" came to be applied to it at an early date. We find the word "philosophy" applied to monasticism in the writings of such fourth-century Christian writers as Gregory Nazianzen, Gregory of Nyssa, and John Chrysostom. It continued to be applied to monasticism in subsequent centuries down to our time. Although it is regarded as the most difficult mode of life, it is asserted to be the one that leads to the highest spiritual attainments. Thus, St. Gregory Nazianzen, who led a monastic life before he was ordained a bishop, says: "Our philosophy is humble in appearance, but sublime in its hidden essence, and leads to God." It is "the greatest and the most difficult of vocations."[41]

Having such a high regard for the monastic life, the Greek Church Fathers call it "the art of arts and the science of sciences" (τέχνη τεχνῶν καὶ ἐπιστήμη ἐπιστημῶν). This characterization is the fifth definition of philosophy given by John Damascene in the *Fount of Knowledge*. He does not, however, identify "philosophy" in this sense with monasticism. This definition was appropriated for monasticism by later writers. We find it, for

---

40. Patrologia Graeca, 94:672B–673A.

41. See my book *Byzantine Thought and Art*, 20. See also Chrysostom: "It became my duty to pursue the blessed life of monks, the true philosophy" ("Treatise on the Priesthood," in *Nicene and Post-Nicene Fathers*, First Series, 9:33); and Gregory of Nyssa, *Opera Ascetica*, 333, 379, 381, 383, etc.

instance, in *The Discourse on Inner Attention and Guarding of the Heart* by Nikephoros the Solitary (fl. 1340), who says: "The monastic way of life has been called 'the science of sciences and the art of arts,' because it promises to us higher and ineffable goods, 'which eye hath not seen, nor ear heard, neither have entered into the heart of man.'"[42] The terms "philosophy" and the formula "art of arts and science of sciences" are still used by Greek religious writers in speaking of monasticism. We find them, for instance, in the writings of Father Philotheos Zervakos (d. 1980), who for more than half a century was abbot of the Monastery of Longovarda on Paros and authored many books. Zervakos says in one of them: "The monastic life is the true philosophy, which is called and in fact is 'the art of arts and science of sciences.'"[43]

So much about the Platonic conceptions of philosophy as they reappear in the Christianized Hellenic East. We shall consider next the utilization there of Aristotelian conceptions of philosophy.

6–10. *The Five Aristotelian Senses of the Term "Philosophy"*

The Aristotelian conceptions of philosophy discussed earlier appear clearly in Damascene's discussion of philosophy. In his *Fount of Knowledge* we find Aristotle's view of philosophy as *organized knowledge in general*. Damascene says here, "Philosophy is divided into the *theoretical* part and the *practical* part. The theoretical part is divided into the *theological*, the *mathematical*, and the *physical*. The mathematical part is divided into the *arithmetical*, the *musical*, the *geometrical* and the *astronomical*; the practical part, into the *ethical*, that of *household management,* and the *political*."[44]

In the last statement, St. John goes beyond what Aristotle explicitly says, dividing the mathematical part of "theoretical philosophy" into four parts. He again goes beyond what Aristotle explicitly says when he subdivides "practical philosophy" into three parts.[45]

Going back to "theoretical philosophy," Damascene gives his own conception of it. The "theological part" of it is, he says,

---

42. *Philokalia*, 4:18–19. See also Kallistos and Ignatios Xanthopouloi, ibid., 210.

43. See my book *St. Arsenios of Paros*, 41, and Zervakos, *Mega kai Thaumaston Proskynema*, 138, 176. See also Louvaris: "Thanks to this action of faith, the monk rises to the level of a 'true philosopher'" (*Athos*, 41).

44. *Patrologia Graeca*, 94:669, 672; see also 533.

45. Ibid., 672.

the consideration of things that are incorporeal and immaterial, that is to say, it is a consideration of God, who primarily and properly is incorporeal and immaterial. But it also treats of angels, demons, and souls, which in themselves are termed immaterial in comparison with the body, although in comparison with that which is immaterial in the true sense, the divine, they are material. This, then, is "theology."[46]

We have in this definition of "theological philosophy" what Aristotle calls "first philosophy" or "theology." Damascene himself does not use the term "first philosophy"; he employs only the term "theology" for this field of philosophy.

"Physical philosophy" according to Damascene, considers "the nature of material things, that is to say, of animals and plants, of stones and the like." The other part of theoretical philosophy, the "mathematical," considers those things which stand midway between immaterial things and material ones. The objects of mathematics "are now considered in matter and now outside matter." The explanation is given that "number in itself is immaterial, but is also found in matter, for we speak of ten measures of grain and of ten pints of wine."[47]

With regard to "practical philosophy," he gives these explanations: Practical philosophy is called "ethics" if it pertains to the guidance of the *individual*. It is called "domestic economy" if it pertains to the guidance of the whole *household*. And it is called "politics" if it pertains to the guidance of the entire *state*.[48]

Aristotle's term "first philosophy" is seldom used by the Church Fathers and modern Greek writers.[49] But his terms "theology," "theoretical philosophy," and "practical philosophy" appear in numerous patristic and modern Greek writings, in the same form or in variants. In patristic texts they acquire new meanings. Thus, Gregory the Sinaite uses the term "theological philosophy," but does not mean what Aristotle means by "theology." For Gregory, "theological philosophy" does not consist in metaphysical discussions and speculations about God, as for Aristotle, but in a precise knowledge of the dogmas of the faith and the actual contemplation of the

---

46. Ibid.
47. Ibid., 672A–B.
48. Ibid., 672B.
49. It is used, e.g., by Photios the Great (see *Patrologia Graeca*, 101:769A) and C. D. Georgoulis (note, e.g., his book *Aristotelous Prote Philosophia*).

The Concept of Philosophy

"divine energies."[50] In Aristotle, the approach is based on sense-experience and reason; in Gregory and other Church Fathers, the approach is grounded in divine revelation, in sacred tradition, and in inner experience, which lift one above the senses and above reason. Thus, Gregory says: "He is a true philosopher who through things knows the Cause of things, or from their Cause knows the things themselves, as a result of a supra-rational union with the Cause and direct faith; by not only having learned about the things that are divine, but also by having experienced them."[51]

Again, the terms "theoretical philosophy" and "practical philosophy" appear in the writings of the seventh-century Church Father Maximos the Confessor. The end of theoretical philosophy is, he says, truth about God, being the simple, indivisible knowledge of all the attributes of God.[52] Sometimes he gives to "theoretical philosophy" a broader meaning, identifying it with the contemplation of suprasensible things in general. Thus, he says that it "lifts the knower above visible things, raising the mind to the intelligible things (τὰ νοητά), which are akin to it."[53] This ascent is viewed as effected with the synergy of God, with the help of divine grace.[54] "Practical philosophy," on the other hand, has as its aim to purify one of the passions and vices, and to develop the virtues.[55]

"Physical philosophy," which occupies an important place in Aristotle's system, is not totally ignored by the Greeks of the Byzantine and post-Byzantine periods; but it is played down, as it was by Socrates and Plato. These Athenian philosophers believed that we cannot gain knowledge in the strict sense of this word (ἐπιστήμη) about the external world, but only opinion (δόξα), hypotheses. Besides, what is important for a man is self-knowledge, knowledge of his nature and destiny, and knowledge about God, who should be for us "the measure of all things."[56] The Greek Church Fathers were in essential accord with this standpoint. And to this day philosophy of nature and physics have not occupied a central place

---

50. *Philokalia*, 4:58. See also, 2:57, where the term is used by St. Maximos the Confessor.

51. *Philokalia*, 4:57.

52. *Philokalia*, 2:131.

53. Ibid., 126.

54. Ibid., 128.

55. Ibid., 126, 131, 185.

56. See Plato's *Phaedo, Gorgias, Theaetetus,* and *Laws* X, and my book *Plato's View of Man*, 15–24.

The Sculptor and His Stone

in Greek thought, as not being among the things that matter most for a human being.

The Greek Fathers have even more reason than Plato for stressing the primacy of knowledge of man over knowledge of the physical cosmos. For they regard man—the inner man, the soul—as a *great* universe and the physical world as a *small* universe. Thus, St. Symeon the New Theologian remarks: "Each one of us has been created by God a second, great cosmos (κόσμος μέγας), within this small visible world, as is testified along with me by Gregory the Theologian."[57] Similarly, Nicodemos the Hagiorite characterizes man as a "great world" (μέγας κόσμος). "God," he says,

> first created the invisible world of angels and second the visible world. After everything else He creates man, of an invisible soul and a visible body. Thus He renders him like a cosmos—not a small cosmos within a great one, as the philosopher Democritos has said, and as other philosophers opine, calling man very pettily only a microcosmos and limiting his dignity and perfection to this visible world; no, but God renders man a great cosmos within a small one. Man is a great cosmos through the multitude of powers which he contains, especially intuitive and discursive reason and the will, which the world that is perceived by the senses (αἰσθητὸς κόσμος) does not have.... For this is what Gregory the Theologian says: "He places man on the earth like a second cosmos, a great cosmos within a small one"; a cosmos adorning both universes, the visible and the invisible, according to the divine Gregory [Palamas] of Thessaloniki.[58]

In the twentieth century, St. Nectarios of Aegina and Nicholas Louvaris have given vigorous expression to this view. Nectarios says:

> Great, indeed, is the spiritual man [the inner man, the spirit or soul], who has been created in the image of his Creator God.... He Who cannot be contained by the universe dwells mystically in the heart of microscopic man. It sounds strange, yet it is true. The manner is mystical, but His revelation is manifest from its results. God is infinite and the universe is in the palm of His hand, and man is a speck of dust; and yet he rises above the cosmos, above the heavens, and views with his mental eyes the grandeur of the creation, examines and searches the universe with his rational

---

57. Symeon the New Theologian, *Ta Heuriskomena Panta*, 483. See also St. Gregory the Sinaite, *Philokalia*, 4:55.

58. *Symbouleutikon Encheiridion*, 20–21. See my book *Modern Greek Thought*, 57–58.

power, discovers the laws that govern the universe, measures the vast distances and dimensions of the heavenly bodies, knows the density, solidity and quantity of the substances that make up the bodies, and in general the nature and the attractive and repulsive force of the enormous giants of the heavenly firmament. Illumined by divine light, his intellect reaches the Creator of the universe, studies the character of the divine Creator and makes assertions about His attributes.[59]

Similarly, Louvaris remarks: "The universe which man encloses within himself is more extensive and more magnificent than the physical universe which surrounds him."[60]

Regarding physical investigations, the following statement of Palamas is characteristic of the patristic attitude towards such investigations: "Not only to know God, and to know man himself and his order is higher knowledge than physics and astronomy and every philosophy about these, but also to know our own mind and its disease and to endeavor to cure this is incomparably better than to inquire about the magnitude of the stars and the nature of physical things."[61]

In modern times, a similar attitude appears in some of the writings of Benjamin of Lesvos (1762–1824), one of the leading Greek philosophers of the early part of the nineteenth century and of the eminent philosopher-theologian Apostolos Makrakes, who flourished during its closing decades. Benjamin remarks, for instance:

> If one does not know how far the sun is from us or the stars and the planets; or whether water or the air are compounds or not, this ignorance will not cause any harm to him, being a matter of mere curiosity. But if one is deficient in his knowledge of his duties, despises his natural duties, is ignorant of his duties to his Creator, this is a loss of everything. Such an individual is indeed an irrational animal, having only the form of a human being.[62]

In the same vein, Apostolos Makrakes observes:

> The anthropological sciences [among which are the philosophical sciences of psychology, logic, and ethics] are vastly superior to

---

59. From my book *Modern Greek Philosophers,* which contains a chapter of selections from St. Nectarios's writings, 60–61.
60. *Symposion Hosion,* 25.
61. *Philokalia,* 4:143. See also St. Antony the Great, *Philokalia,* 1:19.
62. See my book *He Peri Paideias Theoria,* 60.

the cosmological [physical] sciences as regards the value of their object and also their usefulness. Because in the same measure in which the physical world is superior to man in volume and size, man is superior to the physical world in quality and value, being an image and likeness of the supreme and perfect Being.[63]

These passages refer to the secular science of physics. For the Greek Fathers, there is another physics, which they call "physical (or natural) philosophy."[64] This is something different from what Aristotle understands by "physics." It is that part of Christian teaching which pertains to the physical world. Among its cardinal doctrines, derived from Scripture, is that the physical universe is not eternal, but was created by God *ex nihilo*—not out of pre-existing matter—and is a beautiful, very admirable work of divine wisdom and art.

With regard to two of the other Aristotelian terms that we have discussed, "theology," and "philosophy" as *the whole of organized knowledge,* it should be noted that in patristic writings the expression "theological philosophy" is sometimes used instead of "theology," and that "philosophy" is occasionally employed to denote the whole organized secular knowledge apart from grammar. Thus, in his life of Symeon the New Theologian, his disciple Niketas Stethatos says that as a child Symeon "received instruction only in grammatical studies; he did not want to learn the philosophical ones."[65] This connotation of the term "philosophy" appears occasionally in modern Greek writings, most notably in those of the eminent classical philologist Adamantios Koraës.[66]

Six Special Christian Uses of the Term "Philosophy"

We have seen thus far some main classical Greek conceptions of philosophy and their analogues in the Hellenic Christian East. We turn now to some new conceptions of philosophy that were added to these by the Christianized Greeks.

---

63. *New Philosophy*, 1:38, 39.

64. See, e.g., St. Gregory of Nyssa, *De Vita Moysis*, II, 43; Maximos the Confessor, *Philokalia*, 2:57; Gregory the Sinaite, *Philokalia*, 4:58.

65. *Ta Heuriskomena Panta*, 1.

66. See, e.g., Koraës's "Stochasmoi Autoschedioi peri Paideias kai Glosses" (Offhand thoughts on education and language), in *A. Korae Hapanta*.

The Concept of Philosophy

Greek church writers appropriated the word "philosophy," already in the early centuries, for denoting *Christianity*. In order to clarify and justify this appropriation, they drew a distinction between two kinds of philosophy: (1) "external (ἐξωτερική, ἔξω, θύραθεν) philosophy," and (2) "internal (ἐσωτερική, ἔσω) philosophy." The latter they also called "the true philosophy," "heavenly philosophy," "spiritual philosophy," "divine philosophy," "philosophy according to Christ," "sacred philosophy," "philosophy from Above," and "wisdom from Above."

The first kind of philosophy, "external philosophy," comprises for them ancient Greek philosophy and the pagan philosophy of the early Christian centuries. The second kind, "internal philosophy," is identical with the Christian religion. This term is used to denote Orthodox Christian teaching in its totality; lived Christian teaching in general; some interior practice, particularly inner attention and inner stillness; and the monastic life.

1–2. External Philosophy and Internal Philosophy

One will find the distinction between "external philosophy" and "internal philosophy" in Greek patristic texts from the second century on. This distinction continues to be made to this day in Greece.

"External philosophy" is explicitly distinguished by some writers into the authentic and the sham. To give three examples, it appears in the writings of Clement of Alexandria in the second and third centuries, those of the theologian Meletios Pegas in the sixteenth century, and those of St. Nectarios in the twentieth. The authentic, which is inspired by the love of truth, is exemplified by such philosophers as Socrates, Plato, and Aristotle. Although their philosophy contains errors, it also contains many important truths, and thus constitutes, as Clement of Alexandria puts it, a valuable "preparatory training to those who attain to faith through demonstration," "a stepping stone to the philosophy which is according to Christ."[67] Sham philosophy, on the other hand, is exemplified by vainglorious, superficial thinkers: sophists, materialists, atheists, slaves of pleasure. It is this pseudo-philosophy, says Clement, that Paul the Apostle has in mind when he says in Colossians 2:8: "Beware lest any man spoil you through philosophy and vain deceit, after the tradition of men, after the rudiments of this world, and not after Christ."[68]

---

67. *Stromateis*, Bk. 1, chap. 5, *Ante-Nicene Fathers*, 2:305; Bk. 6, chap. 8, ibid., 2:495.
68. Ibid., Bk. 1, chap. 11.

Pegas and Nectarios, both admirers of Clement of Alexandria, make use of this distinction. Thus, Pegas speaks of Socrates and Aristotle as wise and refers to their views approvingly, whereas he characterizes Epicuros and his followers as irrational animals, because they reduced man to an animal, denying him an immortal soul.[69] And Nectarios cites Socrates, Plato, and Aristotle as true philosophers, and the ancient Greek materialists, atheists, hedonists, and sophists as pseudo-philosophers. Thus, he says:

> Behold Socrates, Plato, Aristotle, and Plutarch and the other workers of noble philosophy. What century will ever forget them? Who does not admire the age when they lived as one of glory and grandeur? But behold also the company of the Epicureans. What kind of men were Diagoras, Aristippos, Hegesias and their likes, the co-workers of ancient wretchedness? What were their deeds? History has written black pages about them.[70]

The guidelines for the proper use of "external philosophy" by Christians were given in the early centuries by Clement of Alexandria in his *Stromateis*, Basil the Great in his *Address to Young Men*, and John Damascene in his *Fount of Knowledge*. They advise an *eclectic* use of external philosophy, selecting from heathen books whatever befits a Christian and is allied to the truth, and passing over the rest. Such eclecticism has been practiced continuously in the Hellenic East in Byzantine times and during the post-Byzantine period. There was never a condemnation of it, such as we find in Tertullian in the West, who rejected "external philosophy" in its totality.

The distinction between "external philosophy" and "internal philosophy" has been especially emphasized in times when secularists have sought to ignore it and promote one-sidedly "external philosophy." This happened in Greece in the eighteenth and nineteenth centuries, when materialistic, atheistic, secularistic ideas began to be introduced into Greece from Western Europe. Athanasios Parios (1721/1722–1813), one of the great educators of Greece, reacted strongly. He wrote and published in 1802 a book entitled *Response* (*Antiphonesis*), in which he stressed the distinction between "external philosophy" or "human philosophy," and "internal philosophy" or "divine philosophy." He identified the first with ancient Greek and modern European philosophy; the second, with Christian teaching as contained in Holy Scripture, especially the New Testament, in the writings

---

69. Pegas, *Chrysopege*, 173, 225, 226, 265, 307, 311, 315, 322, 336, 345, 355, 385.

70. From my book *Modern Greek Philosophers*, 85. See also St. Nectarios's book *Peri Alethous kai Pseudous Morphoseos*, 8–21.

of the Eastern Church Fathers, and in the Acts and Canons of the Oecumenical Synods. Parios emphasizes in his *Response* the superiority of divine philosophy over human philosophy, of Christian teaching over secular systems of knowledge. He holds that in Europe the natural hierarchy, where internal philosophy occupies a place above external philosophy, has been overturned, external philosophy having been placed above internal, spiritual philosophy.

3. Orthodox Christian Teaching as Philosophy

The simple term "philosophy," as we have already noted, often appears in Greek patristic texts to denote *Orthodox Christian teaching in its totality*. Use of the term in *this* sense has to be determined by the context in which it appears.

4. Lived Christian Teaching as Philosophy

The word "philosophy" is also used occasionally by the Greek Fathers to denote *lived*—that is, deeply believed in, felt, and practiced—*Christian teaching in general*. Again, use of the term in *this* sense has to be determined by the context in which it appears. This meaning of the term "philosophy," as well as the preceding one, goes back to the early centuries of the Christian era. Thus we find it in the texts of Gregory of Nyssa and John Chrysostom. It is quite apparent in the following passage of Neilos the Ascetic: "Philosophy is a state of character associated with true belief regarding real being. . . . Christ was the first one Who through His life opened its path, having displayed a pure life and always kept His soul above the passions of the body."[71] It is also evident in the remark of Gregory of Sinai that he is a true philosopher who *both knows and practices* the Christian teaching; he "who has not only *learned* things divine, but has *experienced* them."[72] Nicholas Cavasilas, too, uses the term "philosophy" to denote *lived* Christian teaching when he says: "Through meekness, control of anger, not being vexed at those who offended Him, and in many other ways the Savior introduced the

---

71. *Philokalia*, 1:191.
72. Ibid., 4:57.

true philosophy into the world. He set forth far more and greater examples than anyone else through what He did and what He patiently suffered."[73]

5. The Practices of Inner Attention and Inner Quiet as Philosophy

In our discussion of the ἔλεγχος or ἐξέτασις during the Christian period, we saw that one very important form it has assumed is that of inner attention (προσοχή, νῆψις), which Hesychios calls "mental philosophy," "practical philosophy of the mind," and "intellectual philosophy." Other ascetic-mystical Fathers, too, use the term "philosophy" with this connotation. Thus, Philotheos of Sinai says in one of his *Chapters on Inner Attention*: "If, then, we wish to practice mental work which is philosophy according to Christ, the guarding of the mind and exercising inner attention, we must begin by partaking of food and drink with moderation, avoiding excess.... Inner attention may rightly be called a path that leads to the kingdom that is within us and to the future one."[74] The fourteenth-century mystics Kallistos Xanthopoulos and Ignatios Xanthopoulos also call this practice philosophy. They say: "This is philosophy: that one be ever watchfully attentive even in the smallest things that befall him. A person who does this lays up for himself great treasures of inner rest. He does not fall asleep spiritually, lest anything adverse might befall him. He cuts off the causes in advance, suffers a little in small things and thereby banishes great suffering."[75]

Among those who speak of inner quiet or stillness (ἡσυχία) as "philosophy" is St. John Climacos. He says: "Rare are those who are thoroughly versed in secular philosophy; but I assert that those who know well the divine philosophy of true inner quiet are still more rare."[76]

6. The Monastic Way of Life as Philosophy

The use of the term "philosophy" to denote the monastic way of life has already been discussed under the heading "Philosophy as the Way of the Best Life." Much could be added on this subject, but what has been said under that heading is sufficient for the scope of this lecture.

---

73. *Patrologia Graeca*, 150:668C.
74. *Philokalia*, 2:275.
75. Ibid., 4:277.
76. *Klimax*, Discourse 27, 155.

Conclusion

To sum up, we have examined briefly sixteen major senses in which the term *"philosophy,"* alone or together with another word, has been used in the Hellenic tradition. The first ten senses, which we found in ancient Greek philosophy, were (1) philosophy as the love of wisdom, (2) philosophy as μελέτη θανάτου, (3) philosophy as ἔλεγχος, (4) philosophy as dialectic, (5) philosophy as the way of the best life, (6) philosophy as organized knowledge in its totality, (7) theoretical philosophy, (8) practical philosophy, (9) first philosophy, and (10) physical philosophy.

Proceeding from the pre-Christian to the Christian period, we noted the continued use of these terms, though with a modified, deepened, enriched, and more spiritual significance.

Finally, we noted the introduction of the following important new terms or conceptions of philosophy by Christian writers of the Greek East: (1) external philosophy, (2) internal philosophy, (3) philosophy as the whole body of Orthodox Christian teaching, (4) philosophy as lived Christian teaching, (5) philosophy as the practice of inner attention and inner quiet, and (6) philosophy as Orthodox Christian monasticism.

Bibliography

Athanasios of Paros, St. *Antiphonesis.* Trieste: 1802. 2nd ed. Hermoupolis, Syros: 1866.

Burnet, John. *Greek Philosophy,* Part 1. London: Macmillan, 1928.

Cavarnos, Constantine. *Byzantine Thought and Art.* 1968. 2nd. ed. Belmont, MA: Institute for Byzantine and Modern Greek Studies, 1974.

———. *Modern Greek Philosophers on the Human Soul.* 1967. 2nd. ed. Belmont, MA: Institute for Byzantine and Modern Greek Studies, 1987.

———. *Modern Greek Thought.* Belmont, MA: Institute for Byzantine and Modern Greek Studies, 1969.

———. *He Peri Paideias Theoria tou Beniamin Lesviou.* Athens: Ekdoseis "Orthodoxou Typou," 1984.

———. *Plato's View of Man.* Belmont, MA: Institute for Byzantine and Modern Greek Studies, 1975.

———. *St. Arsenios of Paros.* Modern Orthodox Saints 6. Belmont, MA: Institute for Byzantine and Modern Greek Studies, 1978.

Georgoulis, C. D. *Aristotelous Prote Philosophia.* Thessalonike: Alexiou kai Pikopoulou, 1935.

Gregory of Nyssa, St. *De Vita Moysis.* Edited by Herbert Musurillo. In Werner Jaeger and Herman Langerbeck, eds., *Gregorii Nysseni Opera,* vol. 7.1. Leiden: Brill, 1964.

———. *Opera Ascetica*. Edited by Werner Jaeger, J. P. Cavarnos, and V. W. Callahan. In Werner Jaeger and Herman Langerbeck, eds., *Gregorii Nysseni Opera*, vol. 8.1. Leiden: Brill, 1952.

Klimax Ioannou tou Sinaitou (Ladder of John the Sinaite). Athens: Ekdoseis Hieras Mones tou Parakletou, 1979.

Koraës, Adamantios. *A. Korae Hapanta* (All the Works of A. Koraës), vol. 1. Athens: Mpires, 1969.

Laertius, Diogenes. *Lives of Eminent Philosophers*. 2 vols. In *Loeb Classical Library*. Cambridge, MA: Harvard University Press, 1925.

Louvaris, Nicholas. *Athos*. Athens: 1962.

———. *Symposion Hosion*, vol. 1. Athens: Apostolike Diakonia, 1962.

Makrakes, Apostolos. *A New Philosophy and the Philosophical Sciences*, vol. 1. Translated by Denver Cummings. New York: Putnam's Sons, 1940.

Migne, J.-P., ed. *Patrologiae Cursus Completus, Series Graeca*. 161 vols. Paris: 1857–66.

Nectarios of Pentapolis, St. *Peri Alethous kai Pseudous Morphoseos*. Athens: 1894.

Nicodemos the Hagiorite, St. *Symbouleutikon Encheiridion*. 2nd ed. Athens: 1885.

Pegas, Meletios. *Chrysopege*. Edited by G. Valetas. Athens: "Pege Orthodoxou Bibliou," 1958.

Philokalia ton Hieron Neptikon. 5 vols. Athens: Aster, 1957–63.

Photios the Great, St. *The Homilies of Photios, Patriarch of Constantinople*. Translated and edited by Cyril Mango. Cambridge: Harvard University Press, 1958.

Roberts, Alexander and James Donaldson, eds. *The Ante-Nicene Fathers*. 10 vols. Grand Rapids: Eerdmans, 1978.

Schaff, Philip, eds. *A Select Library of the Nicene and Post-Nicene Fathers of the Christian Church*, First Series. 14 vols. Grand Rapids: Eerdmans, 1978.

Symeon the New Theologian, St. *Ta Heuriskomena Panta*. Translated by Dionysios Zagoraios. Syros: 1886.

Taylor, A. E. *Aristotle*. London and Edinburgh: Jack, 1919.

Voulgaris, Eugene. *Diatribe peri Euthanasias*. St. Petersburg: En to Typographeio tes Autokratorikes Akademias ton Epistemon, 1804.

Zervakos, Philotheos. *Mega kai Thaumaston Proskynema eis Palaistinen kai Sina* (Great and wonderful pilgrimage to Palestine and Sinai). Athens: 1959.

CHAPTER 7

Images of the Invisible Beauty: Plotinian Aesthetics and Byzantine Iconography

Archimandrite Patapios

THE IDEA THAT ART imitates nature is a commonplace that can be traced back to Plato; that art is subsequent and inferior to nature is a commonplace of Greek thought in general.[1] Plotinos offers an alternative to such ideas in his fifth *Ennead*: "If anyone despises the arts because they produce their works by imitating nature, we must tell him, first, that natural things are imitations too. Then he must know that the arts do not simply imitate what they see, but they run back up to the forming principles [λόγους] from which nature derives."[2] Plotinos then goes on to make the observation which forms the basis for this paper: "For Pheidias too did not make his Zeus from any model perceived by the senses, but understood what Zeus would look like if he wanted to make himself visible."[3] In his translation of Plotinos, A. H. Armstrong labels this the "Pheidias commonplace" and notes that it goes back at least to the age of Cicero; he also cites the *Life of Apollonios* by Philostratos.[4]

---

1. Close, "Philosophical Theories," 164, 169.

2. V.8.1.33–36. Unless otherwise indicated, all quotations from and references to Plotinos are taken from the Loeb translation by A. H. Armstrong.

3. Ibid.

4. *Plotinus*, 5:240, n. 1. Compare Cicero, *Orator*, II.8–9; Philostratos, *Vita Apollonii*, VI.19. As we shall see from a closer examination of the relevant passages in the *Enneads*, Plotinos does not consider imagination, so much as intuition, to be the formative principle of artistic creation. For his part, too, Cicero goes on to discuss the ideals or patterns with reference to Plato's Forms, which suggests that he did not think of imagination as

When I first came across this passage, I was struck by the resemblance that it bears to the Byzantine and Eastern Orthodox notion of Icons as "spiritual vision reified," to use the title of a perspicacious paper on this topic by Archbishop Chrysostomos of Etna.[5] Now it may seem paradoxical, if not perverse, to draw any kind of connection between Plotinos and Byzantine iconography. After all, does not Porphyry inform us in the opening chapter of his *Life* of the philosopher that Plotinos seemed ashamed of being in the body and that he strongly objected to having his friend Amelios paint his portrait, on the ground that he did not want to leave behind him "a longer-lasting image of the image [εἰδώλου εἴδωλον], as if it was something genuinely worth looking at"?[6] Surely this suggests that Plotinos had as negative a view of the visual arts as Plato.[7] Indeed, from even the most cursory reading of the *Enneads* it is clear that Plotinos had an ardent desire to attain unity with the One, and that he took a rather dim view of matter and things physical. But if we look more closely at what Porphyry says, we shall see that in his estimation Plotinos *seemed* [ἐῴκει] ashamed of being in the body. Moreover, his reluctance to sit for a portrait could have been a sign of shyness or even humility on his part.[8]

When removed from the context of his philosophy as a whole, such a passage as this does appear to indicate that Plotinos had a negative attitude towards art and artists. However, the section quoted at the beginning of this paper belies such an attitude, as do other passages that we shall examine subsequently. This is not to say that Plotinos was entirely consistent in his thinking about art; it is possible to find places in the *Enneads* where he speaks quite disparagingly of artworks. Plotinos was, in fact, far from being a systematic thinker, and so we should not be too surprised if he sometimes contradicts in one place what he says elsewhere.

---

actually constituting the suprasensible ideals [*species*] of artworks. Similarly, although Philostratos uses the term φαντασία to characterize the artist's perception of noetic reality, he subsequently talks of the artist envisaging an εἶδος of Zeus.

5. "Iconography," 184–91.

6. *On the Life of Plotinus*, 3.

7. *Republic*, X. 597b.

8. According to H. P. R. Finberg, however, Plotinos's attitude towards art underwent a considerable development from the time when the above incident took place, at some point between 246 and 253. In Finberg's opinion, it was a series of conversations between Plotinos and his fellow Platonist Origen that helped him reach a more positive view of art than the one he originally held. ("Filiation of Aesthetic Ideas," 150–51.)

For purposes of this paper, the most important Plotinian treatises are "On Beauty" (I.6) and "On the Intelligible Beauty" (V.8). There are remarks on art and beauty scattered throughout other treatises, to which I shall refer during the course of my exposition. After setting forth those aspects of Plotinos's aesthetics that pertain to iconography, I shall discuss how these provide a philosophical context for the Christian practice of representing holy persons by means of Icons.

First, then, let us turn to the treatise "On Beauty." Armstrong comments that Plotinos's concern in this treatise "is not to provide its readers with an aesthetic philosophy but to exhort them to ascend through all the visible and invisible beauties of derived reality to the source of all beauty, the Good, on that journey of the mind to God which was always [his] main concern."[9] Plotinos begins by calling into question the Stoic view[10] that beauty consists in good proportion [συμμετρία] of the parts to each other and to the whole on the ground that it tends to exclude simple things like colors and the light of the sun from participation in beauty, to say nothing of ways of life, studies, or branches of knowledge.[11] It would be absurd to suppose that virtue is beautiful on account of good proportion. Iconography—at least of the traditional Eastern Orthodox kind—is sometimes criticized by modern aestheticians for distorting the natural proportions of the human anatomy and for representing nature in a highly stylized manner. Perhaps some of this criticism rests on the assumption that an object is beautiful only if its parts display good proportion.

Plotinos then states that "the soul speaks of" the primary beauty in bodies "as if it understood it, recognizes and welcomes it and as it were adapts itself to it."[12] In other words, the soul intuits beauty, just as it recoils from ugliness. Since in its higher aspect the soul is "related to the higher kind of reality in the realm of being," it experiences delight when it encounters something akin to itself or the higher reality. It is reminded of its true, noetic homeland, which is composed of Forms. It is by participation in these Forms that things in this world possess beauty, which is to say that

9. *Plotinus*, 1:231.

10. As Armstrong points out, "That good proportion was an essential part of beauty was a general Greek conviction, accepted by Plato and Aristotle; but it was the Stoics who defined beauty strictly and exclusively in these terms" (Ibid., 234, n. 1). Compare Plato, *Philebus*, 64e, *Timaeus*, 87d–e; Aristotle, *Metaphysics*, XIII.3, 1078a36–1078b1, *Politics*, III.13, 1284b8–13.

11. I.6.1.22

12. I.6.2.4–5.

in them matter has "submitted to be completely shaped according to the form [εἶδος]."[13] Form is the principle that gives unity and order to material objects: "So then the beautiful body comes into being by sharing in a formative power which comes from the divine forms."[14]

In order to judge whether a given object is beautiful, the soul has recourse to the forms residing within it. The beauty of anything, be it simple or complex, is nothing other than "the inner form divided by the external mass of matter."[15] The extent of beauty is determined by reference to the form in the soul. This presupposes that the person doing the judging has some internal, "formal" knowledge of what he is evaluating: "Only those can speak about the beauty of ways of life who have accepted the beauty of ways of life."[16] The invisible beauty of virtue, for example, can only be appreciated by one who is "passionately in love with the invisible."[17] But the question still remains: Why do those who have *eros* for true beauty take delight in greatness of soul, a righteous life, a pure morality, and other kinds of moral beauty?[18] Plotinos asks us by way of contrast to consider the case of an ugly soul. "Dissolute and unjust" as it is, "full of all lusts, and all disturbance, . . . thinking mean and mortal thoughts as far as it thinks at all, altogether distorted, loving impure pleasures, living a life which consists of bodily sensations," its perception of reality is so warped that it regards ugliness as beauty.[19] It is incapable of seeing what a soul ought to see because it is sunk in the darkness of matter. Such internal or spiritual ugliness can only be removed if one is willing to "wash and clean himself and so be again what he was before."[20]

A necessary condition, then, for advancing towards union with—that is, knowledge of—the One is the cleansing of one's noetic faculties. "So the soul when it is purified becomes form [εἶδος] and formative power [λόγος], altogether bodiless and intellectual [νοερά] and entirely belonging to the

---

13. I.6.2.18.

14. "Οὕτω μὲν δὴ τὸ καλὸν σῶμα γίγνεται λόγου ἀπὸ θείων ἐλθόντος κοινωνίᾳ" (I.6.2.28–29).

15. I.6.3.8–9.

16. I.6.4.8–9.

17. I.6.4.20.

18. I.6.5.9–18.

19. I.6.5.26–32.

20. I.6.5.47–48.

divine, whence beauty springs and all that is akin to it."²¹ According to Armstrong's rendition of the ensuing sentence, the soul is only truly soul when it becomes perfectly conformed to intellect. The next sentence is of great importance: "For this reason it is right to say that the soul's becoming something good and beautiful is its being made like to God, because from Him come beauty and all else which falls to the lot of real beings."²² This is reminiscent of the exegesis found in some of the Greek Fathers of Genesis 1:26, which in the Septuagint reads as follows: "καὶ εἶπεν ὁ Θεός, Ποιήσωμεν ἄνθρωπον κατ' εἰκόνα ἡμετέραν καὶ καθ' ὁμοίωσιν." This text was commonly understood to mean that man, who since the Fall has tarnished the divine image in him, must strive to regain his original beauty and attain thereby to the divine likeness.²³ According to the teaching of the Orthodox Church, one very important means for achieving this end is the contemplation of holy men and women as they are depicted in sacred images. The definition (ὅρος) of faith of the Seventh Oecumenical Synod states that "the more frequently they are seen in iconic representation, the more those who behold them are awakened to the memory of their prototypes and to a yearning for them."²⁴

In the final three chapters of this treatise on beauty, Plotinos exhorts his readers to "ascend again to the Good, which every soul desires."²⁵ In words of lyrical rapture he maintains that one who has beheld the Good "glories in its beauty and is full of wonder and delight, . . . loving with true passion and piercing longing."²⁶ One who wishes to attain to such a vision must eschew the beauty in bodies, in the realization that these are mere

---

21. I.6.6.13–16.

22. I.6.6.19–21.

23. The distinction between the image and likeness of God—a distinction commonly found in the writings of the Greek Fathers—is very clearly articulated by St. John of Damascus: "For the phrase 'according to the image' denotes man's noetic aspect and his free will, whereas the phrase 'according to the likeness' signifies likeness [to God] in virtue as far as that is possible" (*Exact Exposition of the Orthodox Faith*, II.12, in *Patrologia Graeca*, 94:920B). Compare St. Diadochos of Photike: "We human beings are all created in the image of God; but to be in His likeness belongs only to those who through great love have rendered their own freedom subject to God" (*Ascetic Discourse*, 4, in *Philokalia*, 1:236).

24. Mansi, *Sacrorum Conciliorum Nova et Amplissima Collectio*, 13:377D.

25. I.6.7.1–2.

26. I.6.7.15–18.

images, traces, and shadows.[27] He must shut his eyes, "and change to and wake another way of seeing, which everyone has but few use."[28]

Inner sight alone can lead us to a vision of the Good. We have to look inside ourselves, clearing away all impurity and whatever else impedes our ability to see the Good, until we have become sight; then we will already have ascended to a point at which we need no one else to show us the way.[29] Anyone who "comes to the sight blear-eyed with wickedness, and unpurified, . . . sees nothing, even if someone shows him what is there and possible to see."[30] The following words sum up everything that Plotinos is trying to put across in this treatise: "No eye ever saw the sun without becoming sun-like, nor can a soul see beauty without becoming beautiful. You must become first all godlike and all beautiful if you intend to see God and beauty."[31]

Removing from our souls everything that sullies, distorts, or otherwise clutters our inner sight is a prerequisite for making any kind of spiritual progress. This insight can profitably be applied to the sacred art of iconography. According to Archbishop Chrysostomos, "It is in the inner life, in the transfigured vision of those united to the spiritual world, that we can best understand the nature of the Icon."[32] An authentic Icon "portrays that which we see when we have become habituated to the spiritual world and have attained spiritual vision."[33] One twentieth-century iconographer whom many consider to have attained great spiritual vision was Photios Kontoglou (1895–1965). Almost single-handedly he championed traditional Byzantine art at a time when most iconographers were content to imitate the naturalistic art of the Renaissance and the following epochs. In his view, sacred or spiritual art is concerned with inner beauty, which is deep and imperishable. "With regard to the creation of works of spiritual art, Kontoglou holds that there is presupposed a certain inward state . . . .

---

27. I.6.8.6–9.

28. I.6.8.26–27.

29. I.6.9.16–25.

30. I.6.9.26–28.

31. "Οὐ γὰρ ἂν πώποτε εἶδεν ὀφθαλμὸς ἥλιον ἡλιοειδὴς μὴ γεγενημένος, οὐδὲ τὸ καλὸν ἂν ἴδοι ψυχὴ μὴ καλὴ γενομένη. Γενέσθω δὲ πρῶτον θεοειδὴς πᾶς καὶ καλὸς πᾶς, εἰ μέλλει θεάσασθαι θεόν τε καὶ καλόν" (I.6.9.30–34).

32. "Iconography," 185.

33. Ibid., 189.

Such works . . . can be produced only by an artist, even though he be unlettered, who fasts, prays, and lives 'in a state of contrition and humility.'"[34]

At the beginning of this paper I quoted a famous passage from *Ennead* V.8 about the artist's access to the intelligible world. At the beginning of the chapter from which this comes, Plotinos asks how it is "possible for anyone to contemplate the beauty of Intellect and of that higher world."[35] He pictures two lumps of stone, one of which is shapeless and untouched by art, while the other has been hewn into the statue of a god or a man of outstanding beauty. It is the form imposed by the sculptor that endows the otherwise crude lump of matter with beauty. This form pre-existed in the mind of the artist "because he had some share of art [τέχνης]."[36] The beauty of the form, however, undergoes some diminution to the extent that it is imposed on matter. More precisely, the beauty that is in the art abides there, while "another comes into the stone which is derived from it and less than it."[37] No matter how beautiful an external object may be, such en-mattered beauty cannot compare with the beauty inherent in the art that produces it.

Plotinos believes that the sculptor has a vision of ideal beauty. According to A. N. M. Rich, "What Phidias creates is not based merely upon some insubstantial mental figment, but is, in fact, an imitation of 'the immaterial ideal world of the *noeta* in the soul of the artist.'" Art is a *mimesis,* but one that "dispenses altogether with a sensible pattern and works straight from the Idea."[38] For this reason, Plotinos maintains that one should not despise the arts because they produce their works by imitating nature; after all, "natural things are imitations too."[39] As Rich puts it, "the natural world is itself an imitation, in so far as it is an image of the Intelligible."[40] The arts "run back up to the forming principles [λόγους] from which nature derives."[41] "By concentrating, not on the outward appearance of his model, but on its inner, intelligible essence," the artist "is capable of producing

---

34. Cavarnos, *Byzantine Thought and Art*, 77.
35. V.8.1.6–7.
36. V.8.1.18.
37. V.8.1.20–22.
38. "Plotinus," 236. The quotation is from Pistorius, *Plotinus and Neoplatonism*, 150.
39. V.8.1.33–34.
40. "Plotinus," 237.
41. V.8.1.36–37.

something that is logically no further removed from truth than the natural object itself."⁴²

In the remaining chapters of *Ennead* V.8, Plotinos attempts to give us a vision of the intelligible world, of those realities that the arts are said to imitate. As in the previous treatise (I.6), he emphasizes that true beauty consists in form, "which comes from the maker upon that which he has brought into being, as in the arts it was said to come from the arts upon their works."⁴³ The beauty evident in "studies and ways of life and generally in souls" makes it clear that true beauty has nothing to do with size. The λόγος of beauty makes a noble soul beautiful "by adorning the soul and giving it light from a greater light which is primarily beauty" and "makes us deduce by its very presence in the soul what that before it is like."⁴⁴ This principle of beauty is itself Νοῦς. Now, what kind of image could there be of Intellect, since any image of it would have to be derived from inferior things? "[I]t is from the intellect in ourselves when it has been purified, or, if you like, from the gods, that we apprehend what the intellect in them is like."⁴⁵ As in the treatise "On Beauty," we must purify ourselves of everything that could blur our inner vision if we are to apprehend the noetic realm.

Everything in the world of Intellect is transparent; there is no darkness or opacity. "Everything and all things are clear to the inmost part to everything; for light is transparent to light."⁴⁶ This theme of light is of great importance for understanding how images can portray their prototypes. According to D. N. Koutras, Plotinos uses the image of light to describe the relation between the source of light (ἰδέα) and the lighted body (εἰκών). Citing *Ennead* I.6.3.17–19,⁴⁷ he argues that the source of sensible beauty, whether artistic or natural, is the light: "The degree of the perceptible object's beauty depends on the light-absorbing capacity of the *hyle*, or the latter's degree of submission to the illuminating idea. Thus, the work of art,

---

42. "Plotinus," 237.
43. V.8.2.14–17.
44. V.8.3.5–8.
45. V.8.3.17–19.
46. V.8.4.5–6.

47. "The simple beauty of colour comes about by shape and the mastery of the darkness in matter by the presence of light which is incorporeal and formative power and form."

as an *eikon* depending on form approaches it more or less, according to its capacity of receiving the form's light."[48]

Just as color, which is the light in bodies, needs another light in order for it to appear; so also in the case of intelligible realities, which have a greater degree of light than bodies, there is need of another greater light for them to appear.[49] "When anyone, therefore, sees this light, then truly he is also moved to the Forms, and longs for the light which plays upon them and delights in it, just as with the bodies here below our desire is not for the underlying material things but for the beauty imaged upon them."[50] St. John of Damascus makes a similar point in his defense of the holy Icons: "Now that God has been seen in the flesh consorting with men, I depict that aspect of God which is visible. I do not worship matter; I worship the Creator of matter, Who became matter for my sake.... We venerate Icons, not offering veneration to matter, but through the Icons to those depicted in them. The honor accorded to an Icon ascends to the prototype, as the divine Basil says."[51]

Only one whose mind has been enlightened and purified can attain to a vision of the noetic or spiritual world. Such a person is the artist. "As a maker and a creator of a work of art, the artist participates in the *art* and the *wisdom* which identify with the being of the ideas and the true essence of the intelligible world . . . being inspired as he creates the sublime art, [the artist] is elevated to the realm of Intellect, art, wisdom and true beauty."[52]

How does all this relate to Byzantine iconography? Gary Gurtler provides an excellent summary of Plotinos's ideas in *Ennead* V.8.4–6: "Intelligible objects have a pure movement, rest, and beauty, by which they both keep their identity and blend with one another . . . . As this intellectual vision eliminates the spatial dimension of the objects contemplated, so the resulting contemplative union eliminates the temporal dimension within the subject." Gurtler sees a similar suppression of spatial and temporal dimensions in Byzantine art, in which "Bodies are shown elongated and thus spiritualized. The heads of the saints are slightly enlarged to convey the

48. "Essence," 149.
49. VI.7.21.13–17.
50. VI.7.22.1–5.
51. "First Apologetic Discourse Against Those Who Decry the Holy Icons," 16, in *Patrologia Graeca*, 94:1245A; "Third Apologetic Discourse Against Those Who Decry the Holy Icons," 41, in *Patrologia Graeca*, 94:1357C.
52. Koutras, "Essence," 151–52.

purity and insight of their minds." The aim of this art is to effect a transformation of the viewer's own interior character.[53]

Gurtler also points out that "[t]he artist contemplates the image in the intellectual world, reproducing it in the mirror of material things, so that others will in turn be drawn to the contemplation of intellectual truth."[54] If by "intellectual" we may understand "noetic" or "spiritual," then this is a perfect representation of what happens when one contemplates an Icon. An Icon both "conveys in some real sense the presence of that which is pictured" and points beyond itself to a higher reality, as we can see from the earlier quotation from St. John of Damascus.[55] As Constantine Cavarnos puts it, the Icon must be spiritual in its mode of expression, "pointing to a reality beyond the physical, lifting those who see it to a higher level of thought, feeling and consciousness, denoted by the term spiritual."[56]

The connections that I have been attempting to draw between Plotinian aesthetics and Byzantine iconography are admittedly not grounded in any specific text from the Byzantine period. Nevertheless, aside from the fact that the *Enneads* enjoyed considerable popularity in Byzantine intellectual circles—most notably among savants like Michael Psellos, who compiled a florilegium of excerpts from Plotinos, Theodore Metochites, George Nikephoros Gregoras, and George Gemistios Plethon[57]—it has been argued that his aesthetics may have influenced Byzantine art.[58] Steven Runciman, in a lucid summary of Plotinian aesthetics, points out that since, according to Plotinos,

> the artist should not be concerned with copying nature but with interpreting ideas. The bonds of a naturalistic technique are no longer relevant. As a result the individual work of art begins to be downgraded. Art has no business to concern itself with individual objects; its products should be parts of a universal whole. The artist too begins to lose his individual identity. He becomes instead

53. "Plotinus," 281–82.
54. Ibid., 282.
55. Ibid.
56. *Orthodox Iconography*, 36–37.
57. "Plotinos appealed to this select group of Christian intellectuals because of his emphasis on the existence, beyond this world, of an immaterial world (the 'fatherland' of the soul), an emphasis that, while avoiding a dualistic opposition of the two worlds, called the soul to a virtuous life that would lead it to transcend its materialistic preoccupations" (*Oxford Dictionary of Byzantium*, 3, s.v. "Plotinos").
58. For example, by Grabar, in his *L'art*, 1:15–29.

one of a team of interpreters of the divine. That is why we know the names of so few Byzantine artists.[59]

Runciman goes on to observe that "[i]n other ways, too, Plotinus foreshadowed later taste."[60] To take just one example, Plotinos asserts that "the simple beauty of colour comes about by shape and the mastery of the darkness in matter by the presence of light which is incorporeal."[61] "The Byzantines," says Runciman, "agreed with this. They held light, the first-created element, in supreme regard. They were fascinated by its varying effects, and, like Plotinus, they equated colour with the intensities of light."[62]

Even in the absence of direct textual evidence for my thesis, the parallels between Plotinian and Byzantine aesthetics set forth in this paper are striking enough to warrant the conclusion that the latter was in some sense influenced by the former, if only at a subliminal level. Until a closer literary connection can be established, let the following words of St. Dionysios the Areopagite serve as a fitting conclusion to this paper:

> In the realm of perceptible images, the artist gazes unwaveringly upon the archetypal form [εἶδος], not being drawn away towards any visible object or in any way divided in attention. . . . Thus it is with those artists who love beauty in the mind: their steadfast and unswerving contemplation of fragrant, hidden beauty will yield an unerring and godlike image. Naturally, therefore, when these divine artists unfailingly form their minds in accordance with a transcendently fragrant and noetic pulchritude . . . they sacredly behold, as in an image, the most sacred and hidden mysteries of the Church . . . [and] gaze solely upon the archetypal conception. Not only do they not look at things dissimilar [to God], but not even are they themselves dragged down to the sight thereof.[63]

---

59. *Byzantine Style*, 37.

60. Ibid.

61. I.6.3.17–19. Armstrong comments that for Plotinos, "light is the incorporeal *energeia* of the luminous body" (*Plotinus*, 1:241, n. 1).

62. *Byzantine Style*, 37.

63. *On the Ecclesiastical Hierarchy*, IV.3, in *Patrologia Graeca*, 3:473C–476A.

Bibliography

Cavarnos, Constantine. *Byzantine Thought and Art*. 1968. 2nd. ed. Belmont, MA: Institute for Byzantine and Modern Greek Studies, 1974.

———. *Orthodox Iconography*. Belmont, MA: Institute for Byzantine and Modern Greek Studies, 1977.

Chrysostomos, Archbishop. "Iconography and the Inner Life: Icons as Spiritual Vision Reified." *The Patristic and Byzantine Review* 7 (1988) 184–91.

Close, Anthony J. "Philosophical Theories of Art and Nature in Classical Antiquity." *Journal of the History of Ideas* 32 (1971) 163–84.

Finberg, H. P. R. "The Filiation of Aesthetic Ideas in the Neoplatonic School." *Classical Quarterly* 20 (1926) 148–51.

Grabar, André. *L'art de la fin de l'Antiquité et du Moyen Âge*. 3 vols. Paris: Collège de France, 1968.

Gurtler, Gary M. "Plotinus and Byzantine Aesthetics." *The Modern Schoolman* 66 (1988–89) 275–84.

Kazhdan, Alexander P., ed. *The Oxford Dictionary of Byzantium*. 3 vols. Oxford: Oxford University Press, 1991.

Koutras, D. N. "The Essence of the Work of Art according to Plotinus." *Diotima* 14 (1988) 147–53.

Mansi, G. D., ed. *Sacrorum Conciliorum Nova et Amplissima Collectio*. 31 vols. Florence: Expensis Antonii Zatta Veneti, 1759–98.

Migne, J.-P., ed. *Patrologiae Cursus Completus, Series Graeca*. 161 vols. Paris: 1857–66.

Philokalia ton Hieron Neptikon. 5 vols. Athens: Aster, 1957–1963; reprint, 1974–1977.

Pistorius, P. V. *Plotinus and Neoplatonism: An Introductory Study*. Cambridge: Bowes & Bowes, 1952.

Plotinos. *Plotinus*. Translated by A. H. Armstrong. 7 vols. Cambridge: Harvard University Press, 1966–88.

Rich, A. N. M. "Plotinus and the Theory of Artistic Imitation." *Mnemosyne* 13 (1960) 233–239.

Runciman, Steven. *Byzantine Style and Civilization*. Harmondsworth, UK: Penguin, 1975.

CHAPTER 8

In Defense of Piety: Respect for Words and Respect for *"The Word"*

J. C. B. Petropoulos

Ἀναγίνωσκε πολλὰ καὶ μαθήσῃ πολλά. Καὶ εἰ οὐ νοεῖς, θάρσει· πολλάκις γὰρ διελθόντι σοι τὴν βίβλον παρὰ Θεοῦ γνῶσις δοθήσεται καὶ νοήσεις αὐτήν.

(Read much and you will learn much. And if you do not understand, take courage; for by reading a book several times through, you will receive knowledge from God and you will understand it.)[1]

THE LEARNED SCRUTINY OF the literature of the Orthodox Church is one of the most pressing needs facing the Church and Western society as a whole. In our "decibel-culture" of "post- or sub-literacy"[2] (in which general literacy, let alone that of the religious and scriptural variety, is diminishing drastically) patristic exegesis, as well as the reading of ascetic and hagiographic works, must be conducted with more general concern and, as I hope to argue, with a philological tact and respect that cannot be separated from spiritual piety.

The discipline and act of scriptural exegesis necessarily implicate an activity of the mind that is at once philological and religious and that is, in the ultimate analysis, ineradicably spiritual. The reading of any literary

---

1. Cecaumenos, *Strategicon*, 212.
2. Steiner, *In Bluebeard's Castle*, 86.

text presupposes an attentiveness, a vigilant awareness of its surface structure—its phonetic and formal devices, tropes, grammatical, syntactical and even prosodical constructions, etc. The generic serious reader must also be a generic φιλόλογος: he must trust and love (φιλεῖν) the word (λόγος). Or to quote the critic and philosopher George Steiner, Professor of Comparative Literature at the University of Geneva: "In its authentic sense, philology is, indeed, the working passage, via the arts of scrupulous observance and trust (*philein*), from the uncertainties of the word to the stability of the *Logos*."[3]

The serious reading of literature, then, inescapably involves philology in its root sense. In the case of the elucidation of Scripture the need for philological scrupulosity is likewise unavoidable and arguably even more urgent, calling for vigilance and concentration (compare the analogous ascetic states of νῆψις, προσοχή) and even devotion bordering on love (compare the divine ἔρως of St. Symeon the New Theologian). The religious exegete should be a philologist who works with the selfsame tools as any other literary exegete but with the important difference that his ultimate criterion is not aesthetic judgment, nor even intellectual satisfaction, but rather an apprehension of the divine *Logos*. The student of Byzantine religious literature, in executing a *lecture bien faite*, strives to discern the *Logos* beneath the superficies of his text. Understandably *qua* reader "in depth" and Christian he has a vested interest in positive rigor. An explicator of religious Scripture, he stands in direct line of descent from the Judaic and Hellenic-Byzantine textual commentators; and no less persistently than the Church Fathers[4] will he be concerned with vexed questions of interpretation, summoning every philological method at his disposal.

It is interesting to remark that the student of Orthodox literature will have to invoke a faculty—one might say a sensitivity—that an ordinary

---

3. "Viewpoint," 1262.

4. The Byzantines were astute φιλόλογοι in the positive sense. The Church Fathers, from St. Basil and St. Gregory Nazianzos onwards, were men of literary taste who were trained in (and often practiced) textual criticism and exegetics in general. The fifth-century school at Antioch, represented by Theodore, Bishop of Mopsuestia, and Theodoret, Bishop of Cyrrhus, is probably the earliest example of scholars who applied historical and other positive criteria to the interpretation of the Bible. Byzantine scholars carried out a creditable effort at compiling and editing, and thereby preserving, the Greek classics for posterity (via Renaissance Italy). The Patriarch Photios is an example of an omnivorous Byzantine reader, a dogged philologist and inventor of the book review. With a few rare (and eccentric) exceptions, the Byzantines, be it noted, never banned or burnt pagan texts. See N. G. Wilson's authoritative account of Byzantine scholarship, mainly classical, *Scholars of Byzantium*; also, Reynolds and Wilson, *Scribes and Scholars*.

philologist may not necessarily rely on: faith and piety in the sense of St. Gregory of Nyssa's εὐσέβεια.[5] In his discourse *On The Life of Moses*,[6] St. Gregory aptly outlines this faculty as a prime defense against heretical interpretations (αἱρετικαὶ ὑπολήψεις):

> Ἡ γνῶσις τῆς εὐσεβείας φῶς γίνεται παρὰ τὴν πρώτην οἷς ἂν ἐγγίνηται. Διότι τὸ ἐξ ἐναντίας τῇ εὐσεβείᾳ νοούμενον, σκότος ἐστίν· ἡ δὲ ἀποστροφὴ τοῦ σκότους, τῇ μετουσίᾳ τοῦ φωτὸς γίνεται. (The knowledge of the correct belief [and piety] becomes a light from the outset for those by whom it is perceived. For that which is conceived as contrary to the correct belief [and piety] is darkness; whereas the rejection of darkness occurs through participation in the light.)[7]

St. Gregory is here laying down a methodology of κατάφασις, using the Prophet Moses' experiences on Mt. Sinai as a paradigm for Christian virtue and in particular the mystical approach to God. From the terms of his discussion, however, we might extrapolate an operational model which may apply equally well for Byzantine Studies. Εὐσέβεια may be likened to a light illuminating the pious reader's ascent through the cloud of opaqueness (γνόφος) which surrounds the Unseeable (ἀθεώρητον, ἀθέατον) and Unknowable (ἀκατάληπτον), i.e., the divine determinant of meaning.[8] By contrast, disrespect for a text may be likened to darkness: We might say that without the light of the sun or a lamp the student cannot read, far less do so "in depth"; his hermeneutic enterprise ends, literally, in obfuscation.

Without εὐσέβεια hermeneutics becomes sinister, for there can be no struggle and progress towards the *meaning-fulness* of a patristic or hagiographical text when the presupposition of the *Logos* is left in question. St. Gregory's crucial caveat about the prerequisite of εὐσέβεια has a recent (and telling) analogue in Professor Steiner's challenge of the "deconstructionist" vogue. His despair at the self-indulgent polemics of the practitioners of deconstruction has to do in large part with his impatience with their celebration of the "substantive absence" of meaning in a literary text. The end

---

5. On the double sense of εὐσέβεια (piety and correct belief) see Lampe, *Patristic Greek Lexicon*, s.v. εὐσέβεια. Surely the implication must be that what is respected (εὐσεβεῖσθαι) as correct and true becomes an article of faith (εὐσέβεια).

6. *Patrologia Graeca*, 44:297–430.

7. Ibid., 376D.

8. Ibid., 376D–377A.

result of "the astute trivialisations, the playful nihilism of deconstruction"⁹ may be paralleled with the total (and self-serving) obfuscation which St. Gregory imputed to heretics. Herewith, Professor Steiner:

> Without some axiomatic leap towards a postulate of *meaning-fulness*, there can be no striving towards intelligibility or value-judgment, however provisional . . . . Where it elides the "radical"—the etymological and conceptual root—of the *Logos*, logic is indeed vacant play.
>
> We must read as if the text before us had meaning . . . . The true understanding(s) of the text . . . may, during a briefer or longer time-spell, be in the custody of a few, indeed of one witness and respondent. Above all, the meaning striven towards will never be one which exegesis, commentary, translation, paraphrase, psycho-analytic or sociological decoding, can ever exhaust, can ever define as total . . . .
>
> Where we read truly, where the experience is to be that of meaning, we do so as if the text . . . incarnates (the notion is grounded in the sacramental) a real presence of significant being. This real presence, as in an icon, as in the enacted metaphor of the sacramental bread and wine, is, finally, irreducible to any other formal articulation, to any analytic deconstruction or paraphrase. It is a singularity in which concept and form constitute a tautology, coincide point to point, energy to energy, in that excess of significance over all discrete elements and codes of meaning which we call the symbol or the agency of transparence.¹⁰

In Professor Steiner's theory, the reading of a literary text becomes an investigation and interrogation, however incomplete, of a real (i.e., transcendent) presence. *A fortiori*, in the Orthodox view, the reading of a patristic or ascetic text becomes a striving after *the* Real Presence, Christ. We may take up again St. Gregory's terms and images in order to complete our proposed figural model for Byzantine Studies: The reader must begin with the surface structure of his (or her) text, using the incentives and controls of traditional philology as well as modern linguistic-critical approaches. (For instance, the student might use a formalist approach in considering the stylized articulacy of St. John Chrysostom or the imagery in St. John of the Ladder.) Moreover, he must deal in small units of sense. From *explication de texte* he may proceed to further reaches of enquiry—the historical,

---

9. Steiner, "Viewpoint," 1275.
10. Ibid.

cultural and psycho-sociological strata of the work. The text becomes less opaque; it can be contextualized and minutely crossreferenced. The cloud of darkness (γνόφος) begins to scatter. Mental concentration (προσοχή, περίνοια) together with the indispensable faculty of piety help the reader to traverse[11] the density of phonetic and semantic particulars until he arrives at the meaning of the Presence which the religious text incarnates. The pious student reaches an immaterial tent (ἀχειροποίητος σκηνή)—the deepest of "deep structures"—which he now perceives[12] as if it were an archetype (ὡς εἰς ἀρχέτυπον[13]). This stratified hermeneutic method, that proceeded from textuality to mystery, brings Christ to the reader's mind. Most importantly, Christ, the source of the Meaning sought for (τὸ ζητούμενον[14]) was approached and apprehended through the illuminating agent of piety.

The need for philological rigor and the need for piety in Byzantine Studies are largely the same. Both spring from a respect for the verbal components of a textual tradition which itself bears on the *Word*. The unique metaphysical framework of Orthodoxy, and its historical priority, make piety a *sine qua non* for this academic field. The competing school of cynical ultra-positivism can often promote σκότος—a darkening of meaning, a retreat from the *Word*. For example, according to this second school, a hagiographical text is little more than a confection of rhetorical and literary tags and devices, themselves combined with elements of mass fantasy and religious tendentiousness. Reduced in this way, a saint's life becomes a contingent part of literary and sub-literary tradition. On the other hand, under a more traditionalist approach, which is tempered with spiritual reason, the details of a saint's life are seen to be none too schematized or trivial; a *vita*, in fact, is a scrupulously drawn verbal icon of a higher degree of abstraction than a literary fiction or popular legend. The external form of a *vita* is of course susceptible to philological and other kinds of analysis; but its deep, active meaning (its relationship to the *logos*) defies positivist exhaustion.

We may cite a further example of the divergent modes of reading a Byzantine text: The writings of St. Dionysios the Areopagite may, on one view, be described as a mystical corpus that has been wrongly, or even fraudulently, attributed to this contemporary of St. Paul. *Prima facie* the

---

11. "Ὁ δὲ [sc. Δαβὶδ] ἐκεῖ [sc. ἐν τῷ σκότει] γεγονώς, ἃ προεπαιδεύθη διὰ τοῦ γνόφου, πάλιν διὰ τοῦ γνόφου διδάσκεται." *Patrologia Graeca*, 44:377B.

12. The means of perception is not visual. Ibid., 377A.

13. Ibid., 380B.

14. Ibid., 377A.

later date for the manuscript tradition may be defensible on textual and other external grounds. But unless the student tempers positivist dubiety with spiritual caution (a form of εὐσέβεια) he may overlook a consideration that is *philologically* valid: the teachings of a holy man may have been orally transmitted and/or compiled within his milieu, this corpus of precepts being later preserved by individuals who, for reasons of extreme religious humility, transcribed them in the saint's name.

In brief: the lack of εὐσέβεια—the dismissal of correct belief and spiritual sensitivity among the various critical resources which the Church Fathers exemplified—may lead to fragmentary and less than genuine interpretations. If practiced to an extreme, such modes of reading may give rise to pseudo- or sub-literacy in Byzantine Studies. The defense of the word in this field calls for a philological ethos and subtlety that must operate alongside spiritual piety. Indeed our only recourse, especially in the face of the neoteric muddling of Orthodox doctrine and practice, is a return to Byzantine standards of philology.

Bibliography

Cecaumenos. *Strategicon*. Edited by G. G. Litavrin. Moscow: 1972.
Lampe, G. W. H., ed. *A Patristic Greek Lexicon*. Oxford: Clarendon, 1961.
Migne, J.-P., ed. *Patrologiae Cursus Completus, Series Graeca*. 161 vols. Paris: 1857–66.
Reynolds, L. D. and N. G. Wilson. *Scribes and Scholars: A Guide to the Transmission of Greek and Latin Literature*. Oxford: Clarendon, 1974.
Steiner, George. *In Bluebeard's Castle: Some Notes Towards the Re-definition of Culture*. London: Faber, 1971.
———. "Viewpoint: A New Meaning of Meaning." In *The Times Literary Supplement*, Friday, 8 November, 1985, 1262.
Wilson, N. G., ed. *Scholars of Byzantium*. London: Duckworth, 1983.

CHAPTER 9

Free Will, Character, and Responsibility in Classical Greek Thought, the Greek Fathers, and Modern Existentialism

Constantine Cavarnos

THE QUESTION AS TO whether man does or does not have free will, whether he is or is not responsible for his actions and character, is of fundamental importance for ethics. Even those who deny free will and advocate determinism admit that the belief in free will inarguably bolsters moral earnestness and fervor, whereas the acceptance of determinism is conducive to lassitude and lethargy.[1] An excellent example of this is the case of the American philosopher William James, whose acceptance of materialistic determinism led him, at the age of twenty-eight, into a state of agony and despair. He was delivered from this state when he studied the works of the French philosopher Charles-Bernard Renouvier and was persuaded that the human will is free and rejected the theory of determinism.[2]

In the theocentric era of the Middle Ages, when religious faith was prevalent also among philosophers, men believed that they had free will and, consequently, that they were responsible for their actions, both good and bad, and for their character, be it good or bad. There were, to be sure, a few exceptions to this among men of learning, such as St. Augustine, who, in his old age, as a result of his conflict with the heretic Pelagius, arrived

---

1. For example, Ledger Wood observes: "The belief in free-will no doubt fosters moral earnestness, whereas the belief in determinism may, at least in certain persons, induce moral lassitude" ("The Free-Will Controversy," in Enteman, ed., *Problem*, 39).

2. Compare Cavarnos, *To Sympan*, 35, 53–56.

at the doctrine of divine predestination, which the Protestant theologian John Calvin adopted and disseminated many centuries later. In more recent times, however, the positive sciences have displaced religion from the dominant position that it used to possess and have occupied this position themselves. One result of this was the gradual and widespread replacement of the belief in free will, in the freedom of the will, by the belief in determinism. A consequence of this, in turn, was a slackening in moral awareness and the propagation of immoral behavior. The reason for this is that the positive sciences have as their methodological presupposition that everything that happens takes place necessarily, in accordance with the inexorable law of causality, of cause and effect, not only in nature but also in the realm of the inner man and of human actions. This doctrine is certainly useful for scientific inquiry, since without the conviction that there exists a stable order in the universe, there would be no justification for scientific inquiry and the sciences would not have developed, as A. N. Whitehead admirably demonstrates in his book *Science and the Modern World*.[3] However, for many representatives of the positive sciences and for many philosophers who are devotees of these sciences, this principle has not remained merely what it was originally: a simple presupposition and starting point for scientific research. It has become an indisputable metaphysical axiom. Thus, the conviction has become widespread that man is deprived of free will, that in the final analysis no one is responsible for the quality of his character and his deeds. According to this understanding, our character and behavior are determined necessarily by the quality of the organism that we have inherited and by our physical and social environment. It should, however, be pointed out that this supposedly scientific thesis has been somewhat undermined in recent times on account of the findings of physics, which is regarded as the most exact of the positive sciences, and of the opposition on the part of not a few philosophers. The physicists say that, as far as they can ascertain through the most precise methods that they employ in their researches, there is some indeterminacy in matter at the level of electrons and other subatomic particles. This discovery, which was first formulated by the eminent physicist Werner Heisenberg in 1927, has been labeled "the principle of indeterminacy."[4]

William James makes a distinction between two kinds of determinism: "hard" determinism and "soft" determinism. This distinction is useful

---

3. *Science*, ch. 1.
4. Or "the uncertainty principle." Compare Hook, ed., *Determinism*.

for the purpose of clarifying the issue. Hard determinism maintains that human beings are not morally free, and consequently that they are not responsible. There is no such thing as free will. Therefore, we are not responsible either for our character or for our actions. Representatives of hard determinism among philosophers were the American Jonathan Edwards, the Frenchman d'Holbach, and the German Schopenhauer, and others, while among psychologists the most famous is Freud. There are few today who accept hard determinism.[5]

Soft determinism is the doctrine that some of man's actions are free and others are not, and that, in consequence, man is responsible for certain of his actions and not for others. That an action is "free" means, first, that he who performed it was not forced or compelled to perform it—for example, he did not perform it because someone threatened him, hypnotized him, or drugged him; and, secondly, that he performed it out of his own rational desire and choice.[6] The representatives of soft determinism, who are primarily English, such as Hobbes, Hume, Mill, Bradley, and Ayer, assert that this view is in harmony with moral responsibility. We are responsible for the deeds that we perform freely and not under compulsion.

In spite of its apparent difference from hard determinism, soft determinism does not differ profoundly from it. It would be different from hard determinism if it maintained that we bear responsibility for the quality of our character, which usually determines the expression of our desires, passions, and thoughts. On the contrary, however, it shares the view of hard determinism that our character is, in the final analysis, a product of (1) our heredity and (2) our environment, factors that are beyond our control. The exponents of soft determinism avoid expressing this conviction of theirs, whereas the exponents of hard determinism do express and emphasize it.[7] Consequently, soft determinism is a kind of subterfuge. The responsibility that it ascribes to man is groundless and unreal. It is confined to the superficies of human existence, to the level of sentiments and thoughts. It does not advance beyond these to something more basic, to character, and beyond this to man's creative core. Soft determinism rightly distinguishes between "free" (or voluntary) and "unfree" (or involuntary) actions, but provides no deep foundation for this distinction.

5. See the article "Hard and Soft Determinism" by Paul Edwards in the aforementioned work edited by Sidney Hook.
6. Ibid.
7. Compare Edwards, "Hard and Soft Determinism."

The Sculptor and His Stone

The ancient Greek philosophers, especially Plato and Aristotle, and even more so the philosophers and theologians of Byzantium, the Church Fathers, confronted the issue of free will, character, and responsibility with greater acuity and metaphysical profundity. Existentialist philosophy, too, has refuted contemporary determinism at great length.

Perhaps the most important observations of Plato on this subject are to be found in the tenth book of the *Republic*. One of them is the following: "Virtue is sovereign, and each man will have more or less of her as he honors or dishonors her. The responsibility lies with him who chooses; God is blameless."[8] Here, Plato rejects determinism, which transfers responsibility for one's character from man, the individual, to God. The Athenian philosopher ascribes responsibility to each person: "The responsibility lies with him who chooses; God is blameless." Virtue, he says, is good character. It is a "sovereign" thing, something which is not imposed from without, but which one chooses freely; and according as one esteems virtue more or less, one acquires it to a greater or smaller degree. Another important observation of Plato is that the soul develops a definite kind of character or ethos as a result of the way of life that it chooses: "when it chooses a different life, it must of necessity become different."[9] Therefore, virtuous character is a result of the choice of virtue as worthwhile and of the choice of the way of life that leads to the realization of virtue, of good character.

Aristotle, Plato's most important disciple, teaches the same thing in detail in his *Nicomachean Ethics*. He makes a distinction between virtues and vices "according to similarity," that is, the predispositions that we have "by nature," "from birth,"[10] and those that are virtues and vices "strictly speaking" or in a precise sense. We are certainly not responsible for the first, but we are, according to Aristotle, responsible for the second, which constitute one's ethos or character in the strict sense. Genuine virtues and vices are acquired; they are "habits" that we acquire through "habituation," through repetition, through the choice of a particular manner of life. "Moral [ἠθική] virtue comes about through habit," says the Stagirite, "whence it derives its name [ἦθος], by a slight variation from the word 'ἔθος.'"[11]

Each virtue, and also good character, which is the sum of the moral virtues, is developed through habit, through the repetition of virtuous acts,

---

8. *Republic*, 617D.
9. *Republic*, 618B.
10. *Nicomachean Ethics*, VI.13, 1144b4–16; VII.5, 1148b29–1149a9.
11. Ibid., II.1, 1103a17–19.

and it originates from choice [προαίρεσις]: the conscious, rational estimation and selection of the good, under the form of temperance, courage, justice, etc. "For it is by choosing what is good or evil," Aristotle pointedly says, "that we are the kinds of people that we are."[12]

We are, therefore, responsible, according to Aristotle, for the quality of our character, since it is something that we form, a product of our free choices and actions. The predispositions that we have from birth, whether good or bad, do not play a decisive rôle in the formation of our character; they simply constitute part of the matter to which we will give full and abiding form. We give it this form gradually through our deeds in accordance with our choices.

In conclusion, Aristotle observes: "Virtue is within our power, and so likewise is vice. For where it is within our power to act, it is also within our power not to act, and where we are in a position to say No, we are also in a position to say Yes .... If it is within our power to do, and likewise not to do, what is good and what is base, and if this is (as we saw) what it means to be good or evil, it is therefore within our power to be decent or base."[13]

The Byzantine Church Fathers reject fatalism and determinism in general, and affirm the view that man has free will and consequently is responsible for his actions and character. They profess, as also did Aristotle, the existence of "natural virtues." Thus, St. Gregory of Nyssa, interpreting the biblical statement that God fashioned man "in His image and likeness," says that "it is [therefore] within our power to be free from necessity and not to be subject to any natural power," and that God made human nature a "participant in all good" and that "every virtue is in us."[14] Likewise, Abba Dorotheos (fl. sixth–seventh cent.) says: "God made man in the image of God, that is, immortal, endowed with free will, and adorned with every virtue."[15] Similar observations are scattered in the writings of the Greek Fathers, from which it is evident that they affirm both free will and the existence of the natural virtues in man. They differ from Aristotle in this respect: whereas he acknowledges the existence of certain natural virtues, they teach that all of the virtues exist in human nature. Likewise, Aristotle does not explain the existence of the natural virtues, whereas the Fathers ascribe their existence to the fact that the human nature is a creation of the

---

12. Ibid., III.2, 1112a1–2.88.
13. Ibid., III.5, 1113b6–14.
14. *On the Making of Man*, 16, in *Patrologia Graeca*, 44:184B.
15. "Discourse I," in *Patrologia Graeca*, 88:1617B.

all-good God. The Byzantine Fathers also acknowledge, as does Aristotle, the existence of certain evil inclinations in man from birth. But whereas he regards this as a rare phenomenon and does not venture any explanation of them, the Fathers regard them as a common phenomenon and explain them by way of ancestral sin. Thus, St. Symeon the New Theologian says: "From the time of Adam's transgression, all of the natural capacities of human nature have been impaired.... And for this reason a man can think, but he is ill and cannot think straight. He can desire, but his desire is imprudent. He can get angry, but his anger is irrational."[16]

When the Fathers say that God created man adorned with every virtue, they do not mean that the virtues exist in man from birth in actuality, but rather potentially, as "natural seeds," in the words of St. Maximos the Confessor.[17] The God Who created man gave him the seeds of the virtues, capacities of the soul which incline towards the good, but which require cultivation to be formed into attributes that we call virtues in the strict sense. The Fathers frequently emphasize the need for ascesis, exertion, and struggle for the development of these capacities. "For it is not without effort that virtue is achieved by those who pursue it; nor is it painless for men to separate themselves from pleasurable things."[18] Similarly, St. Neilos (fl. 440 AD) observes: "Do not think that you have acquired virtue if you have not stood prepared even to shed your blood for its sake. For it is necessary to struggle uncomplainingly against sin even to death."[19] Thus, the Byzantine moralists concur with the following statement of Aristotle: "Neither by nature nor contrary to nature are the virtues engendered in us; rather, we are naturally able to receive them, though we are perfected in them through habit."[20]

A resolute choice and love of the good and fine is required at the outset for the development of our innate moral capacities, for the formation of a virtuous character, as is the rejection of what is bad and shameful. This is the beginning of an effortful journey towards the acquisition of the virtues proper. "The principle and source of the virtues," observes St. Gregory the Sinaite (fourteenth century), "is a good intention."[21] It must be

---

16. "Discourse XIV," in *Ta Heuriskomena*, 88.

17. "Second Century of Texts on Love," 32, in *Patrologia Graeca*, 90:993D.

18. "Concerning Infants Who Die Prematurely," in *Patrologia Graeca*, 46:169D.

19. "One Hundred and Fifty-Three Sections Concerning Prayer," 136, in *Philokalia: A Second Volume*, 87.

20. *Nicomachean Ethics*, II.1, 1103a23–26.

21. "Very Beneficial Chapters in the Form of an Acrostic," 83, in *Philokalia ton Hieron*

followed by a life which leads, on the one hand, to man's purification from the inclinations to sin, from the passions, and on the other hand, to the development of his moral capacities.

We frequently encounter the term "purification" (κάθαρσις) in patristic texts. Through purification man is exalted to "passionlessness" (ἀπάθεια), that is, to the eradication of all the passions, of all the vices. Passionlessness betokens purity of mind, heart, conscience, and imagination. Such purity constitutes the "restoration" (ἀποκατάστασις), "refashioning" (ἀνάπλασις), and "renewal" (ἀνακαίνισις) of human nature. Man becomes again what the first-formed humans were before the Fall. "Man, this great and precious thing," says St. Gregory of Nyssa, "by falling into the mire of sin, forfeited his being in the image of the imperishable God. . . . But if the earthly covering [of the filth of sin] were to be removed [by the purifying water of the Christian way of life], the beauty of the soul would once again be made manifest. . . . The putting off of an alien accretion is the return to what is proper to oneself and in accordance with nature, to which one cannot attain otherwise than by becoming again such as he was created from the beginning."[22]

Each man is responsible for purifying himself of the passions, insofar as this purification originates with his choice, with his free personal decision, and requires voluntary self-discipline for its realization.

Purification is a very important accomplishment for man. It is, however, preparatory in nature and does not constitute the final goal that man ought to pursue. The final goal is perfection, which consists in the full development of the virtues and deification. As St. Theodore of Edessa (fl. 660 AD) observes, "The object of the endeavor is not only purification from the passions; for this in itself is not, indeed, properly virtue, but is only a preparation for virtue. Besides purification from bad habits, the acquisition of the virtues is necessary . . . , [as are] ascent and *theosis*."[23]

Each man is also responsible, according to the Greek Fathers, for the development of the virtues and the acquisition of a good character. This presupposes, as we have said, the free choice of each man between good and evil, between virtue and vice. It also presupposes a complete turn towards the good, and especially towards the highest Good, the Archetypal Beauty, God, in Whose image man was fashioned. Through the constant movement of the rational (λογιστικόν), the incensive (θυμικόν), and the

---

Neptikon, 4:43.

22. *On Virginity*, 12, in *Opera Ascetica*, 299–300 (=*Patrologia Graeca*, 46:372CD).

23. "*Theoretikon*," in *Philokalia: A Second Volume*, 253–54.

appetitive (ἐπιθυμητικόν) faculties towards God, and through external actions consonant with this movement, we come, through habit, into the possession of every virtue and thus, into likeness to the Creator.

The upward journey of man, his journey to perfection, is not accomplished exclusively through his own internal and external acts, but with the coöperation of God. "Nothing beneficial comes about," says St. John Chrysostomos, "from human exertion (for virtue) without help from on high."[24] Plato recognizes the indispensability of the divine factor, but does not emphasize or elucidate it. Plato's acknowledgment of this factor is confirmed by the following passage, *inter alia*, from the *Phaedrus*, in which Socrates prays, "Beloved Pan and all of the other gods, grant me to become beautiful in the inner man,"[25] and by his observation in the *Euthyphro* that "there is no good that [the gods] do not give us."[26] But whereas the Fathers ascribe divine assistance to one God and one alone, rejecting polytheism, Plato, accepting polytheism, obviously ascribes divine assistance to the many "gods," whom he regards as creations of the supreme Deity that are superior to man. Aristotle seems to consider man self-sufficient in his struggle for virtue, pursuing this without divine reinforcement.

It should be noted that the acknowledgment of the indispensability of divine help, of divine Grace, by the Fathers is in no way contradictory to the ascription of responsibility to man for his character and his actions, as some suppose, since man's will remains voluntary. Divine assistance is not given irresistibly;[27] it is given to those who freely choose the good and call upon God to strengthen them through His Grace in their struggle for virtue. The doctrine that divine Grace acts irresistibly does not belong to the Greek Fathers, but is a fabrication of certain Western theologians.[28]

In the modern era, existentialist philosophy has upheld the sovereignty and freedom of the will and man's responsibility for his actions and character. This philosophy has as one of its basic axioms that existence precedes essence. This means, with regard to man, that the character of each person

---

24. According to a paraphrase by St. Peter of Damascus, in *Philokalia ton Hieron Neptikon*, 3:79; compare St. John Chrysostomos, "Homily 82 on St. Matthew," 4, *Patrologia Graeca*, 58:742.

25. *Phaedrus*, 279B.

26. *Euthyphro*, 15A.

27. "Nothing beneficial comes about," says St. John Chrysostomos, "from human exertion without help from on high. Neither, in turn, does help from on high come to one who does not choose it" (*Philokalia ton Hieron Neptikon*, 3:79).

28. For example, Cornelius Jansen (1585–1638).

is not something given or innate, but his own creation.[29] First I exist, and then, through my choice and my actions, I gradually create my character. This is plainly a reiteration of the views of Plato, Aristotle, and the Fathers.

The general view of existentialist philosophy on this subject is expounded as follows by the French philosopher Sartre, its best-known representative. According to existentialist philosophers, says Sartre, "existence precedes essence."[30] "What does this mean, that existence precedes essence?" he asks. And he replies: "It means that man first of all exists, encounters himself, surges up in the world, and defines himself afterwards."[31] Man, as existentialism understands him, is nothing at the outset. He will become something later, and will become "what he makes of himself."[32] If existence precedes essence, then man is responsible for what he is,"[33] "he is responsible for everything he does,"[34] "he is responsible for his passion."[35]

Thus, according to Sartre, "the existentialist philosopher, when he portrays a coward, says that he is responsible for his cowardice. He is not like that on account of . . . his physiological organism; he is like that because he has made himself such through his actions. . . . [T]he existentialist philosopher says that the coward makes himself cowardly, the hero makes himself heroic,"[36] "by the choice of his morality."[37]

Some existentialist philosophers, such as the Spaniard Ortega y Gasset[38] and Sartre, put forward the assertion that there is no "human nature," and consequently that the formation and development of character is a creation *ex nihilo*. This constitutes a rejection of the important data—such as reason, will, and the natural virtues—about which Aristotle speaks and the existence of which the Greek Fathers of Byzantium affirm. More generally, atheistic existentialism (Nietzsche, Heidegger, Sartre, Camus, *et al.*) teaches the complete moral self-sufficiency of man, since it denies the existence of God, and there is no place in this philosophy for the lofty ideal

---

29. Compare Barrett, *Irrational Man*, 102; Collins, *Existentialists*, 66.
30. Sartre, *L'Existentialisme*, 16–17.
31. Ibid., 21.
32. Ibid., 22.
33. Ibid., 24.
34. Ibid., 37.
35. Ibid., 38.
36. Ibid., 60.
37. Ibid., 78.
38. Barrett, *Irrational Man*, 16, 102.

of purity and perfection, for the attainment of which human capacities are inadequate. The atheistic existentialist philosophy of our era acknowledges and emphasizes the freedom of will and the moral responsibility of man, and refutes and rejects contemporary theories of determinism, but it denies the factor of divine assistance or Grace.

Christian existentialism (Kierkegaard, Dostoyevsky, Berdyaev, Marcel, *et al.*) acknowledges and emphasizes man's free will and his moral responsibility, as well as the divine factor in the regeneration and perfection of man. Therefore, it corroborates more fully than atheistic existentialism the teaching of classical Greek philosophy and also of Byzantine philosophy on the subject of "free will, character, and responsibility."

In general, the phenomenon of existentialist philosophy in our age is important both as an affirmation of the views of ancient Greek and Byzantine philosophy concerning this topic and as a critique and rejection of determinism.

It should, however, be emphasized that existentialist philosophy is not an isolated phenomenon with respect to this subject. Ever since existentialism made its appearance, by way of the Danish philosopher and theologian Kierkegaard, around the middle of the nineteenth century, many other philosophers have criticized the theory of determinism and upheld the freedom of the will and man's responsibility for his actions and character. Among the contemporaries of the founder of existentialist philosophy who refuted and rejected determinism were Petros Braïlas-Armenes and Ioannes Skaltsounes; among our contemporaries, Nikolaos Loubaris, Ioannes Theodorakopoulos,[39] the American Peter Bertocci, and the Scotsman C. Arthur Campbell. I shall summarize certain observations of two of these—Braïlas-Armenes and Campbell—which complement all that I have said in this brief essay.

Braïlas-Armenes asserts that through introspection each of us can ascertain—either during an action, before it, or after it—that unless he has been compelled through external and insurmountable necessity, he is a free agent of his actions. From this internal freedom flow man's personal responsibility, which "is the basis of all of his moral life," and also "the justice or injustice of actions, merit, the praise of virtue and the reproach of vice, good and bad repute, and reward and punishment."[40]

---

39. See Cavarnos, *Modern Greek Thought*, 76.
40. Moutsopoulos, ed., *Braïla-Armene Erga*, 2:119–20.

In response to the determinist assertion that this freedom is an optical illusion and that in reality our actions are determined by compulsive drives, Braïlas-Armenes makes the following observations: No human action is without a reason, and the reasons for our actions are "instincts, feelings, passions, and ideas."[41] But none of these reasons is fixed. Man can and does react against instincts, feelings, passions, and ideas. Furthermore, freedom exists prior to these and contributes to their birth.[42] With regard to the habits that constitute character, Braïlas-Armenes observes that "habit is, above every other factor, a product of free will, since it proceeds from the prolonged repetition of the same actions . . . and this repetition does not occur without the consent of the soul, and we can interrupt it whenever we wish. To be sure, we are sometimes dominated by habits, but only because we allow them to dominate us."[43]

Affirming the existence of God, in opposition to the contemporary German atheist existentialist Nietzsche, Braïlas-Armenes maintains that God is "all-good, our friend and helper,"[44] and that man is perfected "with the assistance of divine Grace."[45]

Campbell upholds the moral responsibility of man and the freedom of the will, which this responsibility presupposes.[46] He admits that heredity and the environment exercise some influence on man's behavior, but maintains that this influence is not decisive, that there exists an indestructible creative nucleus of energy, which neither heredity nor the environment can affect, something to which man contributes exclusively through his own initiative and, consequently, something for which he can rightly be held responsible. This conviction, says Campbell, is extremely widespread and springs from the direct experience of mankind in situations of temptation.[47] One realizes, then, that he can choose and perform action A, which he considers morally right, or choose and perform action B, which is incompatible with action A. He perceives that it is easier to perform action B than action A, because his character impels him towards action B, whereas in order to perform action A he needs to put forth a concerted effort. Fi-

41. Ibid., 121.
42. Ibid., 121–22.
43. Ibid., 121.
44. Ibid., 168.
45. Ibid., 200.
46. "In Defence of Free Will," in Katz et al., eds., *Writers*, 273.
47. Ibid., 276.

nally, he realizes that he is free to put forth or not put forth the requisite effort to perform action A instead of action B. Obviously it depends entirely on the man to choose whether he will put forth the effort of willing or will give in to his already formed character.[48]

Campbell does not deal with the issue of character, the "essence" of man in the terminology of existentialism, or with the issue of the extent to which a man is responsible for it. His concern in the study to which we have referred is to prove that we have free will and are truly responsible for our voluntary acts. From all that he says regarding this subject it is clear that, according to him, and also to Braïlas-Armenes and the other defenders of free will whom we have mentioned, man is able to counteract his habits and is, consequently, able, through his own choice, to change and reshape his character. This entails that man bears responsibility not only for his voluntary acts but also for his character.

Bibliography

Barrett, William. *Irrational Man: A Study in Existential Philosophy*. Garden City, NY: Doubleday, 1962.
Cavarnos, Constantine. *Modern Greek Thought*. Belmont, MA: Institute for Byzantine and Modern Greek Studies, 1969.
———. *To Sympan kai ho Anthropos*. Athens: Aster, 1959.
Collins, James. *The Existentialists*. New York: 1959.
Enteman, Willard F., ed. *The Problem of Free Will: Selected Readings*. New York: Scribner, 1967.
Gregory of Nyssa, St. *Opera Ascetica*. Edited by Werner Jaeger, J. P. Cavarnos, and V. W. Callahan. In Werner Jaeger and Herman Langerbeck, eds., *Gregorii Nysseni Opera*, vol. 6. Leiden: Brill, 1952.
Hook, Sidney, ed. *Determinism and Freedom in an Age of Modern Science: A Philosophical Symposium*. New York: New York University Press, 1961.
Katz, Joseph, Philip Nochlin, and Robert Stover, eds. *Writers on Ethics: Classical and Contemporary*. Huntington, NY: Krieger, 1962.
Migne, J.-P., ed. *Patrologiae Cursus Completus, Series Graeca*. 161 vols. Paris: 1857–66.
Moutsopoulos, Evangelos, ed. *Petrou Braïla-Armene Philosophika Erga*, vol. 2. In *Corpus Philosophorum Graecorum Recentiorum*. Thessalonike: 1971.
The Philokalia: A Second Volume of Selected Readings. Translated by Constantine Cavarnos. Belmont, MA: Institute for Byzantine and Modern Greek Studies, 2009.
Philokalia ton Hieron Neptikon. 5 vols. 1957–63. Reprint. Athens: Aster, 1974–77.
Sartre, Jean-Paul. *L'Existentialisme est un humanisme*. Paris: Éditions Nagel, 1946.
Symeon the New Theologian, St. *Ta Heuriskomena Panta* (All extant works). Translated by Dionysios Zagoraios. Syros: 1886.
Whitehead, A. N. *Science and the Modern World*. New York: Macmillan, 1925.

48. Ibid., 276–7.

CHAPTER 10

The Ancient Greek Heritage

Constantine Cavarnos

THE SUBJECT OF THE Hellenic Heritage—Ancient, Byzantine, and Modern—is one of vital significance, not only for the Greeks, but also for the world at large, the οἰκουμένη. This will become manifest as my discussion proceeds.

The Hellenic Heritage has accumulated over a period of three millennia—from the time of Homer (ninth century BC) to the present. It is an extremely rich heritage, one that encompasses all the Fine Arts, the Sciences, Philosophy, and Religion.

When I say "Fine Arts," I mean literature in its many forms, namely, epic poetry, lyric poetry, comedy, tragedy, fables, stories, and orations. I also mean architecture, sculpture, painting, music, and the dance. When I say "Science," I mean mathematics, astronomy, physics, biology, medical science, and history. By "Philosophy," I mean the various fields into which this discipline is distinguishable, namely, logic, metaphysics, epistemology, ethics, political theory, and aesthetics. Finally, by "Religion" I mean particularly the religion of the Greeks of the Christian era, namely, the Orthodox Christian Faith.

Together, these constitute what the ancient Greeks called Παιδεία and the modern call Πολιτισμός. Westerners—that is, the Europeans and Americans—call this totality "Culture" or "Civilization."

In *all* these areas, the Greeks have made *contributions of the highest order*. Moreover, they have been recognized through the centuries as the *originators* of the majority of them. Thus, Thales is called "the Father of Philosophy"; Herodotos, "the Father of History"; Hippocrates, "the Father of Medicine"; Aristotle, "the Father of the Natural Sciences."

That the Greeks originated them is testified to by the fact that the very *words* by which they are designated in English and other languages are words of Greek derivation. Thus, the word "poetry" is derived from the Greek word ποίησις; "epic," from ἔπος; "lyric," from λυρικός; "tragedy," from τραγῳδία; "comedy," from κωμῳδία; "stories," from ἱστορίαι; "rhetoric," from ῥητορική; "music," from μουσική; "arithmetic," from ἀριθμητική; "geometry," from γεωμετρία; "physics," from φυσική; "biology," from βιολογία; "history," from ἱστορία; "pedagogy," from παιδαγωγία; "philology" from φιλολογία; "philosophy," from φιλοσοφία; "epistemology," from ἐπιστήμη; "ethics," from ἠθική; "politics," from πολιτική; "theology," from θεολογία.

For the ancient Greeks, the Fine Arts, the Sciences, Philosophy, and Religion constituted the *chief* part of *Paideia*, because they pertain to the *soul* or *mind*, which was viewed by them as the higher, chief part of man—as have the Greeks of subsequent ages. Plato called this division of *Paideia* "Μουσική," using this term as a generic one and viewing what is commonly called "music" as a species of this genus. The generic sense of the term music derives from the fact that, according to Greek mythology, the nine sister goddesses who presided over the fine arts, the sciences, and the rest of the disciplines that pertain to the mind were called "Muses" (Μοῦσαι).

The other part of *Paideia*, which pertains to the *body*, was called by the ancients Γυμναστική, "Gymnastic." Today, gymnastic is identified with physical exercises, nothing more. For the ancient Greeks the term Γυμναστική had a broader connotation. It included, besides proper physical exercises, right diet, moderation in food and drink, due rest, and other forms of care of the body.

"Μουσική," *Paideia* of the soul, was directed to the acquisition of the virtues or "excellences" of the *soul*: wisdom, courage, temperance, justice, piety, and so on. "Gymnastic" was directed to the promotion and preservation of physical health, strength, endurance, agility, and grace, which the ancients called "virtues of the body" (σωματικαὶ ἀρεταί).

This twofold ideal of *Paideia* was summed up in the maxim: "A healthy mind in a healthy body" (Νοῦς ὑγιὴς ἐν σώματι ὑγιεῖ).

The culture of the ancient Greeks was one of a *high order*. It was religious, organic, aristocratic, and also popular, in the sense that the common people participated in it. For there was no great gap between the intellectual class and the popular life. It was characterized by the *love of truth and unrelenting quest of it, love of beauty, love of excellence, love of precision, clarity and simplicity of expression, and of moderation—avoidance of excesses.*

The Ancient Greek Heritage

About the great value of ancient Greek culture and the debt to it of the Western world, the famous Anglo-American philosopher Alfred North Whitehead (1861–1947) has made some very noteworthy remarks in his brilliant book *Science and the Modern World*. Thus, he says:

> Greece was the mother of Europe; and it is to Greece that we must look in order to find the *origin* of our *modern ideas* . . . . The Greek genius was philosophical, lucid, and logical . . . . Mathematics interested the Greeks mightily. They invented its generality, analyzed its premises, and made notable discoveries of theorems by a rigid adherence to deductive reasoning . . . . They demanded clear, bold ideas, and strict reasoning from them. All this was excellent; it was genius.[1]

Continuing, Whitehead remarks: "For patient observation, there were the astronomers. There was a mathematical lucidity about the stars, and fascination about the planets."[2]

Then he calls attention to the conviction of the ancient Greeks that there is a *Moral Order* in the universe and an *Order of Nature*. This conviction, he asserts, was transmitted to Europe. The concept of the Moral Order and of the Order of Nature was implanted in the European mind by its contact with the Hellenic East, together with the habit of definite exact thought.[3] The concept and sense of the Order of Nature, along with the habit of disciplined thinking inherited from ancient Greek culture, he adds, made possible the remarkable development of the sciences in the modern age.

Another famous twentieth-century philosopher, Henri Bergson (1859–1941) of France, has made similar remarks. Thus, he says: "Mathematics goes back to the ancient Greeks."[4] More broadly, he remarks, *"precision, exactness, the anxiety for proof,* the habit of distinguishing between what is simply *possible* or *probable,* and what is *certain*—these qualities would perhaps never have appeared in the world at all, had there not existed formerly a small people, in a corner of Greece."[5]

The ancient Greeks sought to *transmit* their culture to other peoples, whom they called "Barbarians," meaning by this term foreigners. This resulted in their *Hellenization,* to a greater or lesser degree. For as the classical

---

1. *Science,* 7. (The italics are mine.) Compare his *Adventures,* 180.
2. Ibid.
3. Ibid., 12.
4. *Mind-Energy,* 98.
5. Ibid., 102. (The italics are mine.)

Greek rhetorician Isocrates remarked, "Those are called Hellenes who are partakers of our culture (παιδεία)."

Alexander the Great, who was the most illustrious pupil of the Athenian philosopher Aristotle, undertook to effect this Hellenization on a grand scale. He was eminently successful in this undertaking. Through his expeditions, Alexander spread Greek culture—the Greek language, fine arts, philosophy, and science into Asia—as far as India—and to North Africa, to Egypt in particular. Egypt became and endured for centuries as a Greek dynasty, that of the Ptolemies, with its capital—Alexandria—named for Alexander the Great.

Through this quite extensive *Hellenization, Alexander prepared the people of those lands to espouse the Christian Faith,* when it was proclaimed by Christ and His Apostles, "when the fullness of the time was come" (Gal 4:4). In his philosophy of history, St. Nectarios of Aegina develops the thesis that the appearance of Alexander and his Hellenizing expeditions occurred *according to Divine Plan,* in order to prepare peoples spiritually for the reception of the gospel.[6]

How Hellenic culture prepares people for the reception of the Christian Faith was explained in the early centuries of the Christian era by St. Justin the Martyr and Philosopher (100–164), Clement of Alexandria (150–211/215), and St. Basil the Great (*ca.* 329–379). In his *Apologies,* his defenses of Christians addressed to the Roman Emperors, who respected Greek philosophy, Justin points out that the teachings of the Greek philosophers Heracleitos, Socrates, and Plato are not altogether different from those of the Christians. He calls attention to some remarkable similarities, such as the doctrines of the immortality of the soul and retribution after death, and the emphasis on living according to reason (λόγος). This similarity attracted Justin himself, and later many other intellectuals, to Christianity. Justin was a pagan philosopher before he became a Christian.

Clement of Alexandria remarks in his *Stromateis*—referred to in English as the *Miscellanies*—that "before the advent of the Lord, philosophy was necessary to the Greeks for righteousness. And now it becomes conducive to piety. It is a kind of preparatory training (προπαιδεία) to those who attain to faith through demonstration.... Greek philosophy, therefore, was a *preparation,* paving the way for him who is perfected in Christ."[7]

---

6. *Melete,* 81–83.
7. Book I, chapter V.

The Ancient Greek Heritage

In his important pedagogical work entitled *Address to Young Men on How They Might Profit from Greek Writings,* St. Basil says that there are many elements in Greek philosophy and other Greek writings that are uttered in *praise of virtue.* So we must apply ourselves especially to such writings. He also points out that by means of many analogies in Greek philosophy that are not entirely different from revealed Christian teaching, the eye of the soul is trained and is enabled to understand the sacred and mystical teaching of Christianity.

With regard to the significance of Alexander the Great in the spread of Greek culture, the following facts are to be noted: His campaign in Egypt resulted in the establishment of the city of Alexandria, of a great university there, and of two libraries—a very large one and a smaller one. The university was established in 296 BC—twenty-eight years after Alexander's death in Egypt—by the first king of the Greek Dynasty of Egypt named Ptolemaios Lagidas (called in English "Ptolemy"). It was named *Mouseion.* The large Library was established at about the same time as the university.

Both the Mouseion and the libraries continued in existence into the Christian era. Thus, Hypatia, the first woman philosopher, is known to have taught at the Mouseion in the early part of the fifth century AD, and the libraries are believed to have existed up to the year 700 AD.[8]

Especially significant about the *spread of the Greek heritage in Egypt* are the following facts: During the Dynasty of the Ptolemies, *Greek was the language of the Palace and the Administration of Egypt.* (When we say "dynasty" we mean a succession of rulers of the same line of descent.) The *official* languages of the *Mouseion, or University of Alexandria, were Greek and Egyptian.* Basically, however, the language of the Mouseion was Greek. All the texts recording the results of the research done there were Greek. Research was extensive, especially in the field of philology, where much work was done to determine the chronology and authenticity of Greek texts, especially as regards the works ascribed to Plato.

The writings of Plato were what we call today "best-sellers." Homer's *Iliad* and *Odyssey* also were extensively studied at the Mouseion. The Greek language as such was studied thoroughly. It was there that the small ("lower case") letters of the Greek alphabet were stylized, and certain new punctuation marks were conceived and put to use, such as the diaeresis and the asterisk. Greek grammar was systematized and used as a basis of other grammars—of Latin, for instance.

---

8. See my book *Cultural and Educational Continuity of Greece.*

The two libraries of Alexandria treasured the works of classical Greek writers—Plato, Homer, Pindar, Sophocles, Euripides, Aristophanes, and others. Much important research pertaining to them was done there.

With regard to the use of the Greek language, of great interest and importance is also the fact that it was the language not only of the Palace and of the Administration, one of the two official languages of the Mouseion, and the language of the Greek population, but also the language of the Jews. The Jews in Egypt had abandoned the Hebrew tongue and adopted Greek. There were about a million Jews in Egypt at that time. Around 285 BC, seventy-two Jewish savants of Alexandria translated the Old Testament from Hebrew into Greek. The Greek version which they produced is known as the *Septuagint*. It was done at the University of Alexandria, the "Mouseion," at the behest of the Greek King Ptolemy II. Named after the approximately seventy (Latin: *septuaginta*) translators, the *Septuagint* has always been the Orthodox Church's official text of the Old Testament. It is the text employed in the original Gospels and the rest of the New Testament. Also, the Septuagint is the version quoted by the Jewish philosopher Philo Judaeus *(ca.* 13 BC–45/50 AD) and the Jewish historian Josephus *(ca.* 37 AD–*ca.* 100).

In addition to the University of Alexandria and the two Libraries in that city, the ancient Greek heritage found in Alexandria a home at the *Christian Catechetical School*. This was established towards the end of the second century *(ca.* 190). The Catechetical School was virtually a Greek Christian University. It was established by Pantainos, a very learned Sicilian Greek, originally a Stoic philosopher. It flourished under the direction of his great pupil Clement of Alexandria, a native of Athens. Like Pantainos, Clement was initially a pagan philosopher. Abandoning paganism, he became a very devout and dynamic Christian. Following his conversion, he continued to esteem classical Greek philosophy, especially Plato. He regarded it as valuable προπαιδεία for Christians, as we noted earlier.

The Catechetical School, or Greek Christian University of Alexandria, prepared teachers and preachers of the Orthodox Christian Faith. It exercised a great influence upon theological science, and numbered among it pupils many celebrated theologians and bishops, such as St. Athanasios the Great. This school continued in existence until the end of the fourth century.[9]

---

9. See my book *Cultural and Educational Continuity*, 61–62.

The Ancient Greek Heritage

Its link with the ancient Greek heritage, particularly philosophy, shows the perennial important value of that heritage, as do the Mouseion of Alexandria and the two Alexandrian libraries.

Bibliography

Bergson, Henri. *Mind-Energy*. Translated by H. Wildon Carr. New York: Holt, 1920.
Cavarnos, Constantine. *Cultural and Educational Continuity of Greece: From Antiquity to the Present*. Belmont, MA: Institute for Byzantine and Modern Greek Studies, 1995.
Nectarios of Pentapolis, St. *Melete peri tes Athanasias tes Psyches*. Athens: 1901.
Whitehead, A. N. *Adventures of Ideas*. New York: Macmillan, 1933.
———. *Science and the Modern World*. New York: Macmillan, 1925.

CHAPTER 11

The Hellenic Heritage in Byzantium

Constantine Cavarnos

COMING TO THE BYZANTINE period, which stretches from 330 AD to 1453, we witness not only the *preservation and utilization of the ancient Greek heritage,* but also many *additions* to it, new creations of great importance and value. These consist most notably in the following:

1. The formulation of the *Divine Doctrines* of the Orthodox Christian Faith by the Seven Great Holy Oecumenical Synods, and of the *Holy Canons* or laws of the Church.

2. The writings, *of the Greek Church Fathers,* which in Migne's famous *Patrologia Graeca* number 161 monumental volumes.

3. The *Liturgical Hymnography* or *Poetry* of the Church—the hymns chanted at its services. They are preserved in many monumental volumes that are used by the *Psaltai* (Cantors), such as the *Octoechos* or *Parakletike,* the *Triodion,* the twelve *Menaia,* and the *Mega Horologion.*

4. *Byzantine Music.*

5. *Byzantine Architecture.*

6. *Byzantine Iconography*—icons in mosaic, in fresco, on panels, and miniatures in manuscripts.

The *preservation* of and *transmission* of ancient Greek culture in a *selective* manner took place particularly at the University of Constantinople, which was founded by Emperor Constantine the Great, but also at cities such as Alexandria, Antioch and Damascus in Syria. These were important centers of Greek culture and Christianity. When I say here Greek culture I mean particularly the Greek language, philosophy, rhetoric, the concepts of

The Hellenic Heritage in Byzantium

Moral Order and Order of Nature, the habits of disciplined thinking, and of clarity and precision of expression.

Greek culture was preserved in Antioch and Damascus by the Christians, and also by the pagans and the Islamic Arabs. The Arabs were particularly fond of the writings of Aristotle. These they translated into Arabic and wrote learned commentaries on them. The Arabic versions and commentaries were translated in Western Europe into Latin; and it was through these that Latin thinkers came to learn Aristotle's philosophy in the Dark Ages. In the eighth century, the Arabs invaded Spain, and they occupied a major part of it until 1492. These Arabs possessed an enormous culture, which they had brought from Syria, particularly Antioch and Damascus. Syria had acquired its culture from the Mouseion of Alexandria, the Platonic Academy and the Aristotelian Lyceum at Athens, and the University of Constantinople. It should be noted that for centuries Syria remained a part of the Byzantine Empire.

I said that in Byzantium a *selective* use was made of the ancient Greek heritage. By this I mean that polytheistic and materialistic teachings were not accepted. They were rejected as being false, quite incompatible with the Christian doctrine of God, man, and the universe. From ancient philosophy, those elements—especially Platonic and Aristotelian—were accepted which could be assimilated into Christian teaching. A new meaning was infused into many of them—they were spiritualized. I discuss the chief of these in the first chapter of my book *Byzantine Thought and Art,* and more extensively in my work *The Hellenic-Christian Philosophical Tradition.*

From ancient Greek *rhetoric* the Byzantines adopted those features and lessons that were suitable for the sermons and hortatory discourses of Christian preachers and writers. These they found in orators such as Demosthenes and Isocrates, not in Protagoras, Gorgias and other Sophists, whose rhetoric was divorced from ethical principles and from concern about the truth.

The Byzantines respected the *scientific contributions* of Greek Antiquity, particularly those in the *medical art* contained in the writings of Hippocrates and Galen. They cultivated the *mathematical sciences* bequeathed by the ancients, most notably by Euclid. And they made contributions to them, which have not been duly studied.

The greatest contributions of the Byzantine Greeks have been in the spheres of *Orthodox religious culture.* By this I mean the following:

1. *Theology*, taking this term in the broadest sense, which includes teaching about God, man's nature and destiny, the spiritual life, and the Divine Dispensation.

2. *The sacred arts* of church architecture, iconography, hymnography, and music.

3. *Law*, both State Law and Church or Canon Law.

Their contributions in all these areas are of the highest order. In all of them, excellent use was made of the lessons provided by the ancient Greeks. But being guided above all by the Orthodox Christian Faith, their contributions are of a higher level, expressive of the Orthodox view of God, man, and the universe, and of Orthodox Christian spirituality.

We see this vividly in Byzantine holy icons. The iconographers of the Byzantine period assimilated certain important principles that are evident in classical Greek art, particularly sculpture—namely, clarity, simplicity, measure, grace, symmetry, appropriateness. Plato regarded these as characteristics of all true art. What distinguishes Byzantine art from classical Greek art is the quality of *hieraticalness*, of *spiritual solemnity*, of *sanctity* that emanates from the holy persons depicted on icons of the Byzantine style.[1]

Regarding Byzantine *Law*, let me refer again to Alfred North Whitehead. He observes, in his book *Science and the Modern World*, that one of the great achievements of the Byzantine Emperor Justinian the Great (sixth century), was the *codification* of Roman Law. This, he says, established the *ideal of legality*, which dominated the sociological thought of Europe in the succeeding centuries. Law is both an engine for government, remarks Whitehead, and a condition restraining government. The Canon Law of the Church, and the Civil Law of the State, established in the Western mind the ideal that an authority should be at once *lawful* and *law-enforcing*, and should exhibit a *rationally* adjusted system or organization. The impress of these ideas upon the Western mind was fostered by the contact of Europe with *the Byzantine Empire*.[2]

The emphasis which Justinian gave to law was due to the heritage he had received from ancient Greece, especially from the Seven Sages, who flourished around 600 BC. The name of one of them, *Solon*, the founder of Athenian democracy, has become synonymous with *lawgiver*.[3]

---

1. See my book *Guide to Byzantine Iconography*, 1:39–41.
2. *Science*, 13–14.
3. See my book *Seven Sages*.

The Hellenic Heritage in Byzantium

One of the major factors that enabled the Byzantine Empire to endure for more than a thousand years—longer than any other state—was the system of *good laws* it had, the fact that these laws *were respected* by the *subjects and by the rulers,* and the fact that these laws were *both Civil and Church laws,* that is, the *holy canons* of the Orthodox Church. The laws of the Church were upheld by the State as laws also of the State.

About the influence of the Greek heritage of the Byzantine period, Whitehead also makes the following noteworthy remark: "In the nonpolitical spheres of *art and learning* Constantinople exhibited a standard of *realized achievement* that acted as a *perpetual spur* to Western culture."[4]

Another English writer, Cecil Stewart, has made this important remark: "For over ten centuries this *Eastern Christian Empire was the guardian of art and civilization* in Europe. Within its extensive boundaries *the culture of Greece prevailed and prospered.* Here alone in the so-called Dark Ages of civilization, *art and architecture flourished and disseminated an influence which endured long after the greatness and glory of the Empire had passed away.*"[5]

During Justinian's reign, among the most tangible examples of Byzantine "realized achievements" in art that acted as a perpetual spur to Western culture were the churches that were built and decorated with superb mosaics at Ravenna, Italy, and the most famous of all churches, Hagia Sophia at Constantinople. These and other Byzantine churches spurred Western Europeans to cultivate the arts of sacred architecture and sacred painting. However, they gradually deviated from the style of the Byzantines and finally abandoned it, both in church architecture and church painting, developing increasingly secular styles. The same thing happened in church music, where one-part sacred music was replaced by four-part music, and purely vocal music was replaced by instrumental music, or singing with instrumental music accompaniment. Hellenic simplicity was replaced by undue Western complexity, and the sublime, spiritual expression of Byzantine art was replaced by a mundane one.

Also to be noted is the fact that Byzantine culture spread to the West via the European students who attended the *University of Constantinople.* There they received instruction in the humanities and the sciences, other than theology.

---

4. *Science*, 14. (The italics are mine.)
5. Stewart, *Byzantine Legacy*, 5. (The italics are mine.)

In Byzantium, *theology* was the queen of the sciences, the highest part of culture. Theology was not taught at the University of Constantinople, but at *monasteries* and at the *Patriarchal Academy*. The Academy was founded in the seventh century by the Byzantine Emperor Heraclios (610–641). Of the monasteries where theology was taught in a comprehensive manner, the best-known example was the *Stoudion*, near Constantinople. This acquired great fame especially through St. Theodore the Stoudite (759–826), a staunch critic of iconoclasm in the early decades of the ninth century.

The impact of Byzantine culture was not limited to the West; it extended to the East and to the North. Of the eastern lands where Byzantium exercised an important influence, besides Syria, which I have already mentioned, were Palestine and Sinai. In the North, important influence was exercised in the Slavic countries. Patriarch Photios the Great, who lived in the ninth century, sent two of his best students and disciples as missionaries to the Slavs. Their names were Constantine the Philosopher, renamed Kyrillos (Cyril), and Methodios. They were natives of Thessaloniki—the most important Byzantine city after Constantinople. Their missionary activities resulted in the conversion of the Serbs and Bulgarians to the Orthodox Faith, and the transmission to them of the related culture, particularly iconography, sacred music, and religious literature.

Further missionary activity resulted in the conversion of the Rumanians and the Russians. The debt of Russia to Byzantium has been duly emphasized by the outstanding nineteenth-century thinker and writer Konstantin Leontiev, who has written this: "What would Russian Christianity be without its Byzantine foundation and forms? . . . Byzantine religious culture has in general produced all those principal types of Saintliness, which later served as examples to Russia. All our Saints were only disciples, the imitators and followers of Byzantine saints."[6]

To this statement of Konstantin Leontiev should be added some observations made by another eminent Russian philosopher and gifted writer, Prince Evgenii Nikolaevich Trubetskoi, who flourished in the early decades of the twentieth century. In his book *Icons: Theology in Color*, Trubetskoi called attention to the important role that was played by Greek icon painters, from the early part of the eleventh century to the early part of the fifteenth, in the iconographic decoration of Russian churches, and in the development of Russian iconography. He mentions as examples Isaiah the Greek and Theophanes the Greek. Theophanes, he explains, "was

---

6. Berdyaev, *Leontiev*, 179.

the foremost Novgorod master and teacher of icon painting," and Andrei Rublev *(ca.* 1370–1430), the most famous Russian iconographer, was one of his pupils.

It is interesting to note in this connection that the icon reputed to be "the Russian icon *par excellence",* namely, "The Vladimir Mother of God," was painted in Constantinople *(ca.* 1125) for a Russian patron.

Byzantine iconography was also transmitted by the Greeks to Serbia, Bulgaria, and Rumania. The transmission took place during the same period that it took place in Russia.[7]

Bibliography

Berdyaev, Nicholas. *Leontiev.* Orono, ME: Academic International, 1968.

Cavarnos, Constantine. *Byzantine Sacred Art.* 2nd ed. Belmont, MA: Institute for Byzantine and Modern Greek Studies, 1985.

———. *Byzantine Thought and Art: A Collection of Essays.* 3rd printing. Belmont, MA: Institute for Byzantine and Modern Greek Studies, 1980.

———. *Guide to Byzantine Iconography.* Vol. 1. Boston, MA: Holy Transfiguration Monastery, 1993.

———. *The Hellenic-Christian Philosophical Tradition.* Belmont, MA: Institute for Byzantine and Modern Greek Studies, 1989.

———. *He Hiera Byzantine Techne.* Athens: Aster, 1995.

———. *The Seven Sages of Ancient Greece.* Belmont, MA: Institute for Byzantine and Modern Greek Studies, 1996.

Stewart, Cecil. *Byzantine Legacy.* London: G. Allen & Unwin, 1959.

Trubetskoi, Eugene N. *Icons: Theology in Color.* Crestwood, NY: St. Vladimir's Seminary Press, 1973.

Whitehead, A. N. *Science and the Modern World.* New York: Macmillan, 1925.

---

7. Regarding Byzantine iconography in these countries see my books *Byzantine Sacred Art,* 70–80, and *He Hiera Byzantine Techne,* 99–117.